WALKING
GREAT BRITAIN

WALKING
GREAT BRITAIN

ENGLAND, SCOTLAND, AND WALES

HEATHER HANSEN

MOUNTAINEERS
BOOKS

For my mom, Ellen Baukney (1941–2018),
adventurous soul, now dancing with the daffodils.

MOUNTAINEERS BOOKS is dedicated
to the exploration, preservation, and enjoyment
of outdoor and wilderness areas.

1001 SW Klickitat Way, Suite 201, Seattle, WA 98134
800-553-4453, www.mountaineersbooks.org

Printed in South Korea
Distributed in the United Kingdom by Cordee, www.cordee.co.uk

First edition, 2022

Copyeditor: Laura Lancaster
Design and layout: Jen Grable
Cartographer: Lohnes+Wright
All photographs by the author unless credited otherwise
Cover photographs: *Sheep on Lord's Seat, Trail 10*; *Mountain path leading to lake at Cwm Idwal, Devils
Kitchen, Trail 38* (istock/fungirlslim); *Seal Cove on Treginnis Peninsula, Trail 45*; *Eas Mòr on the Isle of
Skye, Trail 61*
Frontispiece: *Now-tranquil Janet's Foss (Trail 8) in the Yorkshires was once used to dip sheep before
summer shearing.*

Library of Congress Cataloging-in-Publication Data is on file for this title at https://lccn.loc.gov
/2021043129. LC ebook record available at https://lccn.loc.gov/2021043130.

Printed on FSC®-certified materials

MIX
Paper from
responsible sources
FSC® C140526

ISBN (paperback): 978-1-68051-317-2
ISBN (ebook): 978-1-68051-318-9

An independent nonprofit publisher since 1960

CONTENTS

EASTERN ENGLAND

SOUTHERN ENGLAND

WALES (CYMRU)

SCOTTISH LOWLANDS

SCOTTISH HIGHLANDS

WALKS AT A GLANCE

		DISTANCE	RATING	DIFFICULTY	YEAR-ROUND	
NORTHERN ENGLAND						
LAKE DISTRICT						
1.	Castle Crag	5.4 miles	★★★★	3	•	
2.	Hawkshead to Wray Castle	6.9 miles	★★★	1	•	
3.	Three Lakes Loop	7.6 miles	★★★★★	3	•	
4.	Helvellyn	8.5 miles	★★★★★	5		
5.	Tarn Hows	2 miles	★★★★	1	•	
YORKSHIRE DALES						
6.	Pen-y-ghent	6.5 miles	★★★★★	4	•	
7.	Malham Cove	3.5 miles	★★★★★	3	•	
8.	Gordale Scar & Janet's Foss	4 miles	★★★★	1	•	
9.	Langstrothdale Riverside Walk	6.2 miles	★★★★	2	•	
CENTRAL ENGLAND						
PEAK DISTRICT						
10.	Lord's Seat Loop	6 miles	★★★★	4	•	
11.	Great Ridge Ramble	6.5 miles	★★★★	4	•	
12.	Longshaw & Padley Gorge	3.5 miles	★★★★	2	•	
13.	Stanage Edge	5.0 miles	★★★★	4	•	
14.	Dovedale & The Stepping Stones	5.4 miles	★★★★	3	•	
15.	Cave Dale & Winnats Pass	4.9 miles	★★★	3	•	
THE COTSWOLDS & OXFORD						
16.	Chipping Campden & Dover's Hill	4.2 miles	★★★	2	•	
17.	Winchcombe, Belas Knap & Sudeley Castle	6.3 miles	★★★★	3	•	
18.	Buckholt Wood & Cooper's Hill	4.5 miles	★★★★	2	•	
19.	Bath Skyline	6.2 miles	★★★★★	3	•	
20.	Woodstock & Blenheim Palace	5.2 miles	★★★★★	2	•	
21.	Oxford Blues & Greens	5.5 miles	★★★★	2	•	

	FAMILY-FRIENDLY	DOG-FRIENDLY	WILDLIFE	WOODLAND	BEACH-COMBING	HISTORY	GEOLOGY	WATER FEATURE
	•	•	•	•		•	•	•
	•	•	•	•		•		•
	•	•	•	•		•		
		•				•	•	
	•	•	•	•		•		•
	•	•				•	•	•
	•	•	•			•	•	•
	•	•	•	•		•	•	•
	•	•	•	•		•	•	•
	•	•		•		•	•	•
	•	•		•		•	•	
	•	•	•	•		•	•	•
	•	•	•			•	•	
	•	•		•		•	•	•
	•			•		•	•	•
	•	•	•	•		•		
	•	•				•		
	•	•				•		
	•	•				•	•	
	•	•	•	•		•		•
		•		•		•		•

	DISTANCE	RATING	DIFFICULTY	YEAR-ROUND	
EASTERN ENGLAND					
LONDON & EAST ANGLIA					
22. Parks of London	7.2 miles	★★★★	3	•	
23. Hampstead Heath	5.6 miles	★★★★	2	•	
24. Parkland Walk to Alexandra Palace	7 miles	★★★★	3	•	
25. Grantchester Meadows	4.5 miles	★★★	1	•	
26. Cambridge Parks & Backs	4.3 miles	★★★★	2	•	
27. Holkham Beach	8 miles	★★★★	3	•	
28. Dunwich Beach & Heath	7.3 miles	★★★★	3	•	
29. Greyfriars Wood & Monastery Ruins	5 miles	★★★	2	•	
SOUTHERN ENGLAND					
CORNWALL					
30. The Lizard	4.2 miles	★★★★★	2	•	
31. Kynance Cove to Lizard Point	4.8 miles	★★★★	3	•	
32. Bedruthan Steps to Porthcothan	7.7 miles	★★★★	3	•	
DEVON					
33. Tour of Tors	5.2 miles	★★★★	4	•	
34. Teign Gorge & Fingle Woods	9.5 miles	★★★★	3	•	
35. Valley of Rocks	2.5 miles	★★★	2	•	
DORSET & THE JURASSIC COAST					
36. Branscombe & Hooken Cliffs	4.8 miles	★★★★	3	•	
37. Lulworth Cove & Durdle Door	3.5 miles	★★★★★	2	•	
WALES (CYMRU)					
SNOWDONIA NATIONAL PARK					
38. Cwm Idwal	3.5 miles	★★★★★	4	•	
39. Legends of Beddgelert	1.5 miles	★★★★	1	•	
40. Snowdon (Yr Wyddfa)	8 miles	★★★★	5		
BRECON BEACONS NATIONAL PARK					
41. Three Peaks of the Brecon Beacons	11.4 miles	★★★★★	5		
42. Four Waterfalls of the Brecon Beacons	5 miles	★★★★	3	•	

	FAMILY-FRIENDLY	DOG-FRIENDLY	WILDLIFE	WOODLAND	BEACH-COMBING	HISTORY	GEOLOGY	WATER FEATURE
	•	•	•	•		•		•
	•	•		•		•		•
	•	•		•		•	•	•
	•	•	•	•		•		•
	•	•				•		•
	•	•	•	•	•	•		•
	•	•	•	•	•	•		•
	•	•		•		•	•	•
	•	•	•			•	•	•
	•	•			•	•	•	•
	•	•	•		•	•	•	•
	•	•	•	•		•	•	•
	•	•	•	•		•	•	•
					•	•	•	
	•	•	•	•	•	•	•	•
	•				•	•	•	•
	•	•	•			•	•	
	•	•		•		•		•
	•	•				•	•	
	•	•	•	•		•	•	•
	•	•	•	•		•	•	•

	DISTANCE	RATING	DIFFICULTY	YEAR-ROUND	
PEMBROKESHIRE COAST NATIONAL PARK					
43. St. Ann's Head	7 miles	★★★	3	•	
44. Stackpole Head, Barafundle Bay & Bosherton Lakes	6 miles	★★★★	2	•	
45. St. Davids & Treginnis Peninsula	11 miles	★★★★★	4	•	

SCOTTISH LOWLANDS

	DISTANCE	RATING	DIFFICULTY	YEAR-ROUND	
EDINBURGH					
46. Holyrood Park Loop	3.2 miles	★★★★	3	•	
47. Water of Leith	9.6 miles	★★★★	2	•	
PENTLAND HILLS					
48. Pentland Peaks Triptych	7.6 miles	★★★★	4	•	
49. Turnhouse Hill	3.2 miles	★★★	3	•	
EAST LOTHIAN					
50. North Berwick Law	3.2 miles	★★★	3	•	
51. North Berwick Shore	6.8 miles	★★★★	3	•	
52. Dunbar Cliff Walk	4.3 miles	★★★★	2	•	
53. Aberlady Nature Reserve to Gullane Bents	7 miles	★★★★	3	•	
54. Gullane Bents	3.2 miles	★★★★	1	•	

SCOTTISH HIGHLANDS

	DISTANCE	RATING	DIFFICULTY	YEAR-ROUND	
CAIRNGORMS NATIONAL PARK					
55. Loch an Eilein & Loch Gamhna	4.5 miles	★★★★	1	•	
56. Coire an t-Sneachda	4.3 miles	★★★★★	3		
57. Creag Bheag	3 miles	★★★	3	•	
58. Ryvoan Pass, An Lochan Uaine & Meall a'Bhuachaille	5.5 miles	★★★★	4		
LOCH LOMOND & THE TROSSACHS NATIONAL PARK					
59. Ben Lomond	7.6 miles	★★★★	5		
FORT WILLIAM & GLENCOE					
60. North Face of Ben Nevis	7.5 miles	★★★★★	4		
ISLE OF SKYE					
61. Coire Lagan	6 miles	★★★★★	4		
62. Fingal's Pinnacles & The Quiraing	4.6 miles	★★★★	3		
63. Pass of Killiecrankie	9 miles	★★★★	3	•	

	FAMILY-FRIENDLY	DOG-FRIENDLY	WILDLIFE	WOODLAND	BEACH-COMBING	HISTORY	GEOLOGY	WATER FEATURE
		•			•	•	•	•
	•	•	•	•	•	•	•	•
		•				•		•
	•	•	•			•	•	
	•	•	•	•		•		•
	•	•	•	•		•		
			•		•	•		•
	•	•	•	•		•	•	•
	•		•	•				
	•	•	•	•	•	•	•	•
	•	•	•	•		•		•
	•	•	•	•		•	•	•
	•	•	•	•		•	•	•
	•	•	•	•		•	•	•
			•			•	•	•
	•	•	•	•		•	•	•
	•	•				•	•	•
	•	•				•	•	•
		•		•		•	•	•

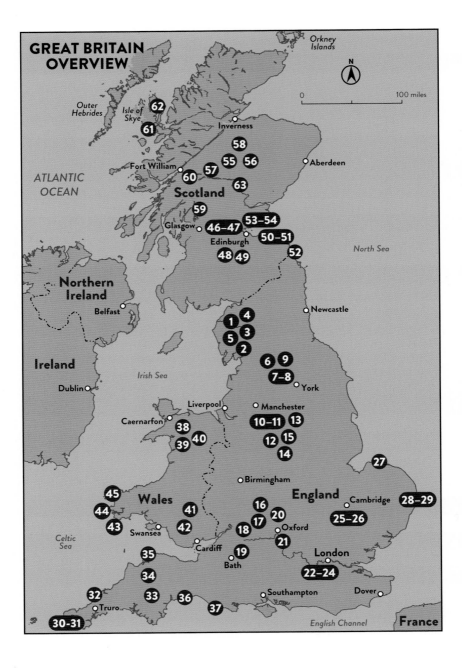

GREAT BRITAIN OVERVIEW

Orkney
Islands

N

0   100 miles

*Outer
Hebrides*

*Isle of
Skye* 62

61

Inverness

58

55 56

Fort William 57

60

Scotland 63

ATLANTIC
OCEAN

59

Glasgow 46–47 53–54

50–51

Edinburgh 52

48 49

North Sea

**Northern
Ireland**

Belfast

Newcastle

1 4

3

5

Ireland

2

Dublin

6 9

7–8

Irish Sea

York

Liverpool

Manchester

Caernarfon

10–11 13

38

12 15

39 40

14

27

Birmingham

45

Wales **England**

Cambridge

41 16 28–29

44

20 25–26

43 *Swansea* 42

17

18 Oxford

35 19 21

Cardiff London

34 Bath 22–24

*Celtic
Sea*

33 36 Southampton Dover

32

37

Truro *English Channel* **France**

30–31

INTRODUCTION

Encompassing England, Wales, and Scotland, Great Britain has remarkable diversity for an island of only 80,000 square miles (roughly the size of Kansas). There are hidden wilds in London, picturesque villages in the Cotswolds, smugglers' coves in Cornwall, broad beaches in Norfolk, stunning cliffs in Wales, rugged peaks in Scotland, and much more. Given its relatively compact size, it's possible to travel from central London to the Scottish Highlands in a day. And with more than 80 percent of the sixty-six million people in Great Britain living in cities, the rest of the island is wide open for exploration.

But that wasn't always true. In April 1932, several hundred people walked up the flanks of 2087-foot Kinder Scout in central England in a bold act of civil disobedience that would become known as "the mass trespass." The peak, and nearby hills and vast moorland, were all off-limits to common folk, reserved instead for the landed gentry to take aim at grouse. Most of the determined ramblers were city slickers who had fled coal-choked environs for a breath of fresh air in the open countryside. On their ascent, they had to physically fight gamekeepers, hired to keep them out. It was a pivotal moment in the "right to roam" movement, as it was later called, which ultimately led to the creation of the first national park in England—Peak District National Park (which Kinder Scout now lies within), in 1951. That park became known as the "lungs of the industrial north."

The access campaign had been waged in some way since 1884, when the first related parliamentary bill was introduced, but it would take until the end of the twentieth century for the Countryside and Rights of Way Act 2000 to become law in Britain. After several years of mapping the countryside and marking rights of way, in 2005, the freedom to roam became a reality. Now walkers can access a 140,000-mile network of public paths in England and Wales (Scotland has its own access rights and code, which apply to nearly all land), including private highland, moor, heath, and down.

In addition to its rights of way, Great Britain has fifteen national parks (ten of which are featured in this guide), each interesting and valuable in its own way. But they differ from national parks in the US. For instance, most national parks in Great Britain are still living and working landscapes. Beautiful places are plentiful, but the distinction between parks and places inhabited by people is often indiscernible; there may be

A greenbelt of commons, where the public still holds land rights, encircles Cambridge.

villages, factories, and even mines within a national park. There is also limited infrastructure, such as signage, visitor centers, or trail markers. I have learned to research areas and to upload or print maps before I leave home (or I buy a map or guidebook in a local shop). A reliable map, and the ability to read it, is essential for navigating trails in Great Britain.

Another major category of open space in England and Wales is property owned by the National Trust, which preserves places of natural or historical interest (their emblem, which you'll see often, is a cluster of oak leaves). The organization has been around for more than a century and stewards over 600,000 acres of land, including nearly 800 miles of coastline and more than five hundred historical homes, castles, gardens, and parks. In the north, the National Trust for Scotland likewise safeguards eighty-eight properties including nearly 200,000 acres of countryside and gardens from battlefields to mountain ranges. Other natural conservation categories in Great Britain include local nature reserves, national nature reserves, Sites of Special Scientific Interest, and Areas of Outstanding Natural Beauty.

There are walks for every level, from easy riverside strolls to mountain summits requiring technical gear, and short rambles to long-distance footpaths (more on that in Long-Distance Paths of Great Britain below). Walking remains something of a national pastime in Great Britain (the term "hiking" is seldom used but rather "walking," "rambling," or "trekking"), regardless of age, gender, or socioeconomic status. Out on the trail, you're as likely to meet a plumber from Liverpool as a banker from London. In a nation whose social structure is still highly influenced by class, the act of ambling is refreshingly egalitarian.

FOR DECADES, I TRAVELED OFTEN TO GREAT BRITAIN FROM MY HOME in Colorado. On those trips, that meant museum-hopping, lingering over tea and tiny, delicious cakes, or seeing a musical in London—never really exploring its outdoor offerings. Then, in 2016, I moved here full time.

Colorado, with its 14,000-foot peaks, has little in common with an island that tops out at about 4400 feet above sea level. For fifteen years, I'd walked happily high and *dry* among the mountains and mesas, plains and desert canyons of the West, concerned mainly with sun, heat, and altitude. The low relative humidity meant I suffered maybe five blisters total during those years. Sweat evaporated before it accumulated. My raingear seldom left my pack.

Where I live near Cambridge, about 70 miles northeast of London, averages 73 percent relative humidity. The sun makes a full appearance sixty-two days per year, and it is considered, without jest, one of the sunnier areas of Great Britain. Some days my weather app calls the outlook (seriously) "dull and dreary." Hills in "the Fens," as this marshy area (drained over the centuries for farming and herding) is known, are referred to as "islands" because, historically, that's all that stayed dry when the fens flooded and the eels multiplied. Most of Cambridgeshire, my home county, lies just several feet above sea level, but in one spot, Holme Fen, it dips down to 9 feet *below* sea level—Great Britain's lowest land point.

I don't particularly like getting wet, especially my feet. But I realized that waiting for the skies to clear above those flatlands was futile if I was going to do the thing I love most—walk. Over the months, and then years, I passed through whatever is the opposite of a "trial by fire." That equaled chaffing and blisters, low-cloud claustrophobia, and vitamin D depletion. It began as an exercise in will, with a lot of whining (often audible, even when I was alone), but it grew into an appreciation for the land's mercurial moods, and much more.

One thing that struck me early on was how civilized Great Britain is. I don't just mean the tea and good manners but the sense that it is firmly built and fully inhabited. The great American transcendentalist Ralph Waldo Emerson wrote in *English Traits* that "under an ash-colored sky" the country seemed to him to have a "finished" quality. "Nothing is left as it was made. Rivers, hills, valleys, the sea itself, feel the hand of a master," he said. This, too, was my first impression of England—it has beautiful, manicured gardens and verdant farms that seem to fill every expanse to the horizon—but the kingdom lacks wildness.

Emerson was drawn to English Romanticism even before he ventured a visit, but he had scorned the work of one of the movement's founding fathers, poet William Wordsworth. He felt that Wordsworth's exuberant voice lacked dignity and called him "an

LONG-DISTANCE PATHS OF GREAT BRITAIN

Few people think of Great Britain as a place where you can walk for days, never mind for weeks or months. Only after exploring for years did I recognize how extensive the long-distance trail network that crisscrosses England, Scotland, and Wales is. In Cambridge (my hometown) alone there are three long-distance paths leading out of the city center, which in turn connect to several more paths—you can walk along footpaths nearly to London!

The British Long Distance Walkers Association defines a long-distance trail as a route at least 20 miles long that is mostly off-road. Among these are 2500 miles along fifteen designated national trails in England and Wales and a new mega-national trail, the 2795-mile England Coast Path, which was partly complete as of this writing. Scotland has an additional twenty-nine Great Trails covering 1900 miles. Many more lengthy trails that don't technically qualify as "long distance" abound.

The best-known long-distance routes in the US, like the Appalachian Trail and Pacific Crest Trail, are prized for their natural seclusion, with remote stretches where a hiker can go days without passing a town or crossing a road. While many long treks in Great Britain also cover spectacular terrain, they often feature spots special for their human history, like Hadrian's Wall Path, an 84-mile route running east-west across England, that follows the barrier built by the Romans roughly 1600 years ago. (The whole trail is a World Heritage Site and passes through some of the prettiest and most historic areas of England.) And while some of these paths tackle remote terrain, especially in Wales and Scotland, many more allow walkers to visit villages with all their amenities. In some cases, long-distance routes begin in, or cut through, major metropolitan areas. One such route is the Thames Path, which spans 184 miles from London's center, along the country's most famous river, to its source in the Cotswolds.

Wherever you are in Great Britain, there is probably more than one lengthy route running nearby. Many of the paths in this guidebook intersect with or even follow sections of these longer paths, offering a tempting glimpse of the tangle of trails that covers England, Scotland, and Wales.

ardent lover of all the enchantments of wood and river and seduced by an overweening confidence in the force of his own genius." But that thinking shifted profoundly when the two spent time together, on a trail in northwest England's Lake District, during Emerson's first journey to Europe in 1833. There, Emerson opened his eyes to a different way of seeing.

Wordsworth, more than thirty years older than Emerson, was lamenting his creative decline, but Emerson began to admire the older man's originality and steadfast belief in the importance of wild places to restore mind and body (both men had suffered tremendous personal losses and sought healing in nature). Wordsworth felt the universe was inherently good and glimpsed that purity in rivers and mountains, meres and moors. "Nature never did betray / The heart that loved her," said Wordsworth in 1798 in one of his most famous poems, "Lines Written a Few Miles above Tintern Abbey." Emerson learned from the Englishman that "wild" is in the eye of the beholder, and later wrote that Wordsworth "has done more for the sanity of this generation than any other writer."

Instead of hiding indoors and missing Colorado, I went to where Wordsworth was born, wrote, and died: England's Lake District, home to the ten highest mountains in the country and its largest and deepest lakes. In his *Guide through the District of the Lakes*, Wordsworth, who had been to the Alps, wrote of his hills that "in the combinations which they make, towering above each other, or lifting themselves in ridges like the waves of a tumultuous sea, and in the beauty and variety of their surfaces and colours, they are surpassed by none." Nonetheless, the area struck me at first as mainly quaint, with still lakes, tumbling hills, stone structures, and seemingly endless rock walls built across the centuries. Not a single acre appeared untouched by human hands, completely unlike the national parks I grew up visiting in the US.

Most woodland tracts across Britain were cleared for use or cultivation over thousands of years. Today forests, ranging from deciduous in the south to coniferous in the north, cover about 10 percent of England, 15 percent of Wales, and nearly 20 percent of Scotland, including plantations managed for logging. The flowers of the island, both wild and cultivated, represent much of the diversity in flora that remains. Gardens, small and large, are something of a national obsession, and wildflower hotspots—where daffodils or bluebells carpet the spring terrain—are well known.

The fauna of Great Britain likewise shifted dramatically as urbanization, industrialization, and climate change have taken their toll. Wolves, brown bears, and wild boar, once common, were hunted to extinction centuries ago. Though seals, dolphins, and whales can often be seen offshore, the largest remaining mammals on the British Isles are in the deer family. (And, honestly, walking without worrying about encountering bears or mountain lions was unexpectedly relaxing.) Reptiles and amphibians are scarce, and there is only one kind of venomous snake—the adder. Great Britain,

Dunwich Heath (Trail 28), on the stunning Suffolk Coast, blushes with fragrant heather in July.

however, remains a birder's paradise with roughly 230 species living in the UK and another 200 flying in seasonally.

I came to learn that the British experience of national parks, open space, and nature in general often centers, not on flora and fauna, but on people, and even celebrates the ingenuity of generations past to thrive in harsh conditions. In Wordsworth's Lake District, nearly 60 percent of the land is privately owned.

Still, there is a freshness, nearly a lushness, to Lakeland. The light is crisp and the fields and hills seem to glow green from within. The lakes are secretive and moody. The daffodils bloom with abandon. And when it stops raining—which happens occasionally—the air smells electric. While there I wanted to walk until sunset, and beyond, to hear the place murmur in the dark.

Wordsworth offered his senses and opened his heart, and nature met him with a lifetime of revelations. He wrote in his Lakes guide: "Days of unsettled weather, with partial showers, are very frequent; but the showers, darkening, or brightening, as they fly from hill to hill, are not less grateful to the eye than finely interwoven passages of gay and sad music are touching to the ear."

In my years of rambling across Great Britain, I began to bring into focus what Wordsworth had seen. I shifted my thinking about how weather *should* be, or what wild places *should* look like, and I listened to what the birds, brooks, and even the bricks, had to say. Melodies began to emerge from the surprisingly varied landscape, along with the history, traditions, and folklore that pepper protected spaces. The "other Britain," as I started to think of it, stood in stark relief to the "Big Ben Britain" I had known, and it was alive with possibility. I have now walked some of the finest miles that the other Britain has to offer, many of which are described in these pages. Happy walking!

KNOW BEFORE YOU GO

Oscar Wilde once wrote that the US and the British Isles are two cultures separated by a common language. British English and American English are different enough that I've embarrassed myself by saying "pants," which means "underwear" in the UK (they say "trousers"). When you're out and about, it's good to know that a "car park" is a parking lot, "petrol" is gasoline, a "torch" is a flashlight, and a "path" generally means a paved sidewalk ("trail" and "track" are more commonly used). English is ubiquitous, but be prepared to hear Welsh in Wales and Gaelic in Scotland, in addition to some fantastic regional accents and dialects. Still, different names for otherwise familiar geography will keep you on your toes—"stream" in England is "nant" in Welsh and "burn" in Scotland. Both Wales and Scotland have vibrant histories and rich cultural traditions separate from those in England. Learning about them will add to your fascination and joy on these walks.

GENERAL TRAVEL TIPS

Walking in Great Britain is a relatively carefree endeavor but, like traveling anywhere, there are certain considerations to keep top of mind on your journey. Plan carefully and take every walk seriously; even short routes can be rolling and deceptively rigorous, especially along the coast. I'd assumed that Great Britain couldn't be as challenging as the Rocky Mountains, but, remember, the folks who first summited Everest trained here!

Beyond mindset, consider the seasons. The dark days of winter are truly dim, with less than eight hours of daylight in December and January. The picture improves from there, however, peaking at over sixteen hours of daylight in July.

Great Britain is full of walker-friendly places to eat and to stay. There aren't many large hotels (except in cities), but there are plenty of bed-and-breakfasts, farm stays (barns, cabins, yurts), self-catering places (such as Airbnbs), guesthouses, and hostels.

When distances are given in kilometers in some sources other than this guide, remember that 1 kilometer equals 0.62 mile. Temperatures will always be given in

Celsius, and the conversion is a bit trickier: multiply the Celsius temp by 1.8, then add 32—or just keep in mind that 16 degrees Celsius is 61 degrees Fahrenheit, and adjust up and down from there! Throughout the driving and walk descriptions, I provide imperial measurements (miles, feet, etc.), which are easy enough to convert online if you are accustomed to thinking "metric."

Credit cards are accepted in most places and cash is rarely necessary—except in the case of some restrooms and parking kiosks that accept only coins. When cash is required, the GBP pound (£) is accepted everywhere. The Scots also print their own currency, which is widely accepted in the rest of Great Britain.

PUBLIC TRANSPORTATION & DRIVING

Travel is seamless between England, Wales, and Scotland, and an impressive network of train lines, bus routes, and ferry crossings serves cities, towns, and villages. When planning an itinerary, the Traveline website is a good place to start. You can also check the National Rail website for trains and the National Express website for buses. (See Resources at the back of the book for contact information.)

Driving is often the easiest way to reach far-flung locations, and car rental agencies abound. That said, driving in Great Britain is rarely easy. Motorways (similar to US highways or interstates), or M roads, are straightforward enough, but A roads (major through-routes with one or two lanes) and B roads (narrow secondary roads) can be more challenging. Be prepared for winding roads barely wide enough for two cars to pass, and get used to relying on "passing places" (or turnouts), where drivers can pull over to let oncoming vehicles proceed.

Despite the dominant metric system, distances are posted in miles, roundabouts are omnipresent, and there are thousands of CCTV (closed-circuit television) cameras—watch your speed. Also, road signs in Wales appear in English and Welsh, and in Scotland they are in English and Scottish Gaelic. And, don't forget, stay to the left!

PERMITS, REGULATIONS & FEES

Permits are not required to walk on any public land in Great Britain. National parks do not charge entrance fees, but both the National Trust and National Trust for Scotland charge fees to park and to tour various historical homes and gardens. If you plan to visit more than a few National Trust sites, join the Royal Oak Foundation, the US membership affiliate of the National Trust, which includes parking as part of its annual membership.

There is very little free parking anywhere in Great Britain, though Scotland has a bit more. Many kiosks accept cards, but some only take coins. No matter how remote a car park may seem, they are generally well patrolled (I learned this the hard way in the Peak District). That being said, never leave valuables in your car, especially near urban centers.

Public restrooms are infrequent and, when they are present, often cost twenty to thirty pence. Restaurants and cafes usually require a purchase to use their facilities.

Camping in Great Britain is usually by fee at private campsites. Many campgrounds are situated in open fields, where tents are generally outnumbered by campers and caravans. Wild camping without the landowner's permission is illegal on private land in England and Wales—this holds true for their national parks, which are often largely composed of private land. Scotland, on the other hand, allows wild camping almost anywhere, within reason (not on a golf course, for example). Check with local authorities before pitching your tent and, if you do wild camp, be respectful by keeping groups small and by packing out trash. *Never* light a campfire, and use camp stoves with utmost caution. Anglers will need a license for certain species of fish. (See Resources for more information.)

Overlooking the Bandstand and Boating Lake on Holme Green in Regent's Park (Trail 22)

The Countryside and Rights of Way Act 2000 allows walkers to pass through any area designated as open countryside. But that doesn't mean it's a free-for-all; walkers must stick to designated paths. Fingerposts mark "public footpaths" and "permissive paths," which often crisscross private land. Scotland has similar rules governed by the Land Reform Act (Scotland) 2003.

ETHICS

England and Wales are governed by the Countryside Code, which emphasizes respect for people and property. Take home litter, bag dog poo, and keep dogs under voice control (or on a leash where required). When traveling near farmland or grazing pastures, be sure to stay on marked footpaths, leave gates as you found them (open if open, shut if shut), and give domestic and wild animals a wide berth. The Scottish Outdoor Access Code, while similar, has one thoughtful addition: "Do not act in ways that might annoy or alarm people, especially at night."

Lake District gem Tarn Hows (Trail 5) has a storied history and a storybook look in every season.

Throughout Great Britain, cyclists must give way to walkers on shared trails and equestrians on bridleways. Mountain biking, while gaining popularity, is still uncommon. Equestrians and walkers should respect each other's space and safety.

Always follow the seven principles of Leave No Trace, as established by the Center for Outdoor Ethics: 1) plan ahead to minimize unexpected impact on natural resources, 2) travel and camp on durable surfaces to protect delicate vegetation and decrease erosion, 3) properly dispose of waste, by packing out your trash and following local guidelines on human waste, 4) leave what you find, by not altering campsites or removing natural or cultural artifacts, 5) be careful with fire and strive to minimize its impact on the surrounding environment, 6) respect wildlife by walking quietly and observing from a distance, and 7) be considerate of other people by hiking in small groups, controlling pets, and avoiding excessive noise.

WEATHER

Most of the British Isles, with the exception of the highest peaks, are walkable year-round. Despite its high latitude, the climate is temperate (generally mild and damp), because warm sea air regularly sweeps across the isles in bands. That said, winter days (November through February) are short and cold. Spring brings a riot of blooms, summer is warm but more crowded, and fall is the "Goldilocks" season, when the tourists ebb but the days are still long enough for a good day's rambling. While the UK can be soggy and windswept much of the time (regardless of the season), the past few summers have also brought record heat.

As a general rule, the higher in latitude you go, and the later in the year it is, the more likely you are to encounter snow. The skies also can be (even more) fickle at higher elevations. It's notoriously wet in the west (think Wales and Cornwall), drying out the farther east you go. But these are not hard and fast rules; the weather across Great Britain is highly variable and preparation is key. British walking icon Alfred Wainwright famously said, "There's no such thing as bad weather, only unsuitable clothing." Whether it's sunny, cloudy, or actively precipitating, bring sunglasses, sunblock, a hat, raingear, and spare socks.

Rain can present significant challenges by making trails and bridges muddy and slippery, which can be dangerous for those on or near a steep slope. Rain can also soak through cotton clothes and leave you shivering—add wind, and hypothermia is a real possibility.

Walkers must be vigilant on escarpments, cliffside coastal paths, and mountains, especially in mist or fog. Snow likewise requires additional caution, especially in high and exposed places, and where it obscures the designated path. Proper equipment and skills are needed to hike where avalanches occur in Scotland in winter.

Storms, which occur throughout the year, can bring lightning and hail. Direct lightning strikes are rare in Great Britain, but elevation and exposure should be limited if a storm is in the forecast or following a period of high humidity. If you hear thunder or see lightning nearby, get safely to low ground, but don't take shelter beneath a tree or in a cave.

Humidity, combined with heat in the summer, can increase your hike time and likelihood of getting blisters, so it's also a good idea to carry a few adhesive bandages—called "plasters" in the UK—in your pack. A good source for forecasts and warnings is the Met Office, the UK's meteorological agency, and the Mountain Weather Information Service (see Resources for contact information).

In addition to preparedness, the key to happiness while walking in Great Britain is to embrace the conditions. Many places are at their brooding best in foul weather, and rain has a cleansing power that can scrub away a sticky summer day. If dry days are by chance your companion, gratitude will be as well.

ROAD AND TRAIL CONDITIONS

Most walks described in this book follow well-designated routes. But things change in dynamic environments. Flooding can, and does, wash away trails and make normally docile streams impassable. Landslides are also a possibility, particularly on coastal stretches where heavy rain can make cliffs unstable. When in doubt, turn around.

Some of these routes, and many hikes across Britain, require you to either cross or follow a road. Always use crosswalks if present and remember to look *right then left*—and then right again. Great Britain, in general, is not big on pedestrian rights, and walkers must wait for vehicles and bicycles to pass.

A few of the featured routes cross coastal areas at low tide. Often the tide table is posted on-site, but they can also be accessed on the Met Office website: www.met office.gov.uk.

In some places, neither trailheads nor trails are well marked with signs or blazes (one of the many reasons I wrote this guide). The spirit and ability to navigate are both useful tools. Despite the often damp conditions, drinking water can be hard to find. Trailheads rarely have water fountains. Always bring enough water and food for the day.

The Ministry of Defence (MOD) owns roughly 1 percent of all land in the UK. While troops often train on that land, it is usually accessible to walkers unless posted. The MOD flies red flags on-site during life-threatening activity and strictly prohibits entry. Ordnance Survey maps also mark potential danger areas with solid red triangles. None of the routes in this book traverse an MOD site, but some are adjacent to such land.

MAPS AND ELECTRONIC DEVICES

The few times I have walked without a map, I've regretted it. Ordnance Survey (OS) maps are the gold standard—they've been making them since the mid-eighteenth century, after all. For each featured route, the relevant OS Explorer map is listed. These have a 1:25,000 scale, which is the best one for walking, and are waterproof (bulky but essential). An online OS subscription allows you to upload maps to a variety of mobile devices.

Taking a fully charged cell phone with local coverage is always a good idea, but keep in mind that you will not have a reliable signal in remote or hilly areas. A GPS device is not necessary, but it can be useful while hiking in pea-soup fog or other tricky conditions.

You can use any map app on a mobile device to locate a trailhead by typing in the location's postcode. Unlike zip codes, postcodes (included in the directions for each route) are generally very specific.

PERSONAL SAFETY

While the lack of predators in Great Britain makes for an overall safe hiking experience, there are still several safety issues worth considering.

Wildlife

Deer, the largest land mammals in Great Britain, pose more risk to drivers than walkers. That said, give all wildlife a wide berth. Of the four snake species in Britain (three native and one non-native), only the adder, or European viper, is venomous.

There are several insects to be aware of: Ticks, which carry a variety of diseases, including Lyme disease, are generally found in areas of dense vegetation. Mosquitoes

Wild Welsh ponies have been grazing Snowdonia's mountain grasslands for centuries.

and gnats are present but rarely overwhelming. Midges, however, can travel in swarms, particularly in Scotland in summer, and cover a person in small, itchy bumps. Horseflies leave a painful bite. There are also bees, wasps, spiders, and hornets.

Along the thousands of miles of coastline, and especially in Wales and Cornwall, gulls can be bold and cunning. They may hover and dive-bomb innocent, cone-licking travelers like something out of an Alfred Hitchcock film.

Domestic Animals

Avid walkers in Great Britain will often encounter livestock and horses. The general rules are: Be aware of your surroundings. Move quietly and quickly past animals, but don't run. Never approach livestock, especially bulls or cows with calves. Leave gates as you find them. Keep dogs on a short leash. If cows, horses, or sheep block the path, you must wait for them to move or give them a wide berth.

Other Humans

I have hiked many miles solo and never felt threatened as a woman on my own. That said, it's better to have a buddy. When you cannot, make sure someone knows your designated route before setting out.

Tales of wolves and wizards intersect in the charming village of Beddgelert (Trail 39).

On the trail, English folks generally offer a friendly, but passing, greeting. In Wales and Scotland, stopping for a short chat is common.

POISONOUS PLANTS

There are many poisonous plants in the UK, but most are only harmful if ingested. Avoid "sampling," and educate yourself on some of the common poisonous varieties, including monkshood, deadly nightshade (with green or black berries), foxglove, lords-and-ladies (with green, red, or orange berries), poison hemlock, and yew (bright red berries). A handful of mushroom species are also deadly, so it's best to leave the wild fungi to the experts.

Many plants may cause skin irritation, but walkers are most likely to encounter stinging nettles, a weedy-looking plant with spiky green leaves covered in tiny "hairs." Brushing up against it will cause a sometimes-delayed burning sensation. They're annoying but critical for butterflies and caterpillars. Also steer clear of giant hogweed, tall with jagged leaves and umbrellas of small white flowers, whose sap can cause burns. There's no poison ivy in the UK, but the sap of English ivy can irritate sensitive skin.

HIKING GEAR

Dressing in layers is the way to go. In the mountains of Scotland, I can be comfortable in a T-shirt one minute and need a warm hat or raincoat the next. Rain jackets, waterproof pants, and gaiters for stream crossings are rarely deadweight in your pack. Sturdy, waterproof boots with good ankle support are a must, as is an extra pair of socks. Other useful items include a waterproof backpack cover, waterproof sacks (like the ones used for canoeing or kayaking) or resealable plastic bags for valuables, and walking sticks or trekking poles, which are particularly helpful on slippery rocks and mud. A light picnic blanket with a water-resistant side can also be handy. And always carry the Ten Essentials, a list developed by The Mountaineers—navigation tool(s), headlamp and extra batteries, sun protection, first-aid kit, knife and repair kit, matches or lighter, emergency shelter, and extra food, water, and clothes.

With your preparations complete, many astounding landscapes, rich in history and stunning scenery, await exploration. As G. M. Trevelyan, British historian and conservationist (who lived and taught at the University of Cambridge from 1927 to 1951), put it: "After a day's walk, everything has twice its usual value."

A NOTE ABOUT SAFETY

Safety is an important concern in all outdoor activities. No guidebook can alert you to every hazard or anticipate the limitations of every reader. Therefore, the descriptions of roads, trails, routes, and natural features in this book are not representations that a particular place or excursion will be safe for your party. When you follow any of the routes described in this book, you assume responsibility for your own safety. Under normal conditions, such excursions require the usual attention to traffic, road and trail conditions, weather, terrain, the capabilities of your party, and other factors. Conditions may have changed since this book was written that make your use of some of these routes unwise. Always check for current conditions, obey posted private property signs, and avoid confrontations with property owners or managers. Keeping informed on current conditions and exercising common sense are the keys to a safe, enjoyable outing.

—*Mountaineers Books*

HOW TO USE THIS GUIDE

These sixty-three walks are arranged geographically by region. Each begins with key information to help you evaluate whether it's a good match for you and your companions in terms of distance, elevation gain, difficulty, amenities, and more. Choose your destination using those highlights and other details on the at-a-glance table (after the table of contents). The walks also have general driving directions for reaching the trailhead and turn-by-turn descriptions featuring relevant points of interest. Finally, some hikes include an option for extending your journey.

KEY WALK INFORMATION

Each walk begins with key stats about the trail and other information to help you quickly evaluate its suitability for you and your companions.

Distance: The walk distance is listed in roundtrip miles, unless otherwise indicated.

Elevation Gain: This category lists the cumulative elevation gain in feet over the entire route.

High Point: This category identifies the highest elevation reached on the route. The value is rounded to the nearest ten unless the walk includes a specific summit or feature with a widely agreed upon elevation.

Rating: This subjective rating, on a scale of one to five stars, is based on the "wow" factor of a hike.

Difficulty: Each walk's difficulty, including overall strenuousness and any required routefinding, is ranked according to five categories: easy, easy to moderate, moderate, moderate to challenging, and challenging.

Year-round: This yes/no is based on whether or not a route can be walked in winter without specialized gear and knowledge of the terrain.

Family-friendly: This description gives a sense of whether the route is appropriate for children, along with potential hazards and on-trail or nearby attractions.

OPPOSITE: *Mist often shrouds the exhilarating approach to the base of Ben Nevis (Trail 60).*

Bath's lush, rolling landscape (Trail 19) is profuse with cheerful wildflowers and fragrant forests.

Dog-friendly: Each trail's suitability for dogs is listed, along with what limitations or restrictions are present.

Amenities: Here the comforts found at trailheads and along the way are listed, including whether or not there are restrooms, spots for food and beverages, and picnic tables. (Some restroom options are porta-potties. Whether or not they are open or clean can never be guaranteed.)

Map: This category identifies the best Ordnance Survey (OS) map available for each route.

Agency: The agency managing the land can provide useful general information (although very few provide detailed maps). Check the Resources section at the back of the book for the agency websites.

GETTING THERE

For each walk, this section covers directions to and GPS coordinates for the trailhead, public transit information, postcodes, and anything else special you need to know before setting out.

GPS: The coordinates for each walk's starting point are based on the World Geodetic System of 1984. In all cases, the latitude is a north value and the longitude is an east value when it is a positive number, and a south value and a west value when it is a negative one.

Postcode: The British equivalent of zip codes, these are often surprisingly specific, and can be paired with a map app to find driving directions to trailheads.

Driving: This field provides a general description of how to reach each walk's starting point by car, including the name of the relevant car park where applicable.

Public Transit: This category provides information for reaching a route's starting point by public transit (when possible).

Before You Go: This category lists important considerations before setting out on each hike, such as trail conditions or livestock potential.

TRAIL DESCRIPTION

The trail descriptions are broken into two sections: the featured trail highlighted on the map and options for extending your walk.

On the Trail: This section includes the main turn-by-turn trail directions, starting from the trailhead, including distances where helpful, as well as landmarks and other features along the trail. It also frequently shares interesting ecological, geological, and historical tidbits about the area.

Extend It: Some, but not all, walks include a suggestion for how to extend your journey.

MAPS

The maps included in this book are intended as an overview of each walk's route. They are not meant for on-the-ground navigation. Use the key stats at the beginning of each walk to gain a more detailed idea of what each route involves and, as always, carefully consider your own abilities. The Ordnance Survey map identified for a particular hike is the most definitive source for navigating on the trail.

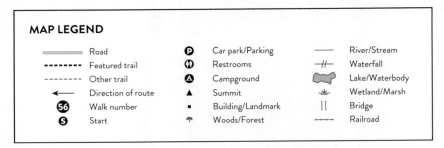

MAP LEGEND

═══	Road	**P**	Car park/Parking	——	River/Stream
- - - -	Featured trail	**WC**	Restrooms	–//–	Waterfall
- - - -	Other trail	**A**	Campground		Lake/Waterbody
←	Direction of route	▲	Summit		Wetland/Marsh
56	Walk number	▪	Building/Landmark	] [	Bridge
S	Start	♠	Woods/Forest	⊢——⊣	Railroad

NORTHERN ENGLAND

Northern England is dominated by the Pennines, an upland land mass with steep western slopes that abandon their fierceness as they dip gently to the east. The steep, rugged Cumbrian Mountains of the Lake District define the west, while farther east lie the sweeping valleys and windswept hilltops and moors of the Yorkshire Dales. The pace of life slows up here among ancient farms, drystone walls, and livestock herds. In the 1970s, England's most famous walker and guidebook author, Alfred Wainwright, plotted out the now classic, and still popular, 191-mile Coast to Coast Walk across northern England. "Give me a map of country I do not know and it has the power to thrill and excite me," he wrote. Indeed.

LAKE DISTRICT NATIONAL PARK

For *lake* country, this is an area of surprisingly diverse topography. It has its lake superlatives, of course, including both the largest natural lake in England (Windermere) and the deepest (Wastwater). Also, all English land 3000 feet above sea level or higher lies within the national park, including its highest peak, Scafell Pike (3209 feet). It's no wonder that British fell-walking ("fell" refers to a hill, mountain, or high common land) and mountaineering were born in this region of Cumbria. Romantic poet Samuel Taylor Coleridge actually launched the country's mountaineering movement in 1802 when he dragged himself up Broad Stand on Scafell (the Pike's slightly smaller neighbor at 3162 feet).

Get the lay of the land in the Lake District (Trails 1–5) by imagining a wheel with spokes emanating from its center—bands of elongated lakes (also called "meres") and stretches of peaks and valleys partitioning the area. Keep in mind that, because of those ups and downs, crossing from fell to fell takes more time than the bird's-eye mileage suggests. This highly varied terrain has an almost endless number of interesting

OPPOSITE: *The curved, limestone crag of Malham Cove (Trail 7) is equal parts calm and drama.*

walks along "becks" (streams), to "forces" (waterfalls), or even up to a "tarn" (small lake in a glacial cirque).

The area was first deposited as seabed sediment five hundred million years ago and then fortified by volcanoes and scoured by ice and water. Later it was uplifted, sculpted, and smoothed over time. That geological activity has resulted in the starkly beautiful, gently sloped valleys and razor-edged ridges that have drawn invaders, residents, and travelers for millennia. The 912-square-mile national park became a UNESCO World Heritage Site in 2017. Despite the 220 days per year that it rains (or snows), the Lake District remains a walkers' paradise with nearly 2000 miles of public footpaths and bridleways.

YORKSHIRE DALES NATIONAL PARK

While garnering less attention than the Lake District, this region (Trails 6–9) is, in many ways, equally captivating, with stark peaks, sheltered valleys, and historical villages. The 840-square-mile national park at the center of the Yorkshire Dales, designated in 1954, straddles the central Pennines. Often referred to as the "backbone of England," the Pennines isn't a mountain range, or even a chain, but a huge upland area characterized by steep western slopes (many forming the peaks in the Yorkshires) that slant gently eastward. Many walks through this dramatic scenery in the Dales follow the ancient tracks of traders and travelers along rambling rivers and across lonely moors. "And he had trudged through Yorkshire dales, / Among the rocks and winding *scars*; / Where deep and low the hamlets lie / Beneath their little patch of sky / And little lot of stars," wrote William Wordsworth in 1798.

1 CASTLE CRAG

This loop in the Borrowdale Valley features some of the most extreme and stunning scenery in the Lake District with a heart-pumping ascent, bewitching oak woodlands, and the tranquil flats of the River Derwent—plus there are caves!

Distance: 5.4 miles
Elevation Gain: 1210 feet
High Point: 951 feet
Rating: ★ ★ ★ ★
Difficulty: Moderate
Year-round: Yes
Dog-friendly: Yes, leashed

Family-friendly: Yes, but some steep sections with final push up Castle Crag traversing slate scree; short rock scramble near route's end with hand chain for balance
Amenities: Restrooms at car park; good picnic spots on Castle Crag and along River Derwent; refreshments at Longthwaite YHA hostel

Map: OS Explorer Map OL4, The English Lakes, North-Western Area

Agencies: Lake District National Park, National Trust

GETTING THERE

GPS: 54.514906°, -3.167178°
Postcode: CA12 5XN
Driving: From Keswick, take Borrowdale Road (B5289) south for 7.6 miles to the National Trust Seatoller car park on your right just past the bus stop sign.

Public Transit: Buses from Keswick stop in Seatoller.
Before You Go: This small car park is in a less crowded part of the Lake District, but still plan to arrive early to find a spot.

ON THE TRAIL

This walk has a bit of zigzagging for the first 0.7 mile. Go through the gate at the back (northeast) corner of the car park and start walking uphill. When the rocky track forks in about 300 feet, go left. In another 300 feet, before crossing the stream, take another left toward towering Scots pines. Follow the track 300 feet more to meet the west-east Coast to Coast Walk, the 182-mile route from the Irish Sea to the North Sea.

Take a sharp right and follow the trail for 0.3 mile as it curves left and heads west through a gate and a coppice. Climb above the glowing green fields and ancient stone walls of Seatoller, a village at the crossroads of two historical packhorse routes—Honister Pass from Buttermere and Sty Head Pass from Wasdale. This is the heart of the Borrowdale Valley, which runs for 10 miles from the high fells (including Scafell Pike, England's highest at 3209 feet) carrying the River Derwent north to Derwentwater. People have been drawn to this idyllic setting—forested crags, oak woods, and river flats—since prehistoric times, and its inhabitants and visitors have included Vikings, monks, and mountaineers. The best-selling 1916 Ward Lock travel guide declared it "the most beautiful valley in England, perhaps in Great Britain."

When the trail forks, veer left and follow this stretch over another stream, ignoring other trails branching right. The nearby village of Seathwaite is known as the wettest inhabited place in the country with double the rainfall of nearby areas. In this more mountainous swathe of Cumbria, rainfall generally exceeds six feet per year. Moisture-laden air blowing in from the Atlantic rises and forms clouds over the mountains, which lighten their load over the valley. Despite it being soggy much of the time, Seathwaite has been, for at least a century, one of the most popular access points for high peaks like Scafell Pike, Glaramara (2570 feet), and Great Gable (2950 feet).

Climb for 500 feet toward a gate at a T intersection where you'll go right onto the wider main track, an old mining road leading to the Honister Slate Mine. Its Westermorland green slate has been quarried since 1728, and some say the Romans cut this path even earlier to transport the unusual rock to coastal ports. Stay on this lush, bracken-lined trail for the next 0.8 mile to the large wooden footbridge spanning Tongue Gill. The crags on the uphill side are too steep even for sure-footed sheep, so

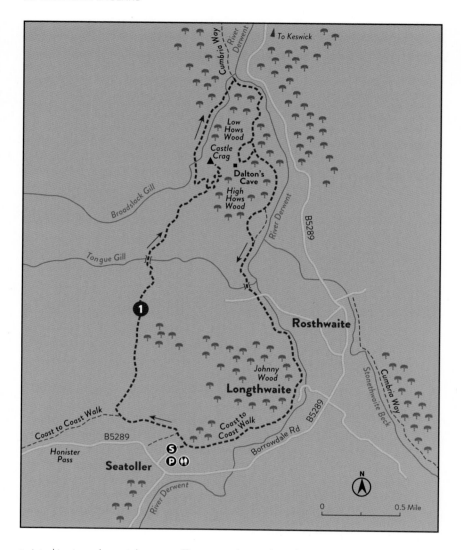

twisted junipers have taken over. They are a haven for many rare and threatened species of birds and insects.

Cross the stream and carry on for 0.3 mile until a minor trail leads off to your right. Look northwest for your first view down-valley at Derwentwater in the distance. (If this track looks too muddy or slippery, you can continue downhill on the main path to another trail a bit farther on.) Pass through a small wooded area and around a minor crag for 0.3 mile. Go over a ladder stile and turn right onto the main path.

From here Castle Crag's formidable shoulders of loose shale are visible. Follow the footpath up the switchbacks for about 500 feet to a clearing. Though technically not the peak, this is the best spot for looking down the valley toward the Lake District's hulking giants. On a clear day, the standouts are Glaramara due south, Great Gable to the southwest, and Scafell Pike, farther south.

To reach the true summit of Castle Crag, continue to a fork in the trail and go right. (The left track dead-ends at an abandoned quarry area where visitors now build stone towers.) Follow the trail past heather-clad rocks, through a carpet of emerald grasses, and beneath enormous Scots pines to the top. Castle Crag, once an ancient hillfort, is now marked by a war memorial and is the only so-called Wainwright below 1000 feet.

Alfred Wainwright, Britain's most famous fell-walker and guidebook author, documented 214 Lake District fells in a seven-volume guide. Wainwright included Castle Crag because it is, he said, "so magnificently independent, so ruggedly individual, so aggressively unashamed of its lack of inches."

Looking north from the summit, the island-studded lake, Derwentwater, dominates, with the town of Keswick and the magnificent fells as its backdrop. If it's clear enough, the stark bedrock massif of Skiddaw (3054 feet) is visible across the lake.

Retrace your steps off Castle Crag but, when you return to the stile at its base, stay on the wider track, walking along a drystone wall and through a lovely forest. From the summit it's a steep 0.3 mile off of the fell to the junction with the main trail. Go right on the main trail, continuing downhill with Castle Crag on your right and through a narrow slot in the valley. Over the next half mile, the rocky track follows Broadslack Gill and passes through a couple of gates.

Once you've reached the tree cover of High Hows Wood, go right at the fork, traveling over a small footbridge across a stream and then along a drystone wall. From that junction walk another 0.2 mile to where the trail ends at the Cumbria Way, a great spot to wander down to the riverside to look for otters. To continue, turn right onto the Cumbria Way and follow it along the River Derwent (a moss-covered wooden fingerpost indicates "Rosthwaite, 1¾ miles").

Over the next 0.5 mile, climb modestly into the trees above the wide, crystalline Derwent, which originates in the Lake District's high country and ultimately flows to the Irish Sea. This section squeezes through the gap between the steep sides of Castle Crag and its neighbor, Grange Fell (1360 feet).

The combination of weather and topography makes the Borrowdale Valley's flora and fauna distinctive, a lush remnant of the tropical rainforests that once blanketed western Britain. The rugged crags shelter peat hollows, and the steep fellsides are cloaked in Atlantic oaks. This part of the walk showcases Borrowdale's reputation as one of the areas in the Lake District with the most native tree species, including its

The dazzling Borrowdale Valley spans 10 miles from the Lakes' high fells to Derwent Water.

famous "hanging oak" woodlands that cling firmly to the sides of the valley. *Derwent* is Old Norse for the "river through the oak woods." Horse chestnut, birch, ash, wild cherry, and more also put on quite a show come autumn.

The climate also encourages a riot of mosses, lichen, liverworts, ferns, and fungi on the valley floor, some of which are considered old growth and are incredibly rare. Pockets of wetland have escaped draining for farmland, showcasing how the area would have looked following the last ice age. Many important specialized plants thrive here, including cotton grass and the fascinating insectivorous sundew, which traps insects with its sticky, spiky arms. Look up for buzzards (a type of hawk in the UK), ravens, and peregrine falcons. Among the trees, the black-and-white pied flycatcher sings a beautiful summer song. Keep an eye out, too, for the elusive, endangered red squirrel.

After that 0.5-mile stretch, carry on straight where the trail appears to divide. (If you have the energy, veer right to take a small, higher loop in the forest, which rejoins the present track.) The eastern flank of the fell harbors many caves, one of which lies nearly alongside the trail. It was the summer home of the self-appointed Professor of Adventure, Millican Dalton, who returned to the spot every year for more than four decades starting in 1903. He was a mountain guide who grew potatoes near the cave, foraged for nuts in the woods, and baked bread (and, apparently, was pretty popular with the ladies). Caveman Dalton was known to bob along the River Derwent to Keswick in a homemade raft to buy tobacco and coffee. His cave is actually two connected caves left over from slate quarrying. On the upper cave's rock he carved, "Don't waste words; jump to conclusions."

Not far beyond the caves, stay right where the trail splits and climb slightly above the river for 0.3 mile. When the paths reconnect, you'll emerge in a clearing. On one of my late summer hikes, a half-dozen large red deer ran across the fellside just as a steady rain started. In fall, the pushy stags can be heard bellowing for mates. Look out for roe deer as well, which are often seen in the woodlands.

The trail drops to hug the riverside lined with wildflowers and blackberry shrubs. Follow it for 0.8 mile (ignoring the path to your left over an impressive stone packhorse bridge) to the Longthwaite YHA (Youth Hostels Association) complex. Beyond that, the trail skims the edge of Johnny Wood, a temperate rainforest with scenery reminiscent of the US Pacific Northwest. Continue straight through forest and field before ending back at the car park.

EXTEND IT
From the junction of this route with the River Derwent, take the Cumbria Way north for a 1.5-mile out-and-back to the village of Grange.

2 HAWKSHEAD TO WRAY CASTLE

The Hawkshead area, set in the Vale of Esthwaite in the South Lakeland, is little touched by modern-day distractions. This easy walk takes in a landscape of gleaming hillsides and flowing valleys, ancient history and colorful folklore.

Distance: 6.9 miles
Elevation Gain: 350 feet
High Point: 320 feet
Rating: ★★★
Difficulty: Easy
Year-round: Yes
Family-friendly: Yes; big adventure play area at Wray Castle; Herdwick sheep and Belted Galloway cattle along the way

Dog-friendly: Yes, leashed near livestock
Amenities: Restrooms at car park; shops, restaurants, and hotels in Hawkshead; cafe, restrooms, benches, and picnic tables at Wray Castle
Map: OS Explorer Map OL7, The English Lakes, South-Eastern Area
Agencies: Lake District National Park, National Trust

GETTING THERE

GPS: 54.374063°, -2.997006°
Postcode: LA22 0NT
Driving: From central Ambleside, take A593 for 1.1 miles to Clappersgate, then left onto B5286 for 4 miles to Hawkshead. Once there, bear left onto B5285 for 0.2 mile to the Hawkshead car park on your right.

Public Transit: Buses run from Ambleside to the Tourist Information Centre in Hawkshead.
Before You Go: During or after significant rain, some sections of this trail can be very boggy.

ON THE TRAIL

Exit the west side of the car park and turn right (north) onto Main Street toward the center of Hawkshead. Take note of the Hawkshead Grammar School, located on the west side of Main Street near the car park, founded in 1585 and long known as the best school for many miles around. After their mother died in 1778, William Wordsworth and his brother were sent there for a free but exceptional "gentlemen's" education. In fact, he wrote his first surviving poems there. There's still a desk inside where naughty Will carved his name, alongside many others.

Walk 0.1 mile along the main drag past whitewashed cottages, cobbled court-yards, and quaint alleyways. Where the road appears to end, continue straight onto

the pedestrian path past the Queen's Head Inn. The center of the village is car-free, making it feel as if time stopped here several hundred years ago. It was around AD 900 that Vikings first settled in Hawkshead, which was named for the Norse warrior Haukr. They ruled for roughly 250 years before the monks of nearby Furness Abbey took over (these popular ruins have been visited by Queen Victoria and, as a boy, Theodore Roosevelt). Hawkshead later grew wealthy as a wool market in medieval times.

Just past the Red Lion Inn, make a right onto Red Lion Yard; there's a blue sign indicating "Wray Castle, 3 miles." Follow the road about 300 feet to the end and go through the wooden gate. Cautiously cross North Lonsdale Road to continue straight through another

Hardy, healthy cows have been a ubiquitous sight in the Lake District for centuries.

wooden gate. Follow the path (Black Beck Road) for roughly 500 feet as it curves right and then left around some houses, before narrowing between shrubs as it approaches Black Beck. Cross through the gate and over the stream on the footbridge, then follow the trail sharply left as it leaves the village. Keeping the stream to your left, walk about 250 feet until the path splits. Take the right branch onto a trail that runs along the edge of a field.

In 0.2 mile, go through a gate and turn left at the wooden fingerpost indicating "Wray Castle, 2 ¾ miles." The trail climbs slightly for a view of the surrounding hills, then dips again into a section lined with huge holly, oak, and larch trees. In 0.5 mile, go left at a T intersection and then veer left again, following the blue signs pointing toward Wray Castle. Follow the well-marked trail 0.1 mile through a meadow toward a wooded area, then veer left into Loanthwaite Coppice, which is carpeted with bluebells in the spring. Continue for 0.1 mile through an enchanting stretch of forest and hillside

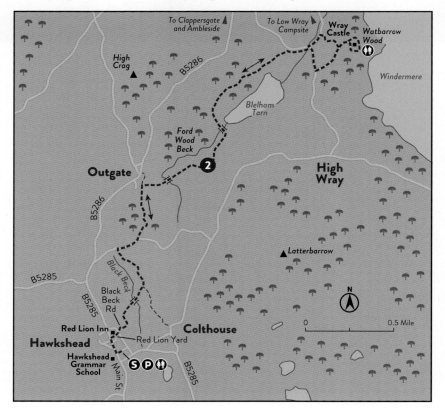

Mock-Gothic Wray Castle on its scenic perch above Windermere, England's largest natural lake

to another gate. Make a right where the sign indicates to head toward "Wray Castle, 2 miles."

For the next 0.5 mile the trail undulates over the hillside, crossing Ford Wood Beck on a footbridge. At this point you've climbed roughly 200 feet in elevation and there are lovely views of the nearby fells, including 800-foot Latterbarrow.

At the T intersection, go left (signed "Wray Castle, 1½ miles"). Ahead and to your right are excellent views of Blelham Tarn. The lake and surrounding bog are a national nature reserve and important for various species of fish (including brown trout and eel), grass, moss, and rare invertebrates. Waterfowl, including great crested grebe and whooper swan, flock to the area. Weave through woods and open meadow over the next mile before reaching a series of footbridges where you'll crisscross over Blelham Beck, which feeds Windermere, the Lake District's largest lake.

The trail reaches a T intersection at an unnamed paved road: take the right branch, which parallels the road, for 0.1 mile. Cross the road when it starts heading uphill to take the Low Wray Campsite road for about 450 feet. Before reaching the campsite, take the path to your right (northeast) through a small but dense set of trees. At the T intersection, turn left and walk another 300 feet to reach Wray Castle.

From the patio, there are stunning easterly views (even on a drenching day) over Watbarrow Wood and out to Windermere. The castle grounds include part of the lakeshore, which is accessible via a short, steep, and well-marked trail. This walk continues on a 0.2-mile clockwise loop around the castle.

The grounds are deceptively lush with sequoias, redwoods, ginkgo biloba, beech, and weeping limes. There's even a mulberry tree planted by Wordsworth in 1845. The castle itself is a curious gothic-revival structure finished in 1840 and almost comically crammed with towers and turrets, crosses and clocks. A retired surgeon from Liverpool built it with his wife's fortune; legend has it that upon setting eyes on it, she declared it "gaudy" and refused to live there!

The most interesting tenant may have been writer Beatrix Potter, whose family rented the estate in 1882 when she was sixteen years old. She reputedly fell in love with the serene setting and, later in life, bought much of the surrounding land (more on this in Trail 5). After completing the green, shady loop around the castle, retrace your steps back to Hawkshead.

EXTEND IT

Many miles of forest and shoreline trails in the area of Wray Castle include the 1-mile loop through Watbarrow Wood, which also gives fantastic views of Windermere.

3 THREE LAKES LOOP

Near the geographic center of the national park, this route takes in some of the Lakeland's best features including fellsides, waterfalls, historical villages, and, of course, lakes: Alcock, Grasmere, Rydal.

Distance: 7.6 miles
Elevation Gain: 1520 feet
High Point: 1220 feet
Rating: ★ ★ ★ ★ ★
Difficulty: Moderate
Year-round: Yes
Family-friendly: Yes; family-friendly beach at Rydal Water; be careful crossing and walking on roads

Dog-friendly: Yes, leashed
Amenities: Numerous restaurants, cafes, and shops in Grasmere; refreshments in Rydal; public restrooms at car park on Stock Lane
Map: OS Explorer Map OL7, The English Lakes, South-Eastern Area
Agencies: Lake District National Park, National Trust

GETTING THERE

GPS: 54.457561°, -3.025222°
Postcode: LA22 9PU
Driving: From Ambleside, take Lake Road (A591) northwest for 4.1 miles to Stock Lane (B5287). Follow it for 0.4 mile as it turns into Red Bank, and look for the Red Bank Road car park on your left.

Public Transit: Check the National Express and Stagecoach websites for buses to and within the Lake District.
Before You Go: Grasmere and Rydal are the epicenter of all things Wordsworth and thus full of "pilgrims." If the recommended parking is full, there are others close by.

ON THE TRAIL

Leave the car park the way you entered and go right on Red Bank Road. Make an immediate left onto Langdale Road and follow as it curves along the outskirts of Grasmere (the village), passing from pubs and inns to stone walls and open fields. Langdale turns into Broadgate before, in 0.5 mile, crossing the bridge over the rushing River Rothay, which replenishes both Grasmere (the lake) and Rydal Water.

Just after the bridge, follow the road, now called Swan Lane, for 0.2 mile as it curves right, and then carefully cross the A591. Bear to the right of the Swan Hotel to follow the narrow, paved road. Straight ahead, the heather-clad hills and craggy top of Stone Arthur (1650 feet) will be visible. Continue for 0.1 mile and, upon reaching a weathered wooden fingerpost indicating "Greenhead Gill, Alcock Tarn," go right. Follow this minor road for about 0.2 mile, first flanked by stone walls and then following Greenhead Gill, until the path reaches a large gate. Cross the gate to enter the fell and

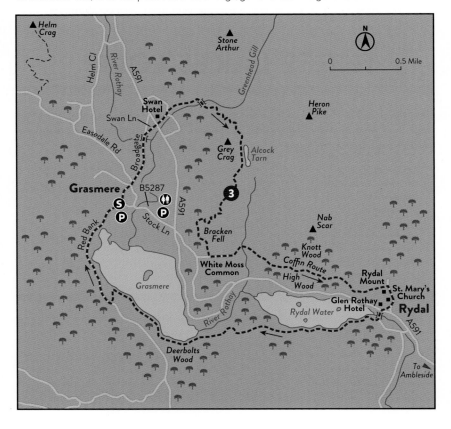

continue straight on the dirt track toward Alcock Tarn (1180 feet). In 0.1 mile, go right over the wooden footbridge crossing Greenhead Gill.

This is where the ascent begins up the western flank of Heron Pike (2010 feet). Ignore minor trails branching left to stay on the rocky, tree-lined trail that runs alongside a stone wall and then weaves up the hillside through crags, bracken, and heather. As you rise above the valley, the views expand—north is Stone Arthur, northeast is Greenhead Gill flowing from Great Rigg (at 2510 feet, Heron Pike's parent peak), northwest is Helm Crag (1329 feet), and west is the verdant Vale of Grasmere. Follow the trail as it rises nearly 750 feet over the next 0.7 mile and levels out through a boggy section near the lake.

Pass through the metal gate and head for the quiet shores of Alcock Tarn nestled in a clearing between the base of Heron Pike and top of Grey Crag. Even with sheets of rain coming down, the thick mosses, soft grasses, and still waters have a certain magic. Thomas West, a priest and historian who was one of the first writers to extol the Lakes' attractions, wrote in the mid-eighteenth century that "whoever takes a walk into these scenes. . . . And such exhibitions of sublime and beautiful objects, cannot but excite at once both rapture and reverence."

Skirt the lake along its western shore for 0.1 mile and head for the gap in the stone wall. From there, spectacular views open up to the south. Beyond Rydal Water, layers upon layers of dark, distant hills rush the horizon. Flowing streams glint from the highest of them, Loughrigg Fell (1100 feet). Follow the trail as it curves around the side of Grey Crag and then zigzags down 650 feet in elevation over 0.7 mile, ignoring many intersecting trails.

Pass through the gate at the entrance to Bracken Fell and make a left. This is a fairytale stretch of trail with towering pine and oak (long ago the area was a landscaped woodland garden complete with a manmade pond). Continue for 0.3 mile through the woods to a worn fingerpost. Go left on the tarmac road along the "Coffin Route to Rydal" as it passes tiny Whitemoss Tarn and then narrows into a dirt track. This is White Moss Common below Nab Scar (1490 feet), a mixed ancient woodland harboring diverse flora and fauna (including deer, badger, fox, and red squirrel) and little changed in the past few centuries. Dorothy Wordsworth (sister of William) wrote in her journal in June 1802: "This White Moss, a place made for all kinds of beautiful works of art and nature, woods and valleys, fairy valleys and fairy tarns, miniature mountains, alps above alps."

Continue along the rolling terrain of the Coffin Route for 1.4 miles, admiring the resident tarns and fells through openings in the woodland tunnels. This stretch is peaceful, despite its grim moniker. Coffin Route or Corpse Road (even worse!) was once literal, a route scraped into the hillside to transport the dead from Rydal to consecrated ground at St. Oswalds' graveyard in Grasmere. It was a route of sadness, no doubt, but also one of love and respect, with large trailside stones where pallbearers briefly set down coffins along the way.

Grasmere is a tranquil haven surrounded by countless spectacular fells.

When the trail ends at a paved road, go right and downhill toward Rydal Mount. From the ninth century or so, the prominent "mount" or mound was used to light beacon fires to warn residents of invaders. More recently it was home to the Wordsworths, from 1813 to 1850, and is still in the family. (The impeccable sixteenth-century Tudor cottage, 4-acre garden, and tea room host visitors.) Across the road is Rydal Hall, a fifteenth-century estate, now a holiday retreat and tea shop that is open and free to visitors.

After 0.2 mile you'll near the A591, with St. Mary's Church on your right. Go through the church gate to visit Rydal's Millennium Garden. From there, pass through to Dora's Field, named for Wordsworth's daughter (with Mary Hutchinson) who died an untimely death. The grieving father, along with family and friends, planted hundreds of daffodils as a memorial, and each year since, the daffodils and bluebells have emerged in the spring.

The poet's best-known work, "I Wandered Lonely as a Cloud," is also known as "Daffodils." In it he captures how even a recollection of sublime nature can soothe a pensive spirit. "I wandered lonely as a cloud / That floats on high o'er vales and hills, /

When all at once I saw a crowd, / A host, of golden daffodils; / Beside the lake, beneath the trees, / Fluttering and dancing in the breeze."

Exit Dora's Field through the gate along the A591 and go right. After about one hundred and fifty feet, cautiously cross the road at the Glen Rothay Hotel and follow the wooden fingerpost indicating "Rydal Water & Grasmere." Take the footbridge over the River Rothay, keeping an eye out for dippers, ducks, and herons, then bear right. Follow the path alongside the southern shore of Rydal Water, bearing right to stay by the lake edge whenever the trail forks.

The view over the open lake is dominated by Nab Scar to the north and, to the west, by the numerous high fells and crags that surround Grasmere like a horseshoe. This is a view that, in part, sparked ideas of conservation for public enjoyment. Preserving a place for its beauty was an unknown concept into the nineteenth century, but the Romantics, like Wordsworth, extoled the virtues of landscape beyond utilitarian purposes and brought a generation of (albeit privileged) people along with them. In his 1810 *Guide to the Lakes*, Wordsworth wrote, "In this wish, the author will be joined by persons of pure taste throughout the whole island, who . . . deem the district a sort of national property, in which every man has a right and interest who has an eye to perceive and a heart to enjoy." That concept ultimately spread throughout Great Britain and beyond, though the Lake District itself did not become a national park until 1951.

Follow the lakeshore for roughly 0.6 mile, passing through the Steps End Wood and along a gravel beach, with plenty of scenic spots to rest along the way. (Beware of beautiful but bold white swans with a taste for trail mix.) Continue straight ahead (west) as the trail climbs gently away from the lakeshore and follows a stone wall.

Roughly 0.8 mile after leaving the edge of Rydal Water, the trail reaches the outlet for Grasmere (lake). Follow the track for another 0.8 mile, first crossing through Deerbolts Wood and then dropping down to the shoreline. Enjoy views of the lake with its large, lonely island, a favorite landing spot of Wordsworth during the dozen-plus years he lived at Dove Cottage in Grasmere. He called the isle "the loveliest spot that man hath ever found."

Curve left away from the lake and climb gently to meet Red Bank road. Pass through the gate and turn right onto the road. Cautiously follow the narrow paved road (still with panoramic views of the Grasmere), past stone walls, historical cottages, and shady pastures, for 1 mile back to the car park.

EXTEND IT

Add an ascent to the Lion and Lamb rock formation on Helm Crag, the most well-known hill overlooking Grasmere. It adds roughly 4 miles round-trip and gains over 1100 feet in elevation. From Grasmere, walk up Easedale Road until the well-worn path to Helm Crag veers right.

4 HELVELLYN

This is a classic loop, done in reverse, to summit England's third-highest mountain, Helvellyn (3117 feet), along Swirral Edge and Striding Edge, arêtes on either side of the peak, which are exposed and require some moderate scrambling.

Distance: 8.5 miles
Elevation Gain: 2930 feet
High Point: 3117 feet
Rating: ★ ★ ★ ★
Difficulty: Challenging
Year-round: No
Dog-friendly: Yes, leashed; walk is exposed with major drops

Family-friendly: No
Amenities: Restrooms, restaurants, and cafes at car park; Red Tarn has level areas with big sitting rocks
Map: OS Explorer Map OL5, The English Lakes, North-Eastern Area
Agencies: John Muir Trust, Lake District National Park

GETTING THERE

GPS: 54.543922°, -2.950584°
Postcode: CA11 0PA
Driving: Glenridding can be reached on A592 from the north (Penrith) or the south (Windermere), and is 13 miles from both. The Beckside car park is next to the tourist information center, which is marked by a brown sign that is visible from the road.

Public transit: Buses run from Penrith and Windermere to Glenridding.
Before You Go: Glenridding is very popular, so arrive early if parking. This is also the starting point for the 20-mile Ullswater Way, which circumnavigates the lakeshore, passing historical bridges, waterfalls, and a castle.

ON THE TRAIL

Head east out of the car park, turn right along A592, cross the Glenridding Beck bridge, and then take another right onto the paved side road (signed toward "Helvellyn"). Walk down the road for about a tenth of a mile until it narrows between stone pillars and passes some homes on your right. At the road's end, continue on the dirt track alongside the stream for 0.4 mile as pastures, high moors, and craggy peaks come into view.

Cross over Mires Beck to reach a T intersection at a camping area. Go left (there's a stone sign in the wall indicating Helvellyn) and continue for 0.2 mile to pass through a gate with a wooden fingerpost that says "Helvellyn via Miresbeck." Instead of following the sign to your left, bear right away from the stream and head up the rocky track (this route ultimately emerges from the gate on your left at the end of the loop). Continue for 0.2 mile and bear left when the trail forks. In another 500 feet bear right when the trail forks again, ignoring the steep uphill route, to continue walking across the hillside.

Curve west-southwest past what is left of the huge Greenside Mine, where lead and silver were excavated for nearly two centuries until the mine closed in 1962 (there's now a youth hostel on its grounds). Past the mine, walking along the roaring waters of Red Tarn Beck, Helvellyn and Catstye Cam (2920 feet) first come into view. The pyramidal peak of Catstye Cam lies in the foreground, with the hulking shoulders of Helvellyn ("pale yellow moorland") looming behind it. Wainwright wrote of the lower hill, "If Catstycam stood alone, remote from its fellows, it would be one of the finest peaks in Lakeland. It has nearly, but not quite, the perfect mountain form with true simplicity in its soaring lines, and a small pointed top, a real summit that falls away on all sides."

Climb about 500 feet in elevation over 1.5 miles to cross a stream on a footbridge. Waterfalls and streams gush down the hillsides, channeling rainfall off the high, lush moors. Continue another 1.2 miles—gaining over 1050 feet in elevation—until the trail branches. Head left to rest a bit on the rock-lined northeast edge of Red Tarn, a large lake formed in the basin of a glacial cirque. Its clear waters are home to herring and trout, while its name is derived from the surrounding reddish scree. From there enjoy impressive views of a good chunk of the Helvellyn range, its 2000-foot peaks running

Walkers tackle Helvellyn's craggy Striding Edge with Red Tarn glinting below.

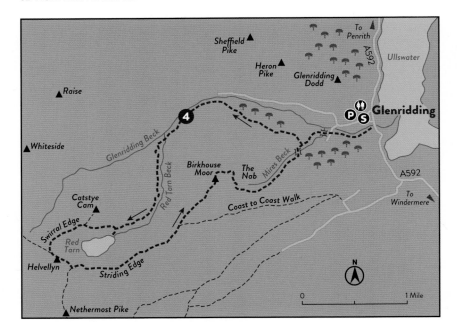

north-south for several miles. Like Helvellyn at its center, these high fells generally fall away to the east in rocky ledges and to the west as gradual, grass-covered slopes.

From the lake's edge there are a number of social trails leading back, but they can be quite boggy. Better to retrace your steps back to the main trail to continue on. From there it's another 350 feet of elevation gain over 0.4 mile to the intersection for the summit trail up Catstye Cam. Head left (west) up the Swirral Edge, one of the two arêtes that stretch and curve from the top of Helvellyn like chiseled, stony arms coming together to collect Red Tarn. The mountain's southern ridge, Striding Edge (your return route), can be seen across the lake.

The Swirral Edge stretches for 0.3 mile, with 350 feet of ascent, and while it's not technical, it does require some focus and scrambling, particularly on a section called The Fangs or during wind, rain, or fog. At the end of the rocky ridge, bear left to continue past the summit pillar to the peak 0.2 mile farther on, at a small cairn near a stone shelter. The summit is thrillingly exposed to the elements. On a clear day the panorama includes Lower Man (3035 feet) and Whiteside (2831 feet) to the north, Skiddaw (3064 feet) and Blencathra (2848) to the northwest, the lanky lake, Thirlmere, to the west, Ullswater and High Street (2717 feet) to the east, and Nethermost Pike (2923 feet) and Dollywaggon Pike (2815 feet) to the south. Roughly 10 miles to the southwest are the only two peaks in England higher than Helvellyn: Scafell Pike (3209 feet) and Scafell (3163 feet).

Continue along the summit plateau as it curves east-southeast toward the Striding Edge. In mist or fog, take care that you are on the steep but well-worn path as it starts to scramble along the razor's edge. Occasionally the trail veers left or right of the rocks, avoiding some of the steepest sections. From the summit, the trail drops about 930 feet over 1.4 miles before reaching a crossroads. Carry on straight along a rolling section for about a half mile over Birkhouse Moor (2356 feet), where Ullswater and the village of Glenridding will come into view.

Descend roughly 1500 feet over the next 1.2 miles along stone stairs and steep slopes. Continue straight as the trail meets and runs alongside Mires Beck, ignoring any trails branching off. Cross Mires Beck and then go through a gate to complete the loop. Turn right to retrace your steps 0.9 mile back to the car park.

EXTEND IT

To add the summit of Catstye Cam, take the trail to your right (instead of left up Swirral Edge) for a 0.5-mile, out-and-back that adds roughly 200 feet of ascent.

5 TARN HOWS

The 37-acre glacial lake and surrounding rocky knolls, emerald hills, and abundant woodland give this easy loop a fairytale feel.

Distance: 2 miles
Elevation Gain: 290 feet
High Point: 771 feet
Rating: ★ ★ ★ ★
Difficulty: Easy
Year-round: Yes
Family-friendly: Yes; path is wide and mostly level

Dog-friendly: Yes, leashed
Amenities: Restrooms at car park; plenty of benches along lake loop
Map: OS Explorer Map OL7, The English Lakes, South-Eastern Area
Agencies: Lake District National Park, National Trust

GETTING THERE

GPS: 54.387204°, -3.038963°
Postcode: LA21 8DP
Driving: Tarn Hows, with its one large car park, is roughly 2 miles northwest of Hawkshead on Oak Street.

Public Transit: Buses run from Coniston to Chapel Cottage via Kendal. Once in Chapel Cottage, walk 0.6 mile to Tarn Hows.
Before You Go: Parking fills up fast. The path can be mucky in spots after heavy rain.

ON THE TRAIL

From the north end of the car park, cross the road and follow the path as it curves right. When the trail splits three ways, bear left and downhill 0.2 mile to the lakeshore. This is the Cumbria Way, a 70-mile long-distance trail, spanning from Ulverston to Carlisle. Follow it along the shoreline through pockets of forest for 0.5 mile. Keep your eyes and ears perked for pied flycatchers, wood warblers, and a couple of woodpecker species.

If you're lucky you may even spot one of the Lake District's iconic and rare red squirrels (English excitement upon spotting one cannot be understated). The red squirrel is native to the UK, while grey squirrels were brought from North America in the 1800s. Competition preferred the interloper and, as a result, red squirrel numbers are perilously low. The Wildlife Trusts, a conservation organization, project that they could be gone from the wild in as little as a decade if not aggressively protected.

There's an unusually diverse selection of conifers and broadleaf trees around Tarn Hows (meaning "lake of rounded hills"), including larch, spruce, willow, cherry, sycamore, beech, and alder, which form a billowy lakeside canopy. That's because, despite its wild feel, the tarn and its environs are largely manmade. In Victorian times, landowner James Marshall built a dam to combine three smaller tarns into the one seen today. He also heavily landscaped it to highlight the beauty of the lakes and hills beyond; the conifers planted to protect the daintier deciduous species were never meant to stay. But before they could be felled, Marshall died. His bold vision endured in some ways, and was softened in others, over the next several decades.

When Marshall's family wanted to sell the land in 1930, it was eyed for major tourism development. Enter the famous children's author, Beatrix Potter, who had fallen in love with the area as a teenager. Many of her beloved stories, including *The Tale of Peter Rabbit*, were inspired by this magical, mythical countryside. Using the profits from her literary success, she first bought the nearby farmhouse and garden called Hill Top and then, twenty-five years later, Tarn Hows. Later, Potter sold or donated large sections of land to the National Trust, its current steward.

As the Cumbria Way branches to your left at mile 0.7, head right to stay alongside the lake. Continue along its northern edge where the tarn is fed by bogs and effusive rainfall channeled by nearby valleys. Ignore a trail that turns left off the main track at mile 0.8 but, when you reach a second fork in another 200 feet, veer left and head uphill into a wooded area. Continue for 0.5 mile and, through the trees, past smaller Rose Castle Tarn, which feeds the main lake. When the trail forks, take the higher track to your left.

Follow the hilltop and climb into a clearing. From there, it's about 0.2 mile and 100 feet of elevation gain to an overlook marked by a couple of boulders. The views are incredible, with forests, crags, and fells extending to the horizon in mellow waves, defying the manicured history of the lake. On a clear day some of the high peaks are also visible—like Wetherlam (2500 feet) to the northwest and even Helvellyn (3118 feet),

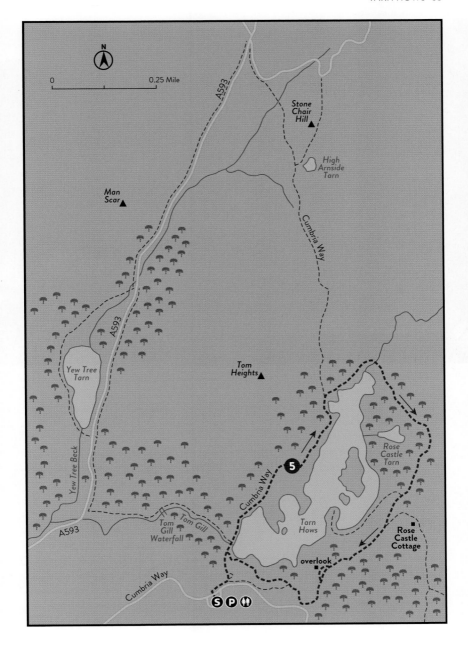

N

0   0.25 Mile

A593

Stone Chair Hill ▲

High Arnside Tarn

Man Scar ▲

Cumbria Way

A593

Yew Tree Tarn

Tom Heights ▲

Yew Beck

Cumbria Way

Rose Castle Tarn

5

A593

Tom Gill Waterfall

Tom Gill

Cumbria Way

Tarn Hows

Rose Castle Cottage

overlook

Cumbria Way

Ⓢ Ⓟ ⑪

The placid waters and diverse woodland of Tarn Hows have soothed visitors for centuries.

nearly 10 miles north. In 1872, guidebook writer George Dixon wrote of this view: "Tarn Hows set wildly amongst the larches and heather slopes, more like a Highland loch than any other water in Lakeland."

Continue past the overlook for 0.1 mile to where the path meets the main road, then veer right and head sharply downhill. Keep right at the many crisscrossing trails over the next 0.3 mile, and you'll return to the first junction on the lakeshore. Retrace your steps back up to the car park.

EXTEND IT

Add 2.8 miles with a side trip to Yew Tree Tarn. After reaching the intersection along the lake at mile 0.1, take the left branch, heading west and then north along Tom Gill. Carefully cross A593 when you reach the bottom of Yew Tree Tarn, cross Yew Tree Beck, then turn left at the intersection to follow the western edge of the lake. Keep heading north to reach the Cumbria Way. Take a sharp right—again crossing over the A593—to follow the Cumbria Way south until it intersects with the main trail around Tarn Hows.

6 PEN-Y-GHENT

Pen-y-ghent (2280 feet), which means "hill of the winds" in Welsh, is the lowest of the Yorkshire Three Peaks but not necessarily the easiest, requiring some light climbing and scrambling to achieve its tremendous views.

Distance: 6.5 miles
Elevation Gain: 1630 feet
High Point: 2280 feet
Rating: ★ ★ ★ ★ ★
Difficulty: Moderate to challenging
Year-round: Yes
Amenities: Restrooms in car park; benches and shelters on summit

Family-friendly: Yes, but light scrambling near summit; use extra caution on spur trail to Hull Pot
Dog-friendly: Yes, leashed near livestock
Map: OS Explorer Map OL2, Yorkshire Dales, Southern & Western Areas
Agency: Yorkshire Dales National Park

GETTING THERE

GPS: 54.148717°, -2.295598°
Postcode: BD24 0HF
Driving: From Settle, follow Duke Street (B6480) for 0.3 mile, then go right on Langcliffe Road (B6479). Continue north 5.9 miles to Horton-in-Ribblesdale car park on the left.
Public Transit: Horton-in-Ribblesdale is a stop on the Settle–Carlisle railway line, with trains coming from Leeds and Carlisle. A bus from Settle stops in the village center.
Before You Go: Arrive early, as this car park fills up fast in the summer and early fall. Dress in layers. While this loop can be done in either direction, the one listed here has a steeper ascent and more gradual descent.

ON THE TRAIL

Head out of the car park and go right on the sidewalk alongside B6479. Walk about a tenth of a mile, following the road as it curves left and passes St. Oswald's Church, then turn left on the second road. Pass a school at 0.4 mile before turning onto a paved path that follows a stream, Horton Beck, through a tunnel of trees. Walk 0.5 mile until you reach a footpath on your left signed to Pen-y-ghent, just before the stone buildings of Brackenbottom Farm.

Head up the wide dirt trail as the landscape opens up to many miles of grazing fields, drystone walls, and stone farm buildings. Climb more than 900 feet, crossing several gates, over the next 1.4 miles. Turn left at the fifth gate, a T intersection, and follow the famous Pennine Way to the summit. From here, the "crouching lion" profile of Pen-y-ghent is visible on a clear day.

The mountain is carboniferous limestone topped with millstone grit. It has a distinctive domed cap and curious lines down its flanks, as if a tidy giant scraped the sides of

Thousands of miles of dry stone walls, like these below Pen-y-ghent, are a distinctive feature of the Yorkshire Dales.

the mountain with a rake. It is instead the result of a tremendous storm in the summer of 1881 when runoff removed much of the topsoil on the hill's southern side. The contrast of grey and green, smooth and rocky, make the mountain appear a more daunting climb than it is.

Make the final push to the summit, gaining another 500 feet or so over the next 0.5 mile. Limestone steps dominate this stretch as you wind your way among bands of rock on steep switchbacks. (These can be quite slippery when wet!) Reach a large boulder field with some rocks to negotiate, as well as slabs of limestone pavement; after this, the steepest part of the climb is behind you. At the top there are stone benches and shelters, and a summit pillar.

If the clouds are high, miles of moorland, valleys, fells, hills, and peaks are visible. Pen-y-ghent forms part of a whaleback ridge—a long, elongated hill shaped like a whale's back—that includes Plover Hill (2230 feet) to the northeast, Ingleborough (2370 feet) to the west, and Whernside (at 2420 feet, the highest spot in Yorkshire) to the northwest. The ridge also functions as a watershed divide; rainfall here flows east to the North Sea and west to the Irish Sea.

Past the pillar on the summit, use the stone steps (also known as a stile) that lead over a low rock wall. Follow the worn wooden fingerpost indicating "Pennine Way, Yorkshire Three Peaks," which heads steeply downhill on the limestone slab steps descending the western side of the mountain. Ignore the paths branching right, and in 0.5 mile take a left at the fingerpost indicating "Pennine Way, Horton-in-Ribblesdale."

Follow a more gradual descent through heather and bracken for 0.7 mile, then pass through a gate and continue straight (west) along the path. In 0.3 mile, cross through another gate and look for a spur trail heading right toward Hull Pot (fingerpost indicates "Foxup"). If you don't mind an extra 0.5-mile out-and-back on level terrain, it's well worth a look. Follow the dirt and grass track to the edge of Hull Pot and continue around its perimeter (use extra caution in mist or fog). Hull Pot measures 300 feet by 60 feet and, at 60 feet deep, is the largest natural hole in England. It's formed by Hull Pot Beck flowing off Plover Hill and percolating through and beneath porous limestone which, over time, collapses. After a heavy rain, it makes for an impressive waterfall. The permeable nature of the limestone in this part of England also means there is a vast network of caves beneath your feet (eek).

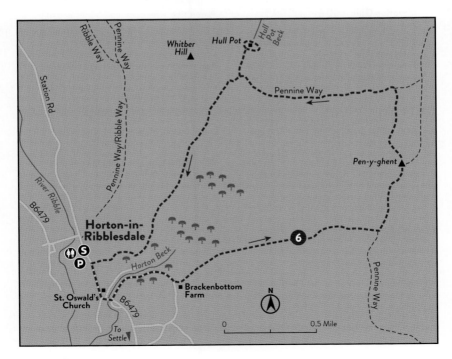

Retrace your steps back to the Pennine Way and continue toward Horton-in-Ribblesdale for 1.6 miles, passing through several gates along the way. Pause for views of Pen-y-ghent to your left across limestone-studded fields and stone walls flanking the wide dirt trail. Head right at B6479 to retrace your steps 0.1 mile to the car park.

EXTEND IT

Take the Three Peaks challenge by adding Ingleborough and Whernside to the day's itinerary. This well-signed, 24-mile route takes roughly twelve hours.

7 MALHAM COVE

Explore a post-glacial landscape of cliffs and dales amid tranquil, ancient countryside in Yorkshire Dales National Park.

Distance: 3.5 miles
Elevation Gain: 600 feet
High Point: 1020 feet
Rating: ★ ★ ★ ★ ★
Difficulty: Moderate
Year-round: Yes
Family-friendly: Yes, but take extreme care above Malham Cove

Dog-friendly: Yes, leashed near livestock
Amenities: Restrooms and picnic area at Malham National Park Centre
Map: OS Explorer Map OL2, Yorkshire Dales, Southern & Western Areas
Agencies: Yorkshire Dales National Park, National Trust

GETTING THERE

GPS: 54.060087°, -2.152796°
Postcode: BD23 4DA
Driving: Malham is most often reached from Settle, roughly 7 miles to the west, or Skipton, 11 miles southeast. The national park center is on your left as you enter the village.

Public Transit: Trains run regularly to Skipton, where a bus goes to Malham.
Before You Go: The wealth of routes and spectacular sites make Malham one of the most popular areas in the Yorkshire Dales. Arrive early to beat the crowds.

ON THE TRAIL

Walk east to exit the car park and turn left on Chapel Gate, heading toward the village of Malham. Pass the Malham Smithy (a traditional blacksmith's forge that is, today, untraditionally run by a woman) and several attractive eighteenth-century stone buildings, now cafes and hotels. Within about a tenth of a mile of the national park center, the road forks: take the right branch—Finkle Street—and follow it to cross over Malham Beck. A few hundred feet from the stream, a wooden fingerpost on your left indicates "Malham Cove, ¾ mile." Follow the stone walls in that direction for a few hundred feet

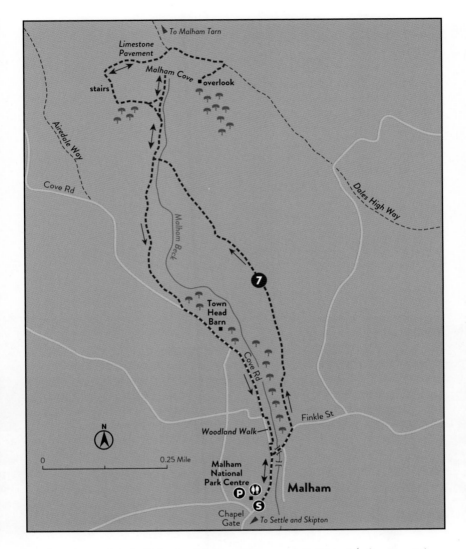

to where the track forks. Take the right branch onto a wide dirt trail (a fingerpost there says "Public footpath"). The path narrows and passes through a wood gate, entering National Trust land that is signed, "Malham Cove Fields."

Walk uphill along a grassy track for 0.5 mile, crossing several more gates. The ascent is modest, roughly 100 feet or so, but it still allows for stunning views of the valley's endless green folds divided by countless stone walls. When the trail forks, bear left (the right branch requires wayfinding across meadows to rejoin the main trail and, in my case once, a lengthy cow delay). Within a few hundred feet, the track crosses Malham Beck on stepping stones, joining up with the main route to Malham Cove. Turn right (north) toward the impressive stone alcove.

Follow the stream 0.2 mile into the cove, a tree-sheltered oasis inside an amphitheater of massive limestone walls roughly 1000 feet wide. Pass through the wooden gate, watching below for slippery stones and above for rock climbers tackling some of the Dales most popular routes.

The limestone, rising 260 feet above the streambed, is an impressive sight that's been captivating writers, artists, and tourists for centuries. For the *General Evening Post* in 1779, Adam Walker wrote, "This beautiful rock is like the age-tinted wall of a prodigious castle; the stone is very white, and from the ledges hang various shrubs and vegetables, which with the tints given it by the bog water . . . gives it a variety that I never before saw so pleasing in a plain rock." Thirty years later, William Wordsworth wondered, "Was the aim frustrated by force or guile, / When giants scoop'd from out the rocky ground— / Tier under tier—this semicirque profound?"

The Great Scar Limestone above Malham Cove holds many fossil corals, shells, and sea lilies.

Ultimately, it was not giants but ice and water that formed Malham Cove at the end of the last ice age, some ten thousand to fifteen thousand years ago. Retreating glaciers dissolved to roaring rivers that eroded the cliff's limestone into the shape seen today. Look for where Malham Beck, which flows through the village, springs from a cave at the foot of the cove.

Retrace your steps back along Malham Beck for roughly 300 feet and take the trail that curves right, following it to merge with another trail (a section of the Pennine Way) heading west. Start up a flight of 400 stone stairs that ascend about 200 feet over 0.3 mile. When you pause for a breather, look for nesting birds, including house martins, jackdaws, and peregrine falcons.

At the top of the stairs, take a hard right to walk east along the top of the cove, taking care on the eroded limestone pavement. This karst landscape is another remnant of scouring ice that swept away soil and exposed underlying limestone to the elements. Over time, rainwater snuck into cracks and dissolved the calcium carbonate of which limestone is made to form grykes (deep crevices) and clints (flat blocks). The microclimate here supports rare plants species; look carefully for ferns, berries, and rare wildflowers growing in the fissures.

Curve around along the cliff's edge for 0.4 mile to an overlook on the east side of the cove. Take extreme care near the edge as you enjoy excellent views into Malham Cove, down the valley to the village of Malham, and uphill toward the higher cracks and crags of Dry Valley. The surreal look of the limestone pavement has attracted many fans over the centuries. Most recently, Harry and Hermione sat atop the limestone in the film version of *Harry Potter and the Deathly Hallows: Part 1*. (Harry also camps in Malham Cove, which is forbidden for Muggles.) From here, you can pick up the challenging 90-mile Dales High Way, which spans the high country of the Yorkshire Dales from West Yorkshire to Cumbria with nearly 14,000 feet of ascent (but that's for another day).

Retrace your steps back to the staircase, although if you're tired of the limestone pavement, there is a somewhat flatter, more predictable track slightly to your right that also leads to the steps. Head down to Malham Cove, then to the bridge across Malham Beck. Instead of crossing the bridge, continue straight (south), crossing three gates over 0.5 mile on your way across the National Trust's Malham Tarn Estate.

Arrive at Town Head Barn just after the third gate. Inside the converted eighteenth-century barn is a museum with information about the nature and conservation efforts of the area. Continue along Cove Road for 0.2 mile to a fingerpost on your left indicating a "Permissive Footpath" that leads through a lovely, lush stretch of trail called the "Woodland Walk." Follow the trail as it runs alongside Malham Beck for 0.2 mile, and exit the woods. Continue straight for 300 feet until Cove Road joins Chapel Gate, then retrace your steps through the village and back to the car park.

EXTEND IT

From the turnaround point above Malham Cove (1020 feet), there is a well-worn route heading north up the Dry Valley for roughly 1.7 miles to the foot of Malham Tarn (1240 feet), Britain's highest marl (mudstone) lake, rich with aquatic life in a stunning setting.

8 GORDALE SCAR & JANET'S FOSS

The stark scale of Gordale Scar has mystified, and even frightened, centuries of visitors, but there's nothing to fear on this easy amble through verdant valley and lush forest to a magnificent gorge.

Distance: 4 miles
Elevation Gain: 400 feet
High Point: 1020 feet
Rating: ★ ★ ★ ★
Difficulty: Easy
Year-round: Yes
Family-friendly: Yes; hunting for fairies and fossils is highly recommended

Dog-friendly: Yes, leashed
Amenities: Restrooms and picnic area at Malham National Park Centre
Map: OS Explorer Map OL2, Yorkshire Dales, Southern & Western Areas
Agencies: Yorkshire Dales National Park, National Trust

GETTING THERE

GPS: 54.060087°, -2.152796°
Postcode: BD23 4DA
Driving: Malham is most often reached from Settle, roughly 7 miles to the west, or Skipton, 11 miles southeast. The national park center is on your left as you enter the village.

Public Transit: Trains run regularly to Skipton, where you can take a bus onward to Malham.
Before You Go: Malham is a popular stepping-off point for many hikes, and parking is limited.

ON THE TRAIL

Take a left from the National Park Centre to head toward the center of Malham. In 0.2 mile, just before reaching the Malham Smithy, go right alongside a stone building to join the Pennine Way (a wood sign points the way to Janet's Foss). Cross Malham Beck on the stone footbridge and turn right. Follow the stream on a dirt and flagstone track for about a quarter of a mile toward rolling green hills. Cross through a gate and head left on the Riverside Path at a fingerpost indicating "Janet's Foss, 1 mile."

After passing through several gates over the next 0.8 mile, the trail enters a surprisingly dense five-acre forest made up of Wedber Wood, Little Gordale Wood, and

Darwin wrote that rock features like Yorkshire's Gordale Scar conceal well the drama of past events.

Stone Bank Wood. Follow the rolling beckside path, shaded by leafy canopies that hide singing wagtails, warblers, and chiffchaffs, and carpeted with bluebells and wild garlic in the spring, through limestone crags thick with ferns and moss. In 0.3 mile veer right to Janet's Foss. "Foss" is a Nordic word for waterfall, and this one was named for the queen of the fairies who, according to legend, lives in a cave behind the curtain of water. The falls are formed by Gordale Beck, which plunges over a smooth limestone terrace and drops roughly 20 feet into a crystalline pool below. Get as close as you like to the grotto, but be careful on the slippery rocks. (Some people even take a dip in the cold waterfall!)

Rejoin the trail and continue through a wood gate to exit the woods. Turn left onto Gordale Lane, a narrow paved road, and walk for 0.1 mile to Gordale Bridge. When you reach the Gordale Scar campsite, turn left (northeast) and pass through a gate to join a path running alongside the campers (a fingerpost indicates "Gordale Scar, ½ mile"). This is also where this route intersects the 90-mile Dales High Way.

Follow the stream as the grass-and-rock knolls on either side start to close in. The trail stays level, but over the next 0.5 mile, the surrounding terrain becomes more extreme, with cliffs flanking the path like huge layer cakes made of stone. Round a curve, and Gordale Scar comes into view. The dark rock, 300 feet high in spots, is studded with iridescent green moss and spongy brown tufa, products of the limey water pouring over the rock ledges. The gorge glistens with three tiers of waterfalls.

It may be this labyrinthine approach, in part, that has made this a storied chasm over the centuries. The surreal, knobby limestone overhanging some parts of the trails troubled writer Thomas Gray, who visited in 1769 and would later popularize Gordale Scar with his writing. If he believed good fairies dwelled in the nearby woods, he may have thought this gash was the domain of mischievous goblins. "I stayed here (not without shuddering) a quarter of an hour, and thought my trouble richly paid, for the impression will last for life," Gray wrote.

Renowned artist J. M. W. Turner was drawn to the Malham area twice, in 1808 and 1816, and set up his easel where you're now standing (some of his sketches and paintings of the area are in the Tate Gallery in London). Both he and William Wordsworth saw Gordale Scar as one of England's greatest natural wonders. "Let thy feet repair to Gordale-chasm, terrific as the lair / Where the young lions couch," Wordsworth wrote in 1819.

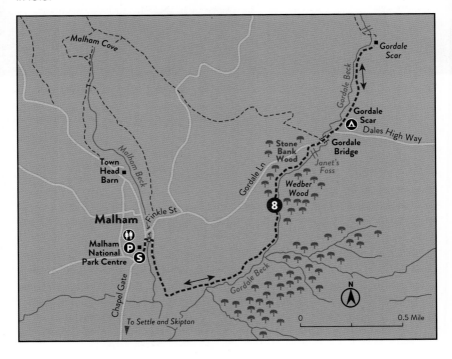

The mile-long scar is at the north end of a 22-mile-long geological fault line called the Craven Fault. The limestone here, carved by ice and water, is made up of the remains of tropical sea creatures that lived three hundred million years ago, making it a great spot to look for fossils imbedded in the cliff walls. When you're finished, retrace your steps to return to Malham.

EXTEND IT

From the turnaround point, look for people picking their way up the rocks and waterfalls. A popular 7.5-mile loop ascends Gordale Scar, cutting across the beck in the process, and heads 2 miles northwest along a well-marked trail to Malham Tarn, a large glacial lake. From there, the loop continues south to the limestone pavement and rock amphitheater of Malham Cove, finishing in the village of Malham. (See Trail 7 for more information.)

Gordale Beck gushes to form several wild waterfalls in a steep limestone ravine.

9 LANGSTROTHDALE RIVERSIDE WALK

Get far from the madding crowd on this riverside walk that climbs above one of the area's iconic dales for views of the glaciated valley.

Distance: 6.2 miles
Elevation Gain: 700 feet
High Point: 1140 feet
Rating: ★ ★ ★ ★
Difficulty: Easy to moderate
Year-round: Yes

Family-friendly: Yes; plan to explore natural pools along river
Dog-friendly: Yes, leashed
Amenities: Upscale pub at The George Inn in Hubberholme

Map: OS Explorer Map OL30, Yorkshire Dales, Northern & Central Areas

Agencies: Yorkshire Dales National Park, National Trust

GETTING THERE

GPS: 54.213025°, -2.166721°
Postcode: BD23 5JJ
Driving: From Kettlewell, follow B6160 3.5 miles west to Buckden, then bear left onto Dubbs Lane, which leads to Stubbing Lane. Continue for 3.7 miles to the tiny hamlet of Deepdale. Look for the small parking area on your left (just before the bridge and village).

Before You Go: The trail is largely grassy and can be muddy or slick in the rain.

ON THE TRAIL

Cross the small Deepdale Bridge (the first road bridge built across the River Wharfe) and take an immediate right to join what the fingerpost calls "Dalesway Footpath to Yockenthwaite." You're on the 80-mile-long Dales Way (not to be confused with the Dales High Way, another long-distance walking route in Yorkshire), which passes through the heart of Yorkshire Dales National Park and the foothills of the southern Lakeland.

Over the next 0.2 mile pass through two gates, and after the second, cross the rocky Deepdale Gill on a footbridge. Follow the well-signed trail for 0.8 mile as it edges pastures (never trampling the would-be hay in the middle) and through several gates with views of the tranquil, tree-studded valley.

This is Langstrothdale, which translates from Old English as "long marsh" or "marshy ground," one of the smaller, but deeper, valleys in the Dales. The "chase," or land, that flanks the river is now moorland and pastureland, but, as the name implies, it used to be hunting ground for medieval noblemen. Where this glacial-carved valley was once covered with trees and wildlife, it's now mainly stone buildings, hay meadows, drystone walls, and a charismatic river.

The River Wharfe originates close to the beginning of this walk, where two streams flow into the hamlet of Beckermonds. Rainfall on the high moors, which form the steep sides of the valley, flows into the becks and gills (such as Deepdale Gill) that drain into the river continuously. Look out for agile dippers and colorful kingfishers along the riverbanks.

Just before reaching Yockenthwaite, the trail dips slightly to a "lip path" alongside the river. Here you'll come across the Yockenthwaite Stone Circle, a rock ring 25 feet in diameter made up of 24 limestone boulders. This is believed to be the perimeter of a burial mound from the Bronze Age. A bit farther on, the trail along the riverbank is dominated by limestone pavement, or flat rocks that make for great picnic spots. The name Wharfe means "fast-flowing," and that's partly true on this stretch, as the river alternates between rapids, gentle cascades, and placid pools.

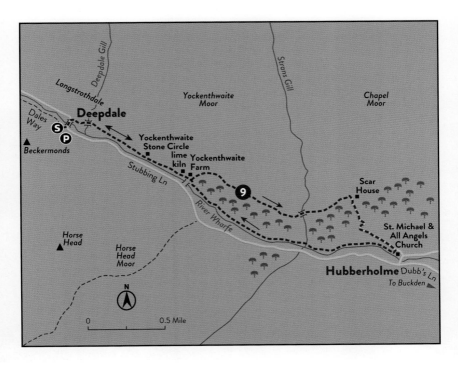

Head toward the tall trees that border Yockenthwaite, pausing at the ruins of a fine lime kiln among moss and bracken. Originally, the area's high acidity made for poor grazing, so farmers "sweetened" the meadows with lime. In June, these meadows are a riot of wildflowers (some of which are left uncut for scientific research) until hay-cutting begins in July.

Walking beside limestone boulders, and beneath ash, hazel, and hawthorn, you'll see the Yockenthwaite pack bridge to your right, an impressive, single-span stone bridge. For centuries, cargo was transported along this former packhorse route from Lancaster to Newcastle upon Tyne. Named for the farming hamlet of Yockenthwaite, this unusual moniker in Scandinavian means "Eoghan's clearing in a wood." Centuries ago, Norsemen overtook Yorkshire in large numbers (they captured the city of York in 866 and made it their capital), and many Nordic names endure from that time.

Reach Yockenthwaite at 1.1 miles and look among the farm buildings for a left turn heading uphill at a sign marked "Cray, 3 miles." Follow a gravel farm road for 200 feet, then turn right at another wood fingerpost indicating "To Hubberholme and Cray." Gradually ascend above Yockenthwaite, gaining views of Horse Head Moor to the southwest and Yockenthwaite Moor to the north.

The fast-flowing River Wharfe, lined with trees, grasses, and limestone, gives the steeply sloped valley a remote, untouched feel.

In 0.2 mile, leave the wide, gravel track and bear right to pass through a gate. Follow the direction of the sign pointing toward "Hubberholme and Cray." The trail narrows, and for the next three-quarters of a mile, you'll trek through fields of tall grass, bracken, and old stone dwellings and walls kept company by a few towering ash trees. After passing through several gates, cross a stone footbridge over Strans Gill, a narrow ravine with low limestone cliffs shaded by sycamores.

From Strans Gill descend slightly over the next 0.5 mile. Go right at the sign indicating "Hubberholme" and pass by Scar House, an impressive seventeenth-century structure visited by George Fox, the founder of the Quaker movement, in 1652 (now a National Trust vacation rental). Carry on downhill on a gravel road, losing about 300 feet over the next 0.6 mile.

A wooden fingerpost on your right indicates "Dales Way, Yockenthwaite" just before Hubberholme. This is your route back, but first take a few minutes to see the small, old village, which consists of St. Michael and All Angels Church, and the George

Inn. The village, which is pronounced "Ubberham" by locals, reputedly takes its name from Hubba the Berserker, a Viking chieftain. It's an unusually fearsome (and comical) connection for such a tranquil, remote-feeling spot.

The typical Norman-style church dates from the early eleventh century and is famous for its rare rood loft, where a cross is displayed. During overzealous religious "reforms" of the mid-sixteenth century, most rood lofts were destroyed as objects of idolatry. Somehow this one survived, with its intricate carvings and even its original paint. The mice carved in the wooden pews are another curiosity.

When you're ready, rejoin the trail. Keep the church on your left and walk 1.6 miles along the gleaming river, through several gates, back to Yockenthwaite. Pick up the same trail you took from Deepdale and retrace your steps to the parking area.

EXTEND IT
Add Horse Head Moor by crossing the river from Yockenthwaite, walking up Stubbing Lane for roughly 0.2 mile, and following the steep uphill track (signed toward Halston Gill) across a wide open area called the Hagg. It's about two miles one way to the pillar on Horse Head and, on a clear day, there are views of the Dales's three peaks: Whernside, Ingleborough, and Pen-y-ghent.

CENTRAL ENGLAND

The middle of the country offers unexpected variety, from the limestone valleys and lonely moors of the Peak District to the fairytale villages and lazy rivers of the Cotswolds. Dramatic landscapes, rich history, and plentiful walks make mid-England an explorers' paradise.

PEAK DISTRICT NATIONAL PARK

The "Peaks," as it's known locally, is a misleading moniker because the Peak District (Trails 10–15) has no mountains, technically speaking. A popular theory is that the area was named for an Anglo-Saxon tribe that once lived there—the Pecsaetan—but no one knows for sure. Still, there are ample high points to summit, ranging from 800 to 2000 feet in elevation.

The Peak District was Britain's first national park, created in 1951 to protect 555 square miles. People have lived at least seasonally in the area for ten thousand years. Some twenty-eight thousand people currently live within the park boundaries, which is home to working farms, mines, and quarries. Another twenty-five million people live within an hour's journey of the Peak District, which leads to its high levels of visitation—more than thirteen million per year explore the park.

At the same time, the Peaks can surprise you with untamed moments. Look to the sky and you might catch a glimpse of the sickle-shaped wings of a peregrine falcon dropping off some gritstone edge (never mind your camera; falcons can dive at more than 200 miles per hour).

THE COTSWOLDS & OXFORD

If anywhere could be described as "classic" English countryside, this is it. Here in west-central England (Trails 16–21), there are undulating pastures, mature woodlands,

OPPOSITE: *The shady recesses of Buckholt Wood (Trail 18) in the Cotswolds have enchanted visitors for thousands of years.*

enchanting churches, grand homes, and postcard-worthy villages. Its human history is long and rich with Romans, Vikings, and Saxons, along with their many battles. But, more than anything, its legacy is sheep. In the thirteenth century there were half a million of them grazing the Cotswold Hills. (A "cot" is a sheep enclosure and a "wold" is a rolling hillside.) By the seventeenth century it had grown into a landscape of wealth and privilege, and it still is.

It's also a walker's wonderland, with hill swells and a steep fringe that runs roughly north-south. The Cotswold escarpment, or "the Edge," as locals call it, is yellow limestone that was uplifted and then tilted to give it a clifflike western face and a gentler eastern slope. The views encompass the many waterways ultimately leading to the River Thames, ancient valleys, the Malvern Hills, and, eventually, the Welsh mountains.

Just east of the Cotswolds lies Oxford, a city that has been of strategic importance since at least the tenth century, when it lay on the border between the kingdoms of Wessex and Mercia. Within a couple of centuries, a university was founded. Over time it rose to prominence as the brain trust of Nobel laureates, prime ministers, and iconic poets. Two rivers wend their way through the city, and several sprawling parks give students plenty of reasons to skip class on a sunny day.

10 LORD'S SEAT LOOP

This walk follows Rushup Edge to a high point of 1800 feet at Lord's Seat, which lives up to its lofty name with a panorama of valleys and hilltops, and then continues to the ancient fort at Mam Tor.

Distance: 6 miles
Elevation Gain: 1230 feet
High Point: 1800 feet
Rating: ★ ★ ★ ★
Difficulty: Moderate to challenging
Year-round: Yes
Family-friendly: Yes, though muddy fields can be tough going

Dog-friendly: Yes, leashed near livestock
Amenities: None, nearby Edale has public restrooms, cafes, and pubs
Map: OS Explorer Map OL1, The Peak District, Dark Peak Area
Agencies: Peak District National Park, National Trust

GETTING THERE

GPS: 53.359354°, -1.839090°
Postcode: S33 7ZL
Driving: From Chapel-en-le-Frith, take Sheffield Road for 3.8 miles, then turn left (just before crossing the River Noe) on an

unnamed, dead-end road. Follow for 0.2 mile to the Barber Booth car park.
Public transit: Trains from Manchester to Edale Village Hall. To join this route, turn

right onto Edale Road, continue 1 mile, and then turn right again at Chapel Gate. **Before You Go:** The twenty free spaces at the car park fill up quickly, but there is pay-and-display parking in nearby Edale. Expect boggy pasture crossings, some short, steep sections, and exposed tor tops and ridges, which can be wet and windy.

ON THE TRAIL

From the car park, walk back down the road you drove in on, with views of Rushup Edge on your right. After passing through the tunnel beneath the railroad at 0.1 mile, continue along the road for another 0.1 mile until you reach a stile on your right that crosses over a fence into a clearing. Farming and grazing have endured for centuries in the Peak District, and its valleys are still dotted with farming hamlets and "booths"—the temporary shelters shepherds would use when tending their flocks.

Cut southwest across the field to cross another stile, then stay left along the edge of the pasture. In autumn berries hang from the holly, elderberry, mountain ash, and hawthorn, while in spring and summer, there is a profusion of wildflowers, like bluebell and buttercup, in the meadows. In between are evergreens, mosses, and yellow gorse, which looks like little sunbursts beaming from the moors.

Follow the track as it curves right for 0.5 mile and then continue onto the wide Chapel Gate trail (ignore the branch to your right). Walk uphill toward the crest of

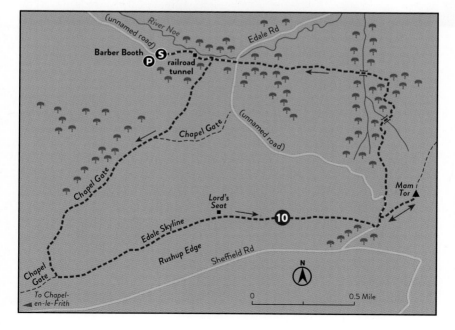

A gorse-lined trail winds through the Vale of Edale, where ancient stone walls and grazing sheep are near-constant companions. (Photo by Juan Nieto Castro)

the ridge for roughly one mile, gaining 550 feet. The trail climbs easily at first, but then steepens as it nears the ridge. Approaching Rushup Edge, the landscape is stark and simple—all sky and spirits. After visiting the area, Charlotte Brontë placed her title character from *Jane Eyre* among these brooding purple moors. (Jane Austen also stayed nearby while writing *Pride and Prejudice*.)

Reach the ridgeline (1610 feet), where there is a junction. Go left and walk uphill alongside the stone wall. Continue straight along Rushup Edge until you reach its high point: Lord's Seat (1800 feet). Here find a roughly circular Bronze Age funerary monument, about six feet high and 30 feet around. The first time I visited this solemn spot, the only people in sight were distant dots along the ridge, and it could have been two thousand years ago (when this mound was likely completed). Being on Rushup Edge feels like floating on a narrow raft, with the cloud-speckled, fingerlike valleys and tree-lined hamlets of Edale and Hope stretching out below and daylight shining off rainfall channels as they course down to join rivers below.

Continue east along the ridge for another 0.5 mile to reach the end of the rock wall, where a trail branches to your right. Follow it downhill for 0.2 mile into a shallow notch with a copse, before hitting the paved, unnamed road passing Mam Tor. Carefully cross the road, pass through a gate, and turn left to walk uphill about 300 feet along a wooden fence. Bear right to follow the paving stones for 0.2 mile to the top of Mam Tor (1696 feet). Here, views open up in every direction: Edale Valley to the north, Hope Valley to the east, and, on a clear day, Manchester is visible 20 miles to the northwest.

The bird's-eye view is why the "Mother Hill" was chosen for a fort around 700 BC. The once-sprawling fortification was occupied for several hundred years and covered roughly 16 acres, making it one of the largest and oldest hillforts in Britain. There is little left of the original structure, but two burial mounds from 1500 BC have endured. (One lies just below the summit and the other is on the top.)

Head back down the walkway, but when you reach the T intersection, go right instead of left. Walk steeply downhill, losing 720 feet in elevation and ignoring the fork that veers uphill to your right. Continue on the winding path for 0.7 mile through bushy gorse and fern-covered banks. Cross a stream, making your way past patchy trees and shrubs, and turn left at the wood sign, heading toward Edale.

In nearby Edale, at the Old Nags Head pub, is the start of the Pennine Way—England's first national trail, inspired by America's Appalachian Trail, and still the best known and reputedly toughest (think mud, routefinding, and extreme weather). It runs north along the country's spine for nearly 270 miles through the Yorkshire Dales and Northumberland National Parks and along Hadrian's Wall, toward the Cheviots, a stretch of rolling uplands straddling the Anglo-Scotch border, before ending near the Scottish border.

Cross another branch of the same small stream in 0.2 mile at Harden Clough, then cross a stile on your left and continue 0.5 mile through an open field to a wooded ravine where you'll cross another bridge. The first time I was here, the clouds loosened as we dropped down into the narrow ravine. Taking shelter in a stand of spindly hawthorn, we soon found we were sharing the space with several chatty, boldly striped meadow pipits. The grey-buff birds are known for their dramatic aerial displays during which they flutter upward from a perch before descending sharply back to earth, trilling a loud, high-pitched tune as they go. Even if you're not forced to by rain, take some time to enjoy this rare pocket of woodland in Great Britain.

Cross two more fields and another small stream over the next 0.2 mile. Pass through a gate and cross Edale Road, then continue straight for 0.4 mile back to the car park by following the River Noe, a 12-mile-long tributary of the River Derwent. This waterway once powered water mills that processed corn and cotton, making it the perfect place to consider the palimpsest character of the Peaks. Imagine the early people who struggled against, and reveled in, the resources of these once-remote hills and dales, such as the nature-revering Celtic people living here around three thousand years ago. They cherished water and showed gratitude by adorning its sources with simple garlands made of vegetation. The practice was banned by early Christians but was revived in the twelfth century. Today dozens of villages in the Peaks practice well dressing by decorating area springs or wells with handmade natural scenes made of flowers, seeds, sticks, and even nuts and berries. They do it to honor their resilient predecessors and, like them, to express thanks for the Peaks' bounty.

EXTEND IT

From Mam Tor, walk the rest of the Great Ridge on a rolling 2-mile route to Lose Hill.

11 GREAT RIDGE RAMBLE

Some of the Peak District's best-known "highs," along with some unusual geology and historical mysteries, are featured on this hike.

Distance: 6.5 miles
Elevation Gain: 1110 feet
High Point: 1560 feet
Rating: ★ ★ ★ ★
Difficulty: Moderate to challenging
Year-round: Yes
Family-friendly: Yes, though low, boggy spots could be a slog

Dog-friendly: Yes, leashed near livestock
Amenities: None, nearby Edale has public restrooms, cafes, and pubs
Map: OS Explorer Map OL1, The Peak District, Dark Peak Area
Agency: Peak District National Park

GETTING THERE

GPS: 53.359354°, -1.839090°
Postcode: S33 7ZL
Driving: From Chapel-en-le-Frith, take Sheffield Road for 3.8 miles, then turn left (just before crossing the River Noe) on an unnamed, dead-end road. Follow for 0.2 mile to the Barber Booth car park.
Public transit: Trains from Manchester to Edale Village Hall. To join this route, turn

right onto Edale Road, continue 1 mile, and then turn right again at Chapel Gate.
Before You Go: The twenty free spaces at the car park fill up quickly, but there is pay-and-display parking in nearby Edale. Expect boggy pasture crossings, some short, steep sections, and exposed tor tops and ridges, which can be wet and windy.

ON THE TRAIL

From the car park, walk back down the narrow road you drove in on for 0.4 mile to the T intersection. Keeping the River Noe on your left, carefully cross the road to the trailhead directly ahead, marked with a green sign that reads "Public Footpath to Castleton, Hope," and go through the gate.

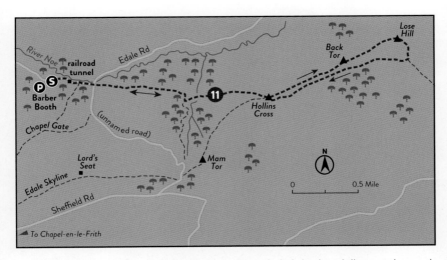

Walk straight across the open field and head slightly downhill toward a path through a copse, giving a wide berth to any grazing animals (or steaming cow patties). Look for the queen and king of British trees—beech and oak, respectively—and for ash, birch, and rowan. The Celts believed the rowans' red berries would ward off evil and, later on, such trees were planted in churchyards for the same reason.

Go over a stile and head slightly uphill for 0.7 mile, following the trail along a fence toward a gate. Pass through the gate and walk downhill toward another dip shaded by more trees. Cross another gate and continue straight, crossing the stream on a wood plank, and join a wide dirt path. Follow that for 0.1 mile, curving right and passing through another gate to intersect a trail with a wooden trail marker. Go left, in the direction marked "Public Bridleway," ignoring the right branch toward "Mam Tor." Cross through another gate marked with a blue arrow and continue on a narrow track flanked by shrubs and small trees. In June and July, wild roses—England's national flower—bloom white or pale pink, while cotton grass blossoms look like clusters of tiny clouds clinging to the ground.

Arrive at a clearing with views of the hills and ridges you'll be tackling. From a distance the gentle curves of the *tors* (or "high rock" in ancient Celtic) look like a sculpture smoothed by unseen hands. They form part of the Great Ridge—a geological oddity in an area dominated by sprawling heathland and gritstone escarpments—which runs for 2 miles east to west and includes the high points of Lose Hill, Back Tor, Hollins Cross, Mam Tor, and Lord's Seat.

Reach upland pastures dotted with farm buildings, and look for thigh-high wood posts—the first one is along the edge of a pasture and to the left of a rock wall. Follow

From Lose Hill, the glorious length of the Great Ridge stretches to the horizon.

the arrows on them to where the wall ends, go over the stile, and stay to the field edge with a line of spindly oak trees to your left. Cross the field and follow two more arrow posts across another field toward a gate on the other side of a dip. Within 0.2 mile of the last stream, you'll cross another stream on a rock slab.

Continue walking straight uphill for 0.6 mile, crossing several fields, gates, and stiles, to arrive at the top of the first Great Ridge hill on this route—Hollins Cross (1280 feet), marked by a cylindrical stone pillar. Travelers from Edale to Castleton used the pass at Hollins Cross, the lowest point on the ridge, for centuries (at least). On a clear day, there are views down-valley to the north and south of the ridge. It's a great spot from which to take in the unique geology of the Peaks. The Great Ridge divides two distinct areas of the park. Its sheer northern flank looks toward the Dark Peak region, with its high moors, gloomy shale, and thick peat. By contrast, to the south lie the narrow vales, bright limestone cliffs, and historical farms of the White Peak. These are the southernmost hills of the Pennines, a nearly 300-mile-long range known as the "backbone of England."

Of the six trails that come together at Hollins Cross, take the rougher one heading uphill and east (opposite the Mam Tor path, which is "paved" with large rock slabs). Follow the wide, rocky track for 0.7 mile as it undulates to the top of Back Tor (1440 feet), pausing to appreciate its stony profile. The final stretch passes through a gate on your left and climbs some rock stairs to the hill's small, flat plateau (a great lunch spot if the weather cooperates).

On a clear day you'll be able to see beyond the crags to your next destination in 0.5 mile—Lose Hill (1560 feet). Continue along the Great Ridge, climbing over a stile, into an area signed "Losehill Pike, Ward's Piece." It's named for GHB Ward, an activist for public land access who founded the first rambling club for working class people from nearby Sheffield. Ward donated to the National Trust the swath of land that bears his name. This stretch of the walk is part of the 21-mile Edale Skyline, a classic loop in the Peaks that circumnavigates Edale Valley along ridges and hilltops. Most of the route is high and exposed along well-worn, rocky footpaths, but other spots are low and boggy.

Find a stone marker atop Lose Hill, with a helpful carved bronze compass marking locations in every direction for several miles, including one for Win Hill (1520 feet—40 feet *lower* than Lose Hill) 2 miles east. This opposing pair is the basis of a colorful, yet historically unsubstantiated, tale that imagines a seventh-century battle between local warring factions.

Head southeast off the summit on paving stones, and follow the trail as it crosses three stiles and curves around to your right, ignoring the three tracks branching to your left. After 0.3 mile from the top of Lose Hill, reach a parallel track below the ridge and begin the hike back toward Hollins Cross. Follow the trail downhill for 0.5 mile to enter a wooded area, the 30-acre Brockett Booth Plantation. This forest stretch lasts just 0.2 mile but is surprisingly dense with coniferous and deciduous trees, including pines, oaks, and ash, which offer a refuge from wind and rain, heat and sun. On spring and summer days the treetops glow viridescent.

After exiting the woodland through a gate, walk straight for 0.7 mile to another gate where the trail reaches Hollins Cross. From there, retrace your steps back to the start.

EXTEND IT
Walk the entire Great Ridge by heading south to Mam Tor from Hollins Cross.

12 LONGSHAW & PADLEY GORGE

This is outstanding walking country with surging streams, peaceful ponds, rolling moors, and ancient woodlands.

Distance: 3.5 miles
Elevation Gain: 500 feet
High Point: 1066 feet
Rating: ★★★★

Difficulty: Easy to moderate
Year-Round: Yes
Family-friendly: Yes; hollowed tree trunk at Longshaw is great for kids

Dog-friendly: Yes, leashed at Padley Gorge and Longshaw Estate
Amenities: Restrooms and cafe at Grindleford Station and Longshaw Estate

Map: OS Explorer Map OL24, The Peak District, White Peak Area
Agencies: Peak District National Park, National Trust

GETTING THERE

GPS: 53.305202°, -1.624471°
Postcode: S32 2HY
Driving: From Grindleford village, take B6521 for 0.6 mile, then bear left onto Midland Cottages, then 0.2 mile to Grindleford Station.

Public transit: Trains to Grindleford Station depart Sheffield and Manchester. Buses from Sheffield stop at the Fox House near Longshaw Estate.
Before You Go: This hike is busy on weekends and public holidays.

ON THE TRAIL

After arriving at the Grindleford Station, walk north on the narrow paved road that crosses the railroad tracks. Walk straight, ignoring a path that branches left, as the road soon turns into a gravel public footpath. Reach a wooden gate in a couple hundred feet, but do not go through it. Instead turn right up a few stone steps at a sign marking "The National Trust, Padley Gorge." At the top of the steps, turn left and start uphill on a wide dirt track, into a wondrous wood.

Ignore the social trails that branch off, and stay left, following the well-worn path over rocks and tree roots, with Burbage Brook on your left. Climb steadily into a dense green canopy of beech and birch, where you're quickly enveloped by a deep, narrow chasm. It's an enchanting place to listen to birdsong and the gushing brook as it plunges steeply among moss-covered boulders.

All of Peak District National Park once looked like Padley Gorge. Oak and birch woodland was common in this part of England—until prehistoric people started clearing it. The tannin in the oak's bark has been used for tanning since Roman times, while the rest of the tree was used for charcoal. Later, widespread livestock grazing impeded regrowth. From the 1850s onward few trees have regrown. Now all that remains are invaluable pockets of trees in valleys and gorges which, though small, still support important species.

Padley Gorge is one such haven. It lies within the 64-acre Yarncliff Wood, which is a designated Site of Special Scientific Interest. Livestock was excluded from an experimental area in 1955, and it rebounded spectacularly. The protected area was expanded in the 1980s, and the results were the same: Grass gave way to bilberry shrubs, then oak, birch, and rowan saplings. Next came alder, holly, and heather, followed by conifers. Then the moss and rare lichen returned. These woodlands are now important habitat for birds including woodpeckers, flycatchers, warblers, and more.

At 0.4 mile you'll arrive at a huge boulder by a wooden footbridge. Take a left onto the bridge over Burbage Brook, which flows from the high moorland near Stanage

Edge into the Derwent River in Grindleford. From there zigzag up a series of stone staircases for about 500 feet to where the trail levels out at a stone bench perfectly positioned to rest tired quads. On a clear day, sunlight flickers through the treetops fluttering in the warm breeze, and the dark, twisting branches of sessile oaks seem to wind and weave all around, almost embracing you. Oaks are a national symbol of strength and endurance in England. Various rulers wore crowns of oak leaves for millennia, and in the seventeenth century couples were wed beneath ancient oaks.

Continue to climb for another 0.2 mile past the bench before passing through a gate. The trail levels out and you will see the edge of the wood in front of you. Continue straight ahead to meet Burbage Brook and, keeping it on your right, emerge onto the exposed, sturdy shoulders of a completely different landscape—the open moors. The forest cover fades and is replaced with gritstone bedrock, dwarf shrub heath, and grass moorland.

Ahead in the distance are the flat-topped, heather-clad hills of Carl Wark (a Bronze Age hillfort) and Owler Tor and the gritstone outcrop of Higger Tor. Continue straight

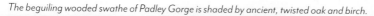

The beguiling wooded swathe of Padley Gorge is shaded by ancient, twisted oak and birch.

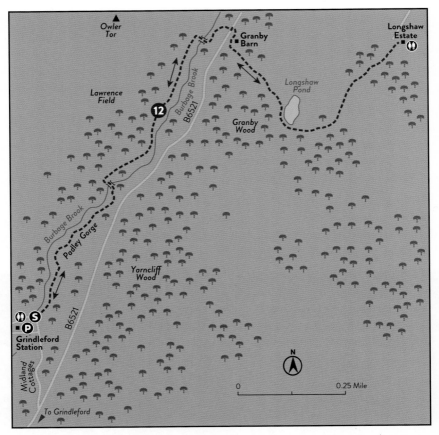

where the stone-slab trail passes between clumps of gorse and heather (in effusive bloom in the summer) for 0.1 mile. To your left is Lawrence Field, with the remnants of a medieval field system and even older longhouses (eleventh or twelfth century). Cross the wooden footbridge on your right where a fingerpost indicates "Longshaw Visitor Centre."

If you visit on a warm summer weekend, this area will likely be crowded with picnickers and stream waders. Head toward the stone wall and staircase roughly 350 feet away, and then carefully cross road B6521 and pick up the trail on the other side (there's a blue sign indicating "Visitor Centre ½-mile").

Stop briefly at the Granby Barn, a stone building on your left, to read about the history and wildlife of Longshaw, before following the wide trail directly out front. Veer right, pass through an opening in a rock wall, and head gently downhill into the woods.

Roughly 0.2 mile after crossing the road, arrive at Longshaw Pond, home to newts, ducks, and water voles, with views of Longshaw Meadow beyond. Opposite the pond, beneath the towering Scots pines of Granby Wood, is a great spot for a picnic lunch.

After resuming the trail, continue left around the lake through a clearing and toward a copse with a gate at its edge. Cross through that gate, and a second one a bit farther on, to where trails branch off in several directions. Make a hard left through a third gate in the direction of the nearby estate buildings.

Walk 0.4 mile from the pond to the complex of old stone buildings at the center of the Longshaw Estate. Now run by the National Trust (there are restrooms and a tea room by the trail), it was built in 1827 by the Duke of Rutland as a hunting lodge specializing in moor grouse. During World War I, it acted as an auxiliary hospital and home to convalescing soldiers. They knew what we've only recently proven with data— that nature heals by reducing blood pressure, heart rate, muscle tension, and stress hormones.

Nobody understood that better than Ethel Haythornthwaite, an environmental activist who agitated tirelessly to save much of what's now Peak District National Park. She was a twenty-two-year-old newlywed during World War I when, in May 1917, her husband was killed in France. Ethel's heart was broken, and her mind and body began to deteriorate soon after. Her family encouraged her to explore the open areas beyond their home in Sheffield, so Ethel went out and walked. Over time she found some equanimity and, lucky for us, a renewed purpose. Later in life Ethel wrote about the importance of that place: "My childhood impressions of the city were a gloomy, noisy, shapeless phenomenon. But outside the city—there one began to live. The escape into clean air, the gradual return to nature—with this came satisfaction, peace, freedom, solitude, excitement. One grew to become conscious of its profounder value, something beyond health and high spirits—something to worship."

In 1924, Ethel helped form the Sheffield Association for the Protection of Local Scenery. When Longshaw Estate went up for sale a few years later, she led the charge to protect the 750-acre site from large-scale development. The campaign was successful—both in preserving the immediate area and making it accessible to the public, the anchor for what would become England's first national park in 1951. Thanks to those efforts, the area around Longshaw remains superb walking country. It is also a critical habitat for many critters, including a herd of red deer, which are often seen on the moors adjacent to Longshaw in the fall when the males bellow for mates.

From Longshaw, retrace your steps back to Grindleford Station.

EXTEND IT

There are a few loops within Longshaw Estate, way-marked by color. The 2.8-mile "blue" loop departs from the main trailhead at the lodge and passes Wooden Pole and Duke's Seat, both with panoramic views of the Peak District.

13 STANAGE EDGE

Amble across open moor and bogland and up onto Stanage Edge for expansive views of the heathland, valleys, and villages below.

Distance: 5 miles
Elevation Gain: 800 feet
High Point: 1510 feet
Rating: ★ ★ ★ ★
Difficulty: Moderate to challenging
Year-round: Yes
Dog-friendly: Yes, leashed

Family-friendly: Yes, but take caution along Stanage Edge
Amenities: Restrooms 0.1 mile east of car park
Map: OS Explorer Map OL1, The Peak District, Dark Peak Area
Agency: Peak District National Park

GETTING THERE

GPS: 53.350344°, -1.645593°
Postcode: S32 1BR
Driving: From Hathersage, take Main Road (A6187) east for 0.2 mile, then turn left onto School Lane. Follow for 0.1 mile and continue onto The Dale. After 1.5 miles, turn left onto an unnamed road (Hook's Carr car park is on your right) and continue for 0.5 mile. Turn right and, in 0.3 mile, look for the entrance to the Hollin Bank car park (coins required).
Before You Go: Stanage Edge is often battered by wind and rain (and snow in the winter) and paths below the escarpment can be muddy.

ON THE TRAIL

From the east end of the car park, pass by a large stone bench and through a cluster of ash, birch, and bracken. Walk uphill into a clearing for a view of Stanage Edge. "Stanage," or "stone edge," is a 3.5-mile stretch of gritstone cliffs that can be seen from miles around. While the dark sandstone, laid down in vast river deltas hundreds of millions of years ago, can be seen at other "edges" in the Peak District, Stanage is considered the finest expanse.

Even though the rock ledge rises just 80 feet at its highest point, its prominence over the surrounding lowlands is striking. There's an air of drama whatever the season—in lashing wind with dark clouds swirling overhead, in a light spring snow, or on summer days of record heat, Stanage Edge has a mood to match. It can look like the ramparts of a hidden castle, the setting of an epic battle, or simply the best place to catch a cooling breeze.

In 0.2 mile from the car park, pass through a gate and enter a thick forest. Walk for 0.1 mile through a stand of deciduous trees planted in the eighteenth century and protected since from grazing animals. Notice the car-sized chunks of rock broken off the "scarp" through erosion and carried by glacial streams to their repose in the shady

A thick carpet of heather blooms in summer on the mesmerizing moors of Stanage Edge.

grove. Continue uphill (north) along the path for 0.3 mile, gaining 200 feet in elevation as you cut through steep moorland slopes covered with rough grass, bracken, and heather, in boisterous bloom in August. Below are views of the Derwent and Hope valleys braided with streams and rivers and dotted with barns, pastures, and villages.

Directly south is Hathersage, where you can see the rooflines and bell towers of historical churches, pubs, and homes. This village has likely been populated since the end of the last ice age over eleven thousand years ago, and its mining, industry, and tourism has drawn people ever since. Tourists in particular have pursued legendary and literary figures—including Robin Hood, whose right-hand man, "Little John" (though he was unusually tall) was rumored to have been born in Hathersage and is buried in St. Michael's graveyard. Charlotte Brontë stayed in the village in 1845 and modeled many of *Jane Eyre*'s locales on the area.

Zigzag up about two hundred feet to the often blustery Stanage Edge plateau, avoiding the social trails. When you reach the top, go left (northwest), where you'll see the western end of the edge in the distance. In about a tenth of a mile, you'll briefly join a wider track. This is the Long Causeway—a route taken by travelers to trade millstones, metals, cheese, ceramics, and salt even before the Romans came. It's a great example of the area's old packhorse trails, so-called hollow-ways, the deep lines cut like memories across the once-remote heath.

Continue along the plateau and, in 250 feet when the trail forks, go right. Watch for buff-colored whinchats and bright yellow siskins perched on the rocks. In 0.7 mile, you'll

A rock climber along Stanage Edge, one of England's most famous gritstone crags

reach High Neb (1510 feet), the loftiest spot along Stanage. The surrounding gritstone moor undulates out in every direction and seems at once solid and unsettled, and altogether remote. The length of Stanage Edge is included in the 53-mile Sheffield Country Walk, which circumnavigates Sheffield by following rivers and crossing farms, woods, and moors.

Look back for views of the southern end of Stanage. Here is where Keira Knightley, as Elizabeth Bennet in a 2005 film version of *Pride and Prejudice*, stood on the stone edge, dress whipping in the wind, contemplating her future. Numbered pools carved into the rock mark basins used to water game birds when people hunted grouse on this moor. It is both a peaceful and haunted—and ecologically critical—landscape.

Continue past High Neb for another mile until the trail forks again. (Just before the trail splits, you have reached Stanage End, the escarpment's northern terminus.) Go left and downhill at a stone pillar with the initials "W.W." carved on it. Also marked "W.M." on the reverse, this spot marks the boundary between Moscar and Hallam Moors once owned by William Moore and William Wilson, respectively. Reach a T intersection soon after and follow the path left for 2 miles, keeping the escarpment on your left. In summer, the bright green bracken can grow chest-high on the boulder-strewn slopes below Stanage, part of the endangered moorland and bog in sharp decline elsewhere in the world. Look out for rock-loving ring ouzels, a.k.a. mountain blackbirds, with a white crescent on their breast and silver-streaked wings, which nest on or below the cliffs. They mark their territory with energetic song and feed on rowan berries, bilberries, and insects.

Along this section you'll also pass below some of Stanage's named rock formations and climbing routes, including Marble Wall and Crow Chin. Rock climbing has been popular at Stanage since the 1890s due to the superior grip offered by the rough rock. Before it was used for climbing, British gritstone was in great demand during the seventeenth century for grind- and millstones. At that time the massive stones were cut on-site and then rolled off the moor. That lasted until the late nineteenth century, when

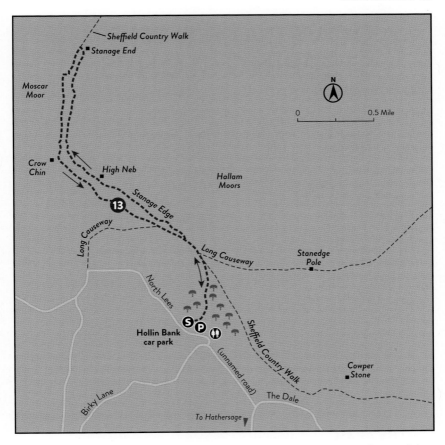

steel replaced stone. Along this section of trail, you will see many huge millstones left in situ, now fulfilling their destinies as benches and picnic tables.

Roughly 1.6 miles from the last T intersection, cross a wooden stile, rejoin the Long Causeway, and start to climb again. After 0.3 mile and 140 feet in elevation gain, the trail takes a downturn and forks. Bear right to rejoin the trail you took to reach the Stanage Edge and, from there, retrace your steps 0.5 mile back to the car park.

EXTEND IT

To complete the Stanage Edge, first walk southeast on the Sheffield Country Walk by making a right instead of a left when you reach the top of the escarpment. Continue 1.4 miles to Cowper Stone, a prominent, solitary block of gritstone, then turn around to rejoin this walk as described.

14 DOVEDALE & THE STEPPING STONES

This loop offers places of refuge and points of inspiration via high grasslands, a rocky gorge, and a surging river, with some rich history to appreciate and a fair bit of tree worship to engage in.

Distance: 5.4 miles
Elevation Gain: 920 feet
High Point: 1010 feet
Rating: ★ ★ ★ ★
Difficulty: Moderate
Year-round: Yes
Family-friendly: Yes, but use extra caution near River Dove

Dog-friendly: Yes, leashed
Amenities: Free restrooms and cafe at Ilam Park and paid restrooms near Dovedale parking
Map: OS Explorer Map OL24, The Peak District, White Peak Area
Agencies: Peak District National Park, National Trust

GETTING THERE

GPS: 53.053623°, -1.805479°
Postcode: DE6 2AZ
Driving: From Ashbourne, take the A515 north for 1.1 miles before turning left onto Spend Lane. Then turn left onto Wintercroft Lane in 1.9 miles and right onto Hall Lane in 0.4 mile. In 0.8 mile, continue onto Thorpe Road for 0.7 mile and then slight right onto Ilam-Moor Lane. The Ilam Park National Trust car park is on your right.

Before You Go: Dovedale is immensely popular in summer. This walk begins at Ilam Hall, a nineteenth-century mansion (now a youth hostel) in the fairytale-like village of Ilam. The fields can be muddy and slippery. Descent into the gorge is fairly steep.

ON THE TRAIL

Leave the car park the way you came in, and cross the road onto the straight path heading east, directly away from the mansion. Already you'll have spectacular views of the White Peak region studded with pale, rocky outcroppings and sprawling green pastures. Slightly to your right you'll see the round top of Bunster Hill (1080 feet), and straight ahead is the well-known, flat-topped Thorpe Cloud (940 feet). They are both reef knolls, the compressed remains of coral reefs from roughly 350 million years ago when a tropical sea covered the area.

Within a few hundred feet, you will reach the Church of the Holy Cross. Its simple Norman-era countenance belies an intriguing history that likely dates back to the tenth century. Inside are both a carved stone Saxon font and the tomb of mysterious Saint Bertram, the son of an eighth century King of Mercia, an Anglo-Saxon kingdom that existed prior to the Viking invasion at the end of the ninth century.

The historical details are sketchy, but the story goes that Bertram traveled to Ireland to seek religious guidance (as Saint Patrick had done before him), found a princess bride, and was traveling back to central England when tragedy struck. His wife went into labor and Bertram left to find a midwife. He returned to the shelter to find that his wife and newborn had been mauled by wolves. Heartbroken, the prince renounced his title and devoted his life to his faith. Bertram became a hermit and lived in a cave near Ilam, but he offered spiritual advice to hopeful pilgrims. Ilam has been a pilgrims' landing ever since.

From the church follow the path 0.2 mile to intersect the Ilam-Moor Road, and take a right onto the sidewalk. Most of the village was built in the 1830s in an alpine style that earned this area the nickname "Little Switzerland." In about 300 feet you'll reach the 32-foot-high Ilam Cross on an island in the middle of the road. This gothic revival monument was installed in 1841 by Jesse Watts-Russell (former owner of the

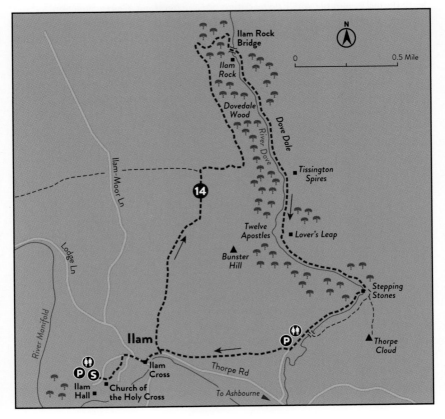

Ilam estate) for his wife, Mary. Another grieving husband, Edward I, had erected similar monuments to his queen, Eleanor of Castile, in 1290, and the Ilam Cross is based on those so-called Eleanor Crosses.

From the Ilam Cross, make a left onto Thorpe Road, keeping the tree-lined bank of the River Manifold on your right. The river is actually named for the many twists and turns it takes over its dozen-mile run (*manig-fald* in Anglo-Saxon meant "many folds"). Walk roughly 500 feet as the road curves right, then cross Thorpe Road where the sidewalk ends. Cross the gate on the other side and take an immediate right to ascend some stairs by a sign saying "National Trust: Bunster Hill." Follow the path for a few hundred feet to a T intersection and go left. Travel that far again and look for a wide rocky trail on your right. Turn onto it and walk uphill for 0.8 mile, ignoring the tracks branching left, following either a rock wall or a line of trees on your left and the steepening slopes of Bunster Hill on your right for most of the way. As you ascend, views of rolling, verdant fields, dotted in summer with billowy cotton grass, extend out in every direction.

Bear left and uphill to reach a sign for "National Trust, Bunster Hill" near the crest. Reach the top in a few hundred feet and cross through a gate along a rock wall. Walk for about a third of a mile, past a barn on your right and other farm buildings on your left to reach a T intersection. Make a right along the narrow gravel road, and carry on for 0.1 mile to a large wood gate that leads to an adjacent gravel road. Pass another smaller gate nearby and go right, away from the farm and onto a grassy knoll. Look for Dove Dale—some of the upper rocky crags of the narrow canyon are now visible—to the east. Watch for buzzards riding the thermals overhead here. Unlike a turkey vulture (what Americans sometimes call a buzzard), the British variety is a medium-sized raptor that, with a four-foot wing span, is the largest bird of prey in the Peak District. Buzzards are regularly seen near the River Dove and over the open moors, hunting rodents and rabbits.

Continue straight for about 350 feet over the crest of the hill. On the other side, follow the direction of the yellow arrow on the wood post to curve left past a "footpath" sign, and head downhill into a wooded area. Pass in and out of tree cover and open hilltop with more views of the dale top over the next 0.3 mile. Enjoy the cool thickets of ash and lime, fungi and ferns, and dogwood and rowan. Rowan, known for its longevity (they can live up to 200 years), stands out in spring with off-white flowers and in autumn with scarlet berries that attract birds.

There are also some wonderful willows at the edge of the woods. Though now often equated with sadness and mourning (we might blame Shakespeare, who drowned Ophelia near a willow in *Hamlet*), their boughs were long used as decorations in British churches in lieu of palm leaves on the Sunday before Easter. The twigs and bark of the willow were also known for centuries (at least) to relieve pain. In the nineteenth century scientists figured out that salicylic acid was responsible; today, its synthetic equivalent is known as aspirin.

Pass through the gate beneath a huge sycamore and continue downhill for 0.4 mile. Go left at the T intersection, descending nearly 350 feet over 0.4 mile to reach the River Dove. Dovedale is home to a number of rare habitats (it became a national nature reserve in 2006) that support rainbow and brown trout and grayling, as well as birds such as dippers, kingfishers, grey herons, and ducks.

Take a right and, in 0.1 mile, cross the river on the Ilam Rock Bridge, where you'll get a good look at what distinguishes the dale. The 3-mile-long limestone gash was formed by glacial meltwater ten thousand years ago. That torrent, now known as the River Dove, easily cut through the limestone base, leaving behind harder bands of rock. The lush, green riverbanks sit beneath rock cliffs, caves, arches, and spires, like the 82-foot-high Ilam Rock. This is the Peak District's most popular dale, and the Dove its most beloved river, and both have been memorialized in poems and prose, paintings and films. The river was made famous initially by writer Izaak Walton in the mid-seventeenth century in *The Compleat Angler*, about fishing on the Dove. Still a hugely popular book, it's a Thoreau-esque contemplation of nature—both human and otherwise. Dovedale got another boost in the early nineteenth century as the railroads brought in tourists. Romantic poet Lord Byron wrote to fellow writer Thomas Moore, "Was you ever in Dovedale? I assure you there are things in Derbyshire as noble as in Greece or Switzerland." In 1882, Lord Tennyson insisted it was "one of the most unique and delicious places in England." By the 1930s, the Dove-lovers wanted the area to be the country's first national park, but it was not designated until 1951.

Make a right and continue along the river's edge for 1 mile to where grey-white rock formations, including the Tissington Spires, appear on the left (east) side of the river (Dovedale Church and Jacob's Ladder is on your right). Climb about 100 feet in elevation over the next 0.3 mile to reach a set of about 100 steps leading to a spot called Lover's Leap. The Twelve Apostles (a dozen rock features on the west side of the river) may be visible, depending on how full the foliage is. If the view is blocked, take heart that Dovedale is an important spot for non-fruiting lime, hawthorn, yew, and ash trees. The tall, graceful ash can live for four hundred years but are now seriously threatened by a fungal pathogen. The mass die-offs affect not just the tree but nearly one thousand species that rely on them.

Continue downhill to rejoin the river for 0.6 mile as it curves to your right before reaching a flat, open area. This is one of the most scenic spots in all the Peaks and, just as it was for Victorian tourists, is a must-see for many visitors today. Nestled in the sculptured limestone gorge of Dovedale, it is a refuge from the speed and cacophony of modern life. Many famous writers and painters over the centuries felt their cares distant when they were on the river. In *The Angler's Ballad*, seventeenth-century English poet Charles Cotton wrote, "But first leave all our sorrows behind us; / If misfortune do come, / We are all gone from home, / And a-fishing she never can find us."

Thorpe Cloud stands sentinel over the pulsing River Dove in the Peaks.

The River Dove widens here to about 60 feet across and kinks as it turns from southeast to southwest. In the clearing you'll see another famous feature of Dovedale, the square-cut Stepping Stones that are used to cross the river's clear, shallow waters. They were installed in 1890 when visitors hired donkeys to ride into the dale.

Cross the Stepping Stones and follow the west bank of the river for 0.5 mile to Dovedale car park. (If you can't cross the stones due to high water, you can follow the east bank of the river to a bridge in 0.4 mile. Cross and turn left to join the main path.) Bear right through a gate and onto a dirt road (also used for parking during the high season). Continue 150 feet ahead to a well-marked path on your right, and immediately ascend a set of stairs. Within a few hundred feet you'll cross through a copse and a gate.

Walk uphill into open fields for about 500 feet to reach a wooden gate at a gap in the stone wall. Continue for 0.2 mile downhill to another gate and pass through to continue along the flank of Bunster Hill. In 0.2 mile pass through a gap in another stone wall and continue on the wide gravel path for roughly 500 feet. Bear left onto the trail where you began this walk, and retrace your steps back to Ilam Park.

EXTEND IT

Add a short but strenuous summit of Thorpe Cloud (about 500 feet ascent in roughly three quarters of a mile). Turn left at the Stepping Stones onto the first path that enters Lin Dale. Soon you'll see two paths that branch to your right; both go to the top, but the second is a bit easier.

15 CAVE DALE & WINNATS PASS

This steep, beautiful hike passes through a hidden valley, across high pastures, and down a popular mountain pass.

Distance: 4.9 miles
Elevation Gain: 890 feet
High Point: 1450 feet
Rating: ★★★
Difficulty: Moderate
Year-round: Yes
Family-friendly: Yes, but the track up Cave Dale can be wet and slippery

Dog-friendly: Yes, leashed
Amenities: Portable restrooms only; services throughout Castleton
Map: OS Explorer Map OL1, The Peak District, Dark Peak Area
Agencies: Peak District National Park, National Trust

GETTING THERE

GPS: 53.342877°, -1.779528°
Postcode: S33 8WP
Driving: The Peak Cavern car park is on the west end of Castleton (roughly 1.5 miles west of Hope and 5.5 miles west of Hathersage). Take the A6187 west from the village center and look for the car park on your left.

Public Transit: Castleton is well served by local buses.
Before You Go: During or after rain, water can flow over the loose rocks on the track up the Cave Dale ravine.

ON THE TRAIL

Walk through a gate at the back of the car park onto a wide dirt path between two stone walls. Cross the paved road directly ahead and go left over the bridge spanning Peakshole Water, a stream which starts nearby at the Peak Cavern and surges through Castleton. Follow the brown sign toward "Peveril Castle" for about a tenth of a mile along a narrow road flanked by distinctive stone structures built with local limestone and gritstone to reach Market Place. This triangular park serves as a war memorial and features a stone cross with Celtic carvings and an enormous lime tree, commonly known as linden in North America.

Ignore the sign for Peveril Castle and continue along the road to where, in about 200 feet, it takes a sharp right at the brown sign for "Cave Dale." Pass through a narrow alley and by an information sign on your left to cross a wide wooden gate leading to a rocky, uphill track. Follow the trail as it snakes up the dale, climbing gradually among dense foliage through the smooth U-shaped valley, its slopes coated with oat grass, sheep's fescue, and meadow rue. Continue straight over the next mile as the dale narrows between near-vertical limestone walls, roughly 160 feet high, as you gain more than 700 feet in elevation.

Keep an eye out for what look like caves but are actually the former entrances to lead mines. Mining for lead was big business for centuries (even the Romans mined nearby). Near the mine openings, where the tailings were tossed, you may see some rare lead-tolerant plants, including yellow and purple mountain pansy and moonwort,

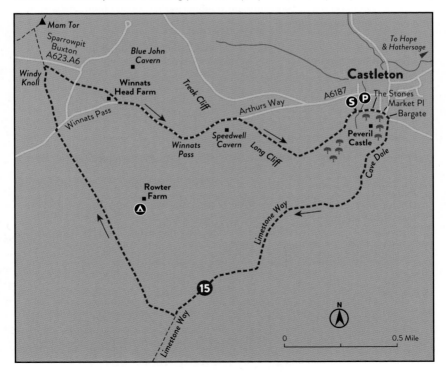

a fern thought to have magical qualities that was popular with alchemists seeking to turn lead to gold.

Pause to look back at the ruins of Peveril Castle. One of England's earliest Norman fortresses, it was built in the tenth century by William Peveril on land granted to him by William the Conqueror, who had enacted a system of forest law (and who some historians think may have been Peveril's father). It was known as Castle of the Peak because its prominence over the Hope Valley made it a great lookout spot.

In medieval times moorland forest covered most of northwest Derbyshire, including what is now Peak District National Park. The so-called Forest of the High Peak was a royal hunting ground, and Peveril was in charge of keeping out the riffraff. Back then royal forests included areas of grassland, wetland, and heath—anywhere the "noble" animals of the chase, including fallow and roe deer, fox and pine marten—would likely be found. Other animals protected by law were red deer, wild boar, hare, and wolves. King Henry II is known to have visited Peveril Castle several times after confiscating the estate in 1155. It fell into ruin in the seventeenth century but is now in the care of English Heritage and can be visited for a fee.

In about a half mile pass through a gap in a stone wall and continue uphill, keeping another stone wall on your right. Cross through three more wall gaps over the next mile as the track leaves the so-called Secret Valley and enters the high pastures. This first part of the route follows the 46-mile Limestone Way, which cuts through some of the most scenic areas of the White Peaks—striking dales, rolling pastures, and storybook villages.

At the next gate go right onto a path flanked by stone walls and, in 0.2 mile, bear right to stay on the trail (ignoring a metal gate straight ahead). Continue straight for 0.5 mile on the wide gravel track, passing large Rowter Farm on your right before turning onto a narrow, unnamed paved road. (Rowter is still a working farm and now also a campsite.) On clear days look north for stellar views of Mam Tor and the Great Ridge. (Here the route runs alongside paved, unsigned Sparrowpit Buxton road, or A623.A6, which snakes through this area.) Pass through the next gate to cross that road and continue north toward the hills along a rocky path.

Continue for 0.3 mile and, just before reaching another section of Sparrowpit Buxton, take a sharp right down a grassy track (near the sign for "National Trust: Windy Knoll"), keeping the road on your left. Enjoy lovely views of the Hope Valley over the next 0.2 mile before passing through a gate, crossing the road a second time, passing through a second gate, and picking up the trail. Head straight (east) through a pasture toward another gate and cross it. Stay to your right along the edge of the pasture, passing large Winnats Head Farm on your right.

Descend 440 feet through Winnats Pass, one of the most spectacular limestone gorges in the Peak District. From wild grasses and wildflowers at your feet, the terrain rises steeply to Treak Cliff on your left and Long Cliff on your right. When the sun hits

Walking above Castleton in the High Peak District yields epic views of the Great Ridge, including Mam Tor.

the emerald-hued slopes and high rock faces, the natural ramparts are as impressive as any fairytale castle.

Stay on the path running parallel to the road for 0.6 mile to reach Speedwell Cavern (marked by a gate and a somewhat garish sign where Winnats Pass road becomes Arthurs Way). Cross the paved road and make a left onto the sidewalk, passing the commercial entrance to the cavern. This part of the Peak District is cave country, and the Castleton area has some impressive show caverns, including Speedwell, Treak, Blue John (home to a semi-precious mineral of the same name used in jewelry and vases), and Peak (also known as the Devil's Arse due to the flatulent-like sounds heard within the cave when water drains out). Nearby Titan is Britain's deepest cavern at 464 feet.

Roughly 350 feet after crossing the road, pass through a gate on your right to join a dirt path, following the sign for "National Trust: Longcliff." About a third of a mile from the cavern, go through a gate and make a left, keeping the stone wall on your left. Continue downhill for 0.2 mile through a short, wooded section of trail that merges onto Goosehill Road. Continue straight for 0.2 mile to reach Peakshole Water and the car park where you began.

EXTEND IT

Instead of turning right just before reaching paved Sparrowpit Buxton road, cross that road and continue straight ahead on the path. It's just a mile round-trip to add a summit of Mam Tor (1720 feet).

16 CHIPPING CAMPDEN & DOVER'S HILL

This loop offers a taste of a historical market town, a wander in mature woodland, and spectacular views atop Dover's Hill.

Distance: 4.2 miles
Elevation Gain: 470 feet
High Point: 750 feet
Rating: ★ ★ ★
Difficulty: Easy to moderate
Year-round: Yes
Family-friendly: Yes, but steep ascent of Dover's Hill

Dog-friendly: Yes, leashed
Amenities: Chipping Campden is full of pubs and cafes
Map: OS Explorer Map OL45, The Cotswolds
Agency: National Trust

GETTING THERE

GPS: 52.050736°, -1.780704°
Postcode: GL55 6AJ
Driving: From Broadway, take Leamington Road north for 0.8 mile to a roundabout. Take the third exit onto A44 and continue for 3.2 miles to B4081. Go left and then straight for 2.6 miles to the Market Hall on your left.

Public Transit: Cotswold villages are well served by buses.
Before You Go: Forest and grassy tracks can be muddy following heavy rain. Chipping Campden is the finish line for those walking the Cotswold Way south to north.

ON THE TRAIL

Begin at the Market Hall, the open-air, stone structure in the center of Chipping Campden. Despite its grandeur, it was built in 1627 for a modest purpose—to shelter local traders selling butter, cheese, and chickens. *Chipping* is, in fact, Old English for "marketplace." Head southwest toward the round marker on the ground with an acorn at its center, the official terminus of the 102-mile Cotswold Way. The trail runs from Bath to Chipping Campden, following the jagged western edge of the Cotswold escarpment through pastoral landscapes, picture-perfect villages, and pocket woodlands.

The quote around the marker's perimeter is from T. S. Eliot's poem "East Coker" (from his *Four Quartets*): "Now the light falls / Across the open field, leaving the deep lane / Shuttered with branches, dark in the afternoon." During World War II, with London suffering daily air raids, Eliot walked frequently around Chipping Campden while visiting a friend. A famously cantankerous city slicker, Eliot found in the countryside a way to process some of the darkness and misery the world was

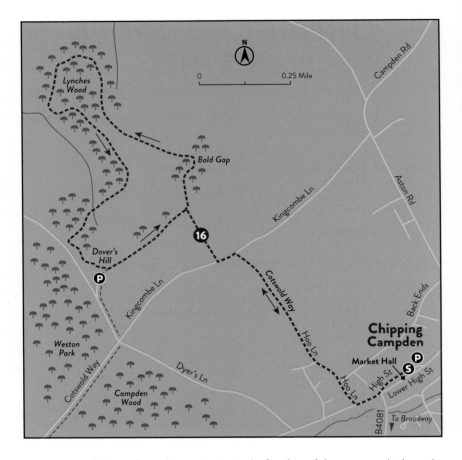

experiencing. Missing from the inscription is the first line of the stanza, which reads, "In my beginning is my end."

Continue along High Street, veering right past the war memorial and around Town Hall (with the clock tower). The honey-colored, terraced buildings that dominate the village were constructed of local limestone called Cotswold stone. Like many Cotswold settlements, Chipping Campden grew prosperous on centuries of wool trading, and looks much like it did four hundred years ago.

At 0.2 mile from the Market Hall, go right at St. Catherine's Catholic Church onto Hoo Lane. Follow the narrow paved road, noting Little Orchard, a stone cottage marked by a circular blue plaque, on your left. This was the home of writer Graham Greene in the early 1930s, and where he penned his first popular novel, *Stamboul*

Train (later made into the movie *Orient Express*). The Cotswolds have inspired countless writers over the centuries including Beatrix Potter, Jane Austen, J. M. Barrie, and J. R. R. Tolkien.

After 0.3 mile Hoo Lane narrows to a dirt track that passes sheep-crammed fields as it starts to climb. Reach Kingcombe Lane in another 0.3 mile, turn left, and walk roughly 300 feet before carefully crossing the tarmac road to join the narrow, blackthorn-lined trail on the other side, signed "Cotswold Way." Continue for 0.2 mile to pass through a "kissing gate" (designed to confound livestock while allowing humans to easily pass through) and bear right. In addition to the Cotswold Way, no fewer than four other long-distance routes pass through Chipping Campden, including the 65-mile Diamond Way, 62-mile Donnington Way, 615-mile Monarch's Way, and 101-mile Heart of England Way. The latter may be the

A stone marker in central Chipping Campden indicates the start of the 102-mile Cotswold Way.

most popular, as it follows the length of the West Midlands through gently undulating farmland and lowland heath, woodland, and riverside paths.

Leave the Cotswold Way here to take the longer, wooded way up Dover's Hill. Follow a line of sycamores for 0.1 mile, then bear right through a gate to take a short detour through a pocket of thick woodland called Bold Gap. In 400 feet follow the trail to veer left, exit via the gate, and rejoin the main track, now heading west along open pasture. On a clear day there are lovely views of the surrounding countryside. Follow the grassy track along the fence line as it curves left around the edge of the field toward another wooded area.

In 0.3 mile, cross through a wooden gate into Lynches Wood, following the trail as it bends in a counterclockwise C shape. Towering sweet chestnut and oak, as well as lanky ash and larch, shelter the trail. In spring and summer the forest floor is a profusion of wildflowers, bracken, and wild garlic. This wood is actually terraced into the hillside, possibly a relic of a Roman vineyard. Follow the signs for "Cotswold Way Circular Route" for 0.6 mile to ascend a long flight of steps and exit Lynches Wood through a gate on its southwest edge.

Stay to your right as you follow the grassy track along the fence that borders the wood. Curve right and then left for over a half mile to ascend roughly 250 feet to the top of Dover's Hill, which is marked by a stone pillar and a toposcope. This is a high point on the Cotswold escarpment, and the amphitheater below the hill is a good example of how water percolates down through the upper limestone layer and erodes the mudstone and clay below. On a good day, western views span the Vale of Evesham to the Malvern Hills and beyond to the Black Mountains of southern Wales. The hill is named for Robert Dover, the lawyer who initiated Dover's Games, or the Cotswold Olimpicks in the early seventeenth century. The competitions were perhaps predictable for the times—horse racing and sword fighting—but there were other more quizzical contests like shin kicking. Drinking, dancing, and feasting were also part of the fun. The games came and went over the centuries but have been played every spring since the 1960s (with the exception of pandemic years 2020 and 2021).

Continue past the toposcope and along the escarpment, passing a National Trust Dover's Hill marker in 0.3 mile. Pass through a gate in another 0.1 mile to complete the loop. Make an immediate right to retrace your steps 1 mile back to the center of Chipping Campden.

EXTEND IT

Continue south for 4.5 miles on the Cotswold Way, from Dover's Hill to Broadway (my favorite village in the Cotswolds), via the Beacon Tower (a.k.a. Broadway Tower), built in 1797. For centuries, the village has been a magnet for the creative and powerful—from King Charles I, Oliver Cromwell, and William Morris to a curious collection of Americans in the late nineteenth century: Henry James, John Singer Sargent, and Francis Millet.

17 WINCHCOMBE, BELAS KNAP & SUDELEY CASTLE

This roundtrip walk from Winchcombe, a charming Cotswold village, passes rolling countryside to an ancient burial ground and a Tudor castle.

Distance: 6.3 miles
Elevation Gain: 930 feet
High Point: 976 feet
Rating: ★ ★ ★ ★
Difficulty: Moderate
Year-round: Yes
Dog-friendly: Yes, leashed

Amenities: Pubs, cafes, and tea rooms galore in central Winchcombe
Family-friendly: Yes, but steep sections and several stretches along paved roads
Map: OS Explorer Map OL45, The Cotswolds
Agencies: English Heritage, Sudeley Castle

GETTING THERE

GPS: 51.952576°, -1.965682°
Postcode: GL54 5LL
Driving: From Broadway, take High Street west for 0.4 mile to Station Road (B4632). Continue for 0.2 mile to Cheltenham Road (B4632). Turn left and continue for 7.7 miles to Abbey Terrace (the war memorial is a

large stone cross in the middle of Abbey Terrace).
Public Transit: Cotswold villages are well served by buses.
Before You Go: Check Sudeley Castle for hours of operation if you plan to visit.

ON THE TRAIL

Start at the war memorial, roughly facing The Plaisterers Arms pub. Here you are in the midst of the 48-mile Winchcombe Way, a long-distance route which forms a figure eight around Winchcombe, crossing some of the prettiest northern Cotswold countryside. (The trail marker is a bright yellow-and-black disc with boot prints at its center.) Head right (west) along Abbey Terrace for 200 feet, then go left onto Vineyard Street in the direction of Sudeley Castle. This area is now dominated by appealing butterscotch-colored cottages made of Cotswold limestone, but Winchcombe once had Roman villas and, when it was an important hub for Anglo-Saxon nobles, protective walls and an abbey. Some timber-framed medieval structures still grace the village.

Follow Vineyard Street for 0.1 mile, over the River Isbourne, to reach a metal gate on your right with a fingerpost indicating the "Cotswold Way." Follow the dirt and grass track straight across the field for 0.1 mile to a wooden gate. Go straight for 0.4 mile to reach another gate at a paved road, Corndean Lane. Carefully cross the road and turn left. Continue about another quarter of a mile to reach a large wooden gate on your right, signposted "Cotswold Way, Belas Knap, 1 ½."

Follow a narrow, paved track for 0.3 mile past the cricket ground toward wooded hills. Pass through a kissing gate on your left to stay on the Cotswold Way, keeping to the left edge of the open field. Over the next 0.4 mile the trail climbs more than 250 feet in elevation. When the trail again meets Corndean Lane, go through the gate and turn right, leaving the Cotswold Way. When the road forks in 0.2 mile, take the higher route to your left. From there climb steadily (about 220 feet over 0.6 mile) until just past Hill Barn Farm, where a fingerpost points left to rejoin the Cotswold Way. Follow that and, sticking to the left edge of the field, walk straight toward the mound of Belas

St. Peter's Church has graced Winchcombe's skyline for more than five hundred years in the scenic Severn Valley.

Knap 0.5 mile in the distance. Watch for kestrels, hanging gracefully on the breeze, scoping for field voles. These remarkable mini-falcons can see something less than an inch long scurrying on the ground from 60 feet overhead.

Belas Knap is a Neolithic burial chamber, also known as a long barrow, and excavations have found the remains of thirty-one people estimated to have died five thousand to six thousand years ago. Go over the stone stile to circumnavigate the oblong structure. The impressive front opening here is a false entrance, meant either to deter thieves or, more likely (since there was little of value buried in the vault), to act as a spirit door for the dead. (The practical entrances to the tomb were on its flanks.)

Cross the stone stile on the opposite side of the barrow to follow the trail left through a metal kissing gate and into the trees. Pass through several gates over the next three-quarters of a mile as you wind downhill, with views across flower-studded meadows to Winchcombe. A normally sleepy hamlet, Winchcombe made the news when, in March 2021, fragments of a meteorite crashed down in the village. The carbonaceous chondrite, leftover from the formation of the solar system 4.6 billion years ago, was a rare find.

After a section of dense woodland, the track once again meets Corndean Lane. Take a right and walk along the road for 0.4 mile to a signpost indicating "Winchcombe Way." Turn left, and then left again at a T intersection. Go straight across the open hillside for 0.8 mile, passing farm buildings and crossing over several stiles, before reaching a bridge. In the spring, the wild garlic in this spot is profuse with fragrant, white bouquets. Cross the bridge and continue straight for 0.2 mile. Look right for views of Sudeley Castle as you cross another stile and dirt road before continuing straight through a field. In about a quarter mile, cross over a footbridge and pass through a gate.

In 0.1 mile, pass through another gate and make a left along Old Brockhampton Road. In 0.2 mile, the road intersects with the road to Sudeley Castle. If you'd like to visit the castle (there is a fee), take a right and walk 0.3 mile to a road that branches off left to the entrance. If you'd like simply to see some of the exterior, continue on this route for another 0.2 mile to the open field. Sudeley is a grand Tudor castle with a colorful history and 15 acres of celebrated gardens. It was visited by King Henry VIII and Anne Boleyn (his second wife) in 1535 when the monarch was meeting with Thomas

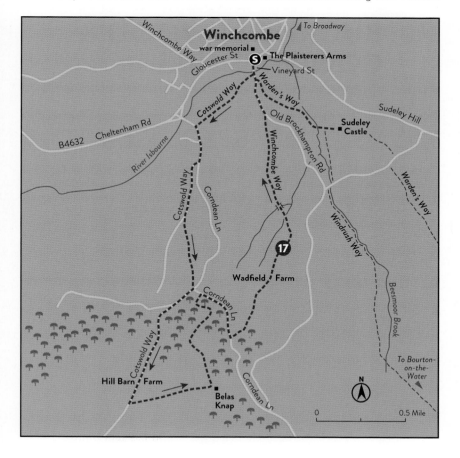

Cromwell to plan the English Reformation. On the castle grounds is St. Mary's Church, the final resting place of Queen Katherine Parr, Henry's sixth wife. She lived and died in the castle and is the only English queen buried on private land.

Head back to the entrance of Sudeley Castle and continue along what was Old Brockhampton Road, now Vineyard Street, retracing your steps 0.2 mile back to the center of Winchcombe.

EXTEND IT
From Sudeley Castle, continue over the hills along a portion of the 14-mile Windrush Way to Bourton-on-the-Water, a popular and picturesque village.

18 BUCKHOLT WOOD & COOPER'S HILL

This rolling route crosses through dense forest that includes some of the country's most impressive beechwood stands, with views from a hill that hosts a curious contest involving cheese, and a short detour to what remains of a Roman villa.

Distance: 4.5 miles
Elevation Gain: 1000 feet
High Point: 901 feet
Rating: ★ ★ ★ ★
Difficulty: Easy to moderate
Year-round: Yes
Family-friendly: Yes, but short sections along narrow roads require caution

Dog-friendly: Yes, leashed
Amenities: Pubs and facilities in nearby Cranham
Map: OS Explorer Map 179, Gloucester, Cheltenham & Stroud
Agencies: Woodland Trust, Gloucestershire Wildlife Trust, English Heritage

GETTING THERE

GPS: 51.816423°, -2.155676°
Postcode: GL4 8HP
Driving: From Cranham Village Hall, take Sanatorium Road 0.2 mile west to the Buckhold Woods car park on your right.

Public Transit: Cotswold villages are well served by buses.
Before You Go: If the small car park is full, there is additional parking nearby on Painswick Road. From there, you can join the trail roughly one mile into the described route.

ON THE TRAIL
Pick up the trail in the northwest corner of the car park to enter a dense woodland. Buckholt Wood is part of the Cotswold Commons and Beechwoods National Nature

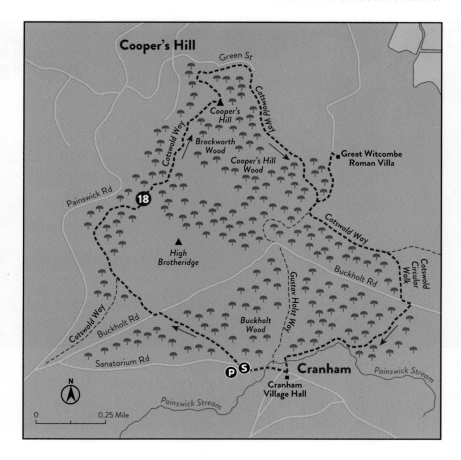

Reserve, an internationally important spot that includes oak, ash, elm, alder, and some of Britain's most abundant beechwoods. Beeches are considered the queen of Britain's trees due to their large domed "crown." Mature beechwoods, like those here, can reach 130 feet.

Go straight along the wide forest track, ignoring all branching paths, for 0.4 mile to reach Buckholt Road. Carefully cross and enter Cooper's Hill Nature Reserve on the opposite side. Continue uphill for 1.1 miles, gaining about 300 feet in elevation, along the flank of High Brotheridge (920 feet) and through thick woods, to join the Cotswold Way, which is well signed throughout the route. Head toward the top of Cooper's Hill (790 feet), ignoring the many side trails, leaving the Cotswold Way on the final stretch to the peak clearing. Keep an eye out for some of the woodland's abundant birdlife,

The edge of Buckholt Wood offers sprawling views of the Gloucestershire countryside.

from the tiny but flashy goldcrest to the huge but stealthy buzzard, and listen for the lyrical trill of the song thrush. There are also many varieties of butterflies that frequent the forest in spring and summer, including the silver-washed fritillary, iridescent in black and orange. The village of Brockworth and the Malvern Hills are visible from the top of Cooper's Hill.

Make a left from the summit to continue along the plateau for 150 feet or so to reach the top of the so-called Cheese Rolling Hill, which is more of a miniature cliff dropping roughly 650 feet. For centuries a festival was staged on Cooper's Hill, where cheese rolling was one of the many traditions celebrating the arrival of warmer days. Today it is the site of a hugely popular annual race in which a seven-to-nine-pound wheel of Double Gloucester cheese is sent careening down the hillside with hordes of lactose-tolerant people in pursuit, few of whom stay upright for long. The goal is to catch the cheese, an impossible get for mere mortals, since it can reach speeds of 70 miles per hour. The first person across the finish line in what's been described as the "world's most dangerous footrace" wins the wheel—and a place in the annals of cheese-chasing.

Leave the hill to continue left (northwest) rejoining the Cotswold Way. Drop down over the next 0.2 mile, wrapping around the base of Cooper's Hill to meet Green Street. Cross through a gate and make a right, then continue along the narrow road for 0.2 mile as it curves and turns into a dirt track. Walk 0.5 mile on the shaded track to reach a wooden signpost, and turn left to take a 0.5-mile roundtrip detour to the Great Witcombe Roman Villa.

The once-expansive complex (AD 150–250) was built on hillside terraces and consisted of living quarters, kitchens, storerooms, and bathhouses. The villa occupants would have been considered wealthy and may have been government officials affiliated with the nearby Roman town of Glevum, now Gloucester. The modern buildings on the site house original mosaics, including a particularly intricate and well-preserved marine scene in the baths, depicting fish and other aquatic creatures with impressive geometric figures on its borders.

Retrace your steps to rejoin the Cotswold Way and follow that for 0.4 mile to a fork at a wooden fingerpost. Turn right (straight ahead follows the Gustav Holst Way) to begin the Cotswold Circular Walk. Climb gradually uphill for 0.3 mile to Buckholt Road, carefully cross over, and turn left to pick up the trail heading back into Buckholt Wood. (When you hit the small car park, walk through it to pick up the "Public Footpath" on its far end.) Veer right where the trail forks, and carry on through the woods for 0.3 mile.

The 250 acres that make up Buckholt Wood host a variety of flora and fauna. There are sturdy woodland shrubs like holly and yew, nearly eight hundred species of wild fungi, and spritely looking primrose, wood anemone, and wild strawberry. Unlike other forests in Britain, this area is believed to have been woodland since the ice sheets retreated thousands of years ago. Back then aurochs (enormous ancestors of modern cattle) and cave bears roamed here, after migrating across Doggerland, the land bridge that once existed between Britain and France. Today's creatures include the less-fearsome fox, deer, badger, weasel, and stoat.

Upon meeting the Painswick Stream, veer right off the main track to follow it downhill. Keep the stream to your left for the next 0.3 mile through some of the oldest, most impressive beech trees on this route. Make a left at the T intersection to rejoin the main track, and continue for roughly 300 feet, crossing the stream on stepping stones. At the paved road (Main Street leading into Sanitorium Road), go right and continue for 0.2 mile to return to the car park.

EXTEND IT

Walk some of the 34-mile Gustav Holst Way, named for the composer who was born and lived in Gloucestershire. Holst, who is best known for his imaginative orchestral composition *The Planets*, took countless walks through the Cotswold countryside, and this route explores spots associated with him.

19 BATH SKYLINE

This loop through tranquil fields and abundant forests offers grand views of the shining and historical city of Bath.

Distance: 6.2 miles
Elevation Gain: 790 feet
High Point: 600 feet
Rating: ★ ★ ★ ★ ★
Difficulty: Moderate
Year-round: Yes
Dog-friendly: Yes, leashed where indicated

Family-friendly: Yes, but a few steep sections; muddy after heavy rain; Family Discovery Trail in Claverton Down
Amenities: None
Map: OS Explorer Map 155, Bristol & Bath
Agency: National Trust

GETTING THERE

GPS: 51.379743°, -2.346097°
Postcode: BA2 6DB
Driving: This walk starts at the corner of Bathwick Hill and Cleveland Walk in Bath. Look for a banner indicating "National Trust, Bathwick Fields."

Public Transit: There is a bus stop at Bathwick Hill and Cleveland Walk, served by the 94, 734, and U1 bus lines.
Before You Go: There is plenty of street parking near the trailhead. The route is well marked as the "National Trust, Bath Skyline."

ON THE TRAIL

Cross Bathwick Hill road from the National Trust site to head north on Cleveland Walk. Continue for 0.3 mile past honey-colored Georgian terraced houses, typical of Bath's stone architecture. Upon reaching Sham Castle Lane, go right to follow the narrow path in between two stone walls for roughly 400 feet. Go right where the path ends at North Road, follow the sidewalk for about a tenth of a mile, and then cross the road to a trailhead at Sham Castle Down. Go through the kissing gate onto the dirt track and then up a long (0.1 mile) flight of stairs. Go through another gate to reach a T intersection.

Take a short detour to the "folly" of Sham Castle by continuing straight for 0.1 mile along a wooded track to a clearing. The "screen wall" here is presumed to have been constructed in the mid-eighteenth century as an elaborate garden decoration. Ralph Allen, who commissioned it, may have been showing off some rock from his nearby limestone quarries. Even as a fake facade, its now-historical arches and turrets are impressive, as are the views of downtown Bath.

Retrace your steps back to the T intersection and go right (north) into Bathwick Wood. The density of the beech and sycamore soaring overhead, with ferns, holly, and ivy on the forest floor, make it hard to believe this is so close to bustling downtown

Bath. In spring and early summer, a profusion of bluebells gives the forest a mythical feel, and wild garlic lends a heady aroma. Keep an eye out for evidence of embankments and terraces etched into the hillside during medieval times, and for stone troughs and markers that channeled clean spring water to Bath during the Georgian era (roughly 1714 to the 1830s).

Continue straight through the wood for 0.3 mile, ignoring trails branching left. Follow "Bath Skyline" signs, veering right as the trail heads a few hundred feet uphill to a gate. Pass through and take a left onto the wide dirt track. Follow the path for 0.6 mile across open meadows as it curves northeast and then east around the base of Bathampton Down (suspected site of the decisive victory of legendary King Arthur over the Saxons around the sixth century) to a kissing gate.

Follow the Bath Skyline trail into Bathampton Wood, where limestone was quarried from the Roman era through the eighteenth century. Its legacy lingers in the sheer rock outcroppings and tramway tracks (built in the 1700s to transport the

Sham castles like this one overlooking Bath were all the rage in the mid-eighteenth century.

stone) seen around the forest. The old mines are now critical to the local bat population. Zigzag for 0.5 mile through the wood to reach another kissing gate.

Cross through to reach Bushey Norwood—two wide, open fields that are part of the Claverton Down limestone plateau. Continue straight for 0.5 mile, with the forested area of Hengrove Wood on your left and an open meadow on your right. Trees were planted in this area in the nineteenth century to create a parkland feel, but this is the site of an Iron Age hillfort near which the Romans later cut a road. (In the eighteenth century, it was also used for horseracing!) Today it's a peaceful spot where wildflowers like cowslips and purple orchids appear in the spring, and nuthatches, tree creepers, and green woodpeckers shelter in tree canopies.

At the end of Bushey Norwood, go through the gate in the stone wall and bear right (southwest). Cross the field in 0.2 mile to reach a wooden gate. Continue along the edge of a wooded area, bearing right and then left to go over the low wall on a stone stile. Take a right to walk along Claverton Hill (road) for 300 feet. Cross the road and go through a gap in the stone wall to resume the Bath Skyline route. Continue straight for 0.2 mile to meet Claverton Down Road, and take a left to walk along the sidewalk. In about 150 feet, cross the road to a wooden gate and pass through to pick up a dirt track.

Follow the path for 0.5 mile in between fences, beneath towering beech trees, and through two gates into Claverton Down. Follow the track as it curves right onto the woodland path, and continue for 0.6 mile to reach a large wooden gate at a gap in the stone wall. Cross through to exit the wood, go left, and cross over the bike path, then make an immediate right to stay on the Bath Skyline trail. Follow the wide dirt track for 0.3 mile to a couple of stone pillars where a trail branches left. Take a quick detour

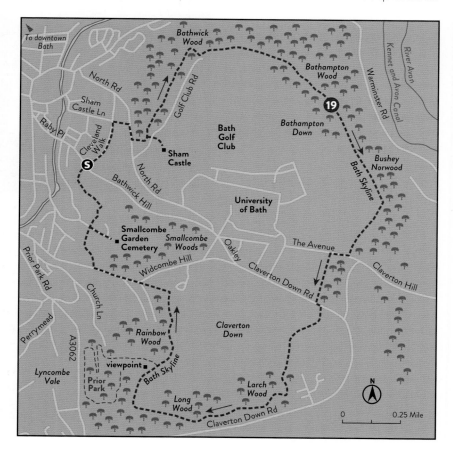

Bath's large green spaces form an appealing backdrop for its many neoclassical structures made of local limestone.

(300 feet or so) to a clearing with excellent views over Lyncombe Vale and Bath, one of the country's prettiest cities, in the valley of the River Avon.

The Romans first built spas and temples in the city below around AD 60, and the popularity of its hot springs has endured. Much of downtown Bath was constructed of Cotswold limestone in the eighteenth century, giving it a distinctive golden glow. During that time, Bath was all the rage for the wealthy and influential. Members of high society soaked in the baths, attended balls, and "took the air" on trails above the city, just as we do today. The writer Jane Austen, in particular, found that the area revived her spirit. While many other places have yielded to scattershot development, Bath, which is a World Heritage site, has maintained its Georgian symmetry and elegance.

Return to the Bath Skyline trail and ascend a long set of stairs leading through Rainbow Wood and across a section of Claverton Down for 0.2 mile. Pass through a kissing gate at the next junction and continue straight on a narrow trail running between stone walls. When the trail ends in less than 300 feet, cross Widcombe Hill Road and make a left to follow the sidewalk for 0.1 mile. Pass through the gate on your right to take the trail marked Smallcombe Vale, then make an almost immediate left to stay on the Bath Skyline route. Continue heading downhill along the edge of the field to a kissing gate at a gravel road.

Go right along the road to take a short detour to the Smallcombe Garden Cemetery. Inside the grounds you'll see two small chapels—the narrow and striking slate-roofed

Church of England Mortuary Chapel, conspicuous with its high bell tower, and the octagonal Nonconformist Smallcombe Vale Chapel, with a pyramidal roof and more modest bellcote. Nonconformist houses of worship were built for Protestant Christians (often Baptists, Methodists, or Quakers) who were not part of the Church of England. Those factions emerged in the sixteenth century from the religious instability of the English Reformation and were called "dissenters" through the seventeenth and eighteenth centuries. Here in Smallcombe, the proximity of these two chapels represents a transition to a (somewhat) more tolerant society. The conformists had their limits, however, and the graveyards for the denominations (which include many prominent members of Bath society from the mid-nineteenth century onward) are strictly divided.

Today the cemetery is a wildlife haven with immense, old-growth trees, including some incredible yew and juniper. Caretakers cut the grass only a few times a year to encourage wildflowers, which support many varieties of bees, butterflies, and birds. It would be easy to pass hours exploring the informal paths through the churchyards and the adjacent, steep ancient wood.

Return to the junction and go right (northeast) through a wooden gate. Continue for about 300 feet, then go left at the T intersection. Follow the trail straight, ignoring branching trails, as it curves around to reach another T intersection. Go left and through a gate to head across the rolling Bathwick Fields. This section offers some of the best skyline views of Bath's landmarks, including the cathedral-like edifice of Bath Abbey, St. John's Church (whose 222-foot spire is a nesting site for breeding peregrine falcons), and the impressive octagonal corner tower of the Empire Hotel. Follow the Bath Skyline trail across the meadow for 0.2 mile to reach the gate at Bathwick Hill road where this walk began.

EXTEND IT

From the viewpoint for Lyncombe Vale, add a 1.8-mile loop around Prior Park to see the eighteenth-century Palladian Bridge and ornate gardens. (There's also a cafe and restrooms on the park grounds.)

20 WOODSTOCK & BLENHEIM PALACE

This rolling loop from Woodstock, "the Gateway to the Cotswolds," to and around opulent Blenheim Palace is a short distance northwest of bustling Oxford, but it feels like it's a world away.

Distance: 5.2 miles
Elevation Gain: 430 feet
High Point: 390 feet
Rating: ★ ★ ★ ★ ★
Difficulty: Easy to moderate
Year-round: Yes
Dog-friendly: Yes, leashed

Family-friendly: Yes, but use caution on roads; plenty of open fields and lawns, kid-oriented activities on palace grounds
Amenities: Pubs and hotels in Woodstock and cafe and restrooms at Blenheim
Map: OS Explorer Map 180, Oxford
Agency: Blenheim Palace

GETTING THERE

GPS: 51.847652°, -1.355780°
Postcode: OX20 1SL
Driving: From Oxford, take A34 2.6 miles and continue on A44 for 7.6 miles to Market Street. Turn left on Market Street and, in 350 feet, the Woodstock Town Hall is on your left.
Public Transit: There are frequent buses from central Oxford to Woodstock.

Before You Go: While the free, on-street parking in central Woodstock is popular with tourists, there's also plentiful parking within Blenheim Palace. Entry tickets to Blenheim are pricey but worth it (a "day" pass can be traded up for an annual pass for free).

ON THE TRAIL

Begin at the historical Woodstock Town Hall, in the heart of the village. Built in 1766 and designed by famous architect Sir William Chambers, the elaborate and color-ful coat of arms above the main entrance reassures onlookers that "Dieu defend le droit," or "God defends the right." If that motto fails to inspire, consider instead the sundial installed in the second-story opening on the south side of the building, which is engraved with the Latin words "Tempus fugit," or "Time flies."

Head straight across the market square and along Park Street, lined with historical inns, pubs, and homes. The Bear Hotel on your left dates from the thirteenth century. A bit farther on, also on your left, is St. Mary Magdalene Church, which is worth taking a few minutes to explore. On its south side is a lovely Norman doorway with a hallmark zigzag, or chevron, pattern. The church was built during the reign of Henry I (1100–1135), when he and his hunting entourage stayed at Woodstock Manor, a royal lodge that sat on the current site of Blenheim Palace.

Woodstock, which means "the clearing in the woods" in Old English, was described as a royal forest in the famous Domesday Book of 1086 that surveyed much of England. The great Wychwood Forest once covered many thousands of acres west of Wood-stock; today the remaining forest, located a few miles away, covers about 1200 acres.

Like his grandfather, Henry II was partial to Woodstock, but hunting game wasn't necessarily his main interest. He kept his mistress, legendary beauty Rosamund Clif-ford, at the manor. "Fair Rosamund," as she was known, has inspired centuries of poems and ballads, and not a little folklore. One popular tale says that, in order to keep the affair hush-hush from the queen, Henry II only rendezvoused with Rosamund within

Blenheim Palace is a masterpiece of Baroque architecture set within a two-thousand-acre parkland.

a complex labyrinth on the grounds of the hunting estate. But, according to legend, the queen tracked down Rosamund within the maze and forced her to drink poison. In reality, the dalliance ended and Rosamund later died around age thirty at a nearby convent in Godstow.

Reach the Woodstock Gate, a.k.a. the Triumphal Arch (1723), at 0.1 mile. Nicholas Hawkmoor modeled it on the arch of the same name in Rome, and it now serves as a pedestrian entrance to the grounds of Blenheim Palace. Pass through the gate and go straight for 0.8 mile along the narrow, paved road, ignoring all turns. The palace is across the vast lawns on your right (southwest). Follow the shady lane as it curves right around the Pleasure Gardens. Continue for 0.5 mile to the neoclassical Bladon Bridge spanning the River Glyme. The riverbank is lined with impressive cedar and copper beech trees. Look for circling raptors and red kites, which were once at risk of extinction but are now on the rebound.

Cross the bridge and carry on for 1.7 miles as the wide trail curves and climbs gently (about 150 feet in elevation) alongside and then through the forested High Park area. There are 2000 acres of mature woodland in Blenheim, including High Park. Named for its prominence on the hillside above The Lake, High Park has nearly one thousand veteran oak trees. At nine hundred years old, this is the oldest continuous woodland in Europe.

At the end of the densely wooded area, just past a section of towering evergreens, emerge at the foot of a grassy knoll surrounded by a wooden fence. Before reaching the fence, leave the main trail and bear right along a grassy track. In 0.2 mile, an arm of The Lake (not an especially creative name, but easy to remember!) will come into view as you reach a junction. Go right to stick to the shoreline along the Wychwood Way. Watch for coots and mallards feeding among the sturdy, abundant reeds. Wind along the lake's edge for 0.7 mile, passing Fair Rosamund's Well near the end. The pool was already well known in the twelfth century, but at that time it was called Everswell because it was rumored never to run dry. Only since the sixteenth century was it named for Rosamund, when pilgrims would journey there to collect water that they believed had curative properties.

Bear right at the junction with the paved track and walk for 0.1 mile to reach the bridge where The Lake, on your right, and the Queen Pool, on your left, come together. Grand Bridge is an impressive stone span, but its original design was, indeed, much grander. Mounting debt required that the plans be scaled back, and

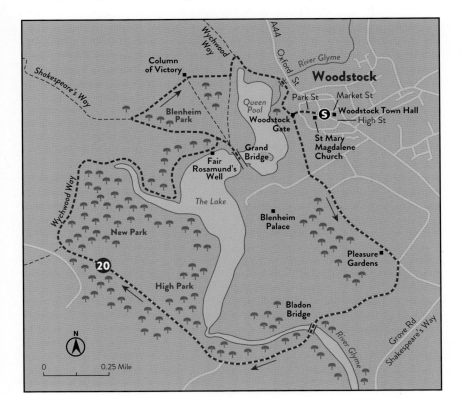

it was finally completed without the planned towers and central arcade. This route does not cross Grand Bridge but pauses on its expanse for views of the pools and palace. The palace is a stellar example of the work of two of England's eminent architects—John Vanbrugh and Nicholas Hawksmoor. The baroque style, in vogue at the time, was meant to be both decorative and awe-inspiring. (Mission accomplished!) After winning his battle here in 1704, John Churchill was granted Woodstock Park by the Crown and became the first Duke of Marlborough. For nearly twenty years after that, public funds allowed this lavish, naturalistic Versailles to take shape.

The structures and grounds were built and rebuilt over centuries to suit the times and the whims of the palace occupants. In the mid- to late-eighteenth century, the lavish landscape was already drawing hordes of tourists (the palace itself was opened to visitors much later, in 1950). The fundamental landscape design has remained largely unchanged since the fourth duke, whose informal style celebrated natural landscapes of tranquil waterways, sprawling lawns, and abundant woodlands, died in 1817. In 1874 beloved wartime prime minister Winston Churchill, grandson of the seventh duke, was born at Blenheim, and he would spend time here throughout his life (he is also buried nearby). The palace and park became a UNESCO World Heritage Site in 1987. The estate has remained in the Churchill family and today is home to the twelfth Duke and Duchess of Marlborough.

From the bridge, retrace your steps to the trail and continue straight to rejoin Wychwood Way. In 0.5 mile, bear right and continue past the Column of Victory on your left. The 135-foot tall Doric column was built between 1727 and 1730 to celebrate the first duke's military prowess. It is topped with stone eagles and a lead statue of the duke, portrayed as Caesar, holding a "winged victory." The clearing to your right, between the trail and the Queen Pool, is where Woodstock Manor once stood. It was destroyed during the English Civil War in the mid-seventeenth century, and much of its stone was used to construct the Grand Bridge.

This stretch of trail is part of the 146-mile Shakespeare's Way, a walking route that spans from the bard's birthplace in Stratford-upon-Avon to London's Globe Theatre. Continue for 0.5 mile across vast sheep pastures to the edge of Queen Pool. Follow the trail for 0.3 mile around its edge and continue straight across the River Glyme. Head uphill through a copse for roughly 0.2 mile and then, at the end of the wooded area, turn left through the Woodstock Gate and retrace your steps back to Woodstock Town Hall.

EXTEND IT

The 36-mile Wychwood Way, which passes through the heart of Blenheim Park, is a circular walk around what remains of the ancient forest of Wychwood.

21 OXFORD BLUES & GREENS

Two of Oxford's best green spaces are at its north and south ends, requiring a trek through the city center—full of history and famous architecture—to see them both.

Distance: 5.5 miles
Elevation Gain: 100 feet
High Point: 215 feet
Rating: ★ ★ ★ ★
Difficulty: Easy to moderate
Year-round: Yes
Family-friendly: Yes, but sections run alongside open water

Dog-friendly: Yes, leashed
Amenities: Innumerable restaurants, hotels, and museums; Speedwell Street Toilets (near Christ Church Meadow's main gate); public restrooms in center of University Parks
Map: OS Explorer Map 180, Oxford
Agencies: Oxford University Parks, Christ Church Meadow

GETTING THERE

GPS: 51.749186°, -1.255911°
Postcode: OX1 1RA
Driving: There are several park-and-ride options on the outskirts of the city, with frequent buses running into the city center, a short walk from Christ Church Meadow.
Public Transit: Buses and trains run frequently to Oxford from central London and the major airports, and many different bus lines serve the city and outskirts.
Before You Go: Oxford University Parks are open sunrise to sunset (gates are locked outside these hours). Christ Church Meadow is open 24 hours a day.

ON THE TRAIL

With the Christ Church Meadow gate at your back, cross St. Aldates road and go right (north) toward the city center. Follow St. Aldates, looking right to see Tom Tower, the distinctive bell tower at the entrance to Christ Church college, which was built in 1681–1682. Designed by famous architect Sir Christopher Wren in the Late Gothic style, it may be better known today as the college where several scenes from the *Harry Potter* movies were filmed (which explains the swarms of tourists in Hogwarts sweatshirts). Christ Church is one of the thirty-nine colleges of the University of Oxford. It is billed as the "oldest university in the English-speaking world," though the university has no clear founding date. Teaching began here around 1096 and started to expand rapidly in 1167, when King Henry II banned Brits from going across the English Channel to study in Paris. In the centuries since, Oxford has become synonymous with academic excellence and has scores of notable alumni, including twenty-eight UK prime ministers.

Oxford's maze-like alleys and awe-inspiring architecture are hemmed in by rolling rivers and parks.

In 0.2 mile, the road curves right, with Queen Street heading left and High Street to your right. Across the intersection is 74-foot-high St. Martin's Tower, also known as Carfax Tower, which is all that remains of a twelfth-century church that once sat on the northwest corner of what is now considered the exact city center. When Oxford was a medieval town encircled by a 2-mile-long wall, all four of the main roads leading to it entered through a tollgate near here (*carfax*, or *quadrifurcus*, means "a place where four roads cross").

Head toward High Street, passing by a pedestrian mall crammed with shops on your left. In a few hundred feet is the Covered Market, marked by an arch over the door-way, which opened in 1774. If time permits, browse its many traditional and eclectic stalls and shops. (Note which door you used to enter the market because it's easy to get turned around in its mazelike alleyways.)

In another 0.2 mile go left just before University Church of St. Mary the Virgin to take St. Mary's Passage. Follow it a few hundred feet to enter Radcliffe Square. Straight ahead is the circular stone hulk of the Radcliffe Camera, one of Oxford's most iconic buildings. The Rad Cam (as it is commonly known), finished in 1749, was England's first circular library, named for a well-known physician who funded its construction. It was originally a science library, but today it is the university's main reading "room." Opposite the Rad Cam is St. Mary's. Its thirteenth-century tower (accessible for a fee), topped a century later with an impressive spire, has panoramic views of the city.

Follow the path around the back of the Radcliffe Camera for about a tenth of a mile to go left on Catte Street, then walk a little under a tenth of a mile to reach the intersection of Broad Street and Holywell Street. Continue straight onto what's now Parks Road, and cross over to the right-hand sidewalk. Follow the tree-lined road past countless academic buildings for 0.2 mile to South Parks Road. Cross South Parks Road and go right. On your left is the Pitt Rivers Museum (housing the university's tremendous anthropological and archaeological collections) and the Oxford University Museum of Natural History.

Continue 0.3 mile along South Parks Road, watching for bikes as the sidewalk becomes a cycling path. A blue sign on your left marks Oxford University Park South Lodge. Pass through the gate to enter University Parks. Here you'll start a 1.3-mile clockwise loop around the park, but there are plenty of side trails to the interior, where huge trees shade countless picnic spots. There are also recreation grounds where rugby and cricket (and Quidditch, at least the Muggle version) are played. The university bought the land, about 90 acres, in the 1850s, back when farmers sowed—and sheep and cattle munched—the surrounding fields. Where there was once only 190 willows, 59 elms, 1 oak, and 1 poplar, the park now has over 1500 trees across 250 species and varieties.

In a few hundred feet, bear left onto the dirt path for South Walk, and follow it around the perimeter of the park. In the warmer months, there are cultivated plants and flowers on your left, leading to pines, chestnuts, cedars, oaks, and more—forming a cocoon of green in bustling Oxford. In 0.3 mile the path bears right onto West Walk (there is a beautiful Japanese pagoda tree on your right) as it runs parallel to Parks Road. This lovely stretch is lined with plentiful benches beneath maple, beech, yew, holly, and one giant redwood. Follow the dirt track for 0.2 mile past another gated entrance on your left as the trail bears right onto North Walk (look for a sign with a park map and the closing time). This particularly leafy area includes, among others, birch, juniper, sycamore, and several varieties of oak.

Continue straight for 0.2 mile, ignoring any tracks branching off, until the turnoff for Lazenbee's Pond. Bear left at the fork and skirt clockwise around the back of the pond for 0.2 mile. An impressive variety of trees flank the pond, including hickory, spruce, coastal redwood, and cottonwood. Bear left again as the path rejoins the main perimeter trail, now called Riverside Walk, alongside the River Cherwell. The 40-mile-long River Cherwell flows southward from its source to join the River Thames in Oxford. Keeping the river on your left, continue straight (south) for 0.3 mile, but bear slightly left at two forks along the way. Soon you'll pass High Bridge on your left (built in the 1920s, and locally referred to as the Rainbow Bridge because of its steep arc), which leads to meadows on the east side of the river. Just past the bridge on your right is the "Tolkien Bench," placed in memory of J. R. R. Tolkien (1892–1973). Tolkien graduated from Oxford in 1915, served in World War I, then returned to teach at the university, where he wrote *The Hobbit* and the first two books of the *Lord of the Rings* trilogy.

Upon reaching the edge of the park, called Cox's Corner, pass beneath some birch and a huge weeping willow and through a metal gate in the southeast corner to reach the Marston Cyclepath. For a short detour to a local favorite (introduced to me by a family living in Oxford), take a left on the cycle path and immediately cross the foot-bridge spanning the Holywell Mill Stream. Just past the bridge on your left is a small greenspace surrounded on two sides by an elbow of the River Cherwell.

This is Parson's Pleasure, so called for a former nude bathing pool at its far end. Nowadays it's marked by the punt rollers that once helped boaters circumnavigate the weir. The all-male spot was used by university fellows for many years and, if that seems sexist, don't despair: a nearby area known as Dame's Delight was women-only. Even though "alfresco" bathing is now banned, this is a delightful spot to sit and watch punts and ducks float by.

Go back across the bridge, past the University Parks gate you exited through, and continue straight along the bike path. In 0.1 mile you'll reach the gate through which you entered the park. Take a sharp left to walk along St. Cross Road, past old stone rowhouses and walled college recreation grounds. In 0.4 mile follow the road as it bears left and becomes Longwall Street, skirting the east side of the city. The street is suitably named for the fifteenth-century stone wall on your left marking the western edge of Magdalen College. Follow Longwall for 0.2 mile to a T intersection at High Street.

Cross High Street via the crosswalk on your right, then turn left to follow it for a few hundred feet toward the octagonal turret-topped Magdalen Tower. Between a stone wall and a hedge, turn right onto Rose Lane. Follow the narrow lane for 0.1 mile, past the visit-worthy University of Oxford Botanic Garden on your left, to where it ends at a metal gate. Cross through the gate to reach Merton Field, then make a right to follow the footpath as it skirts around the top of the field.

This stretch has been known as Deadman's Walk for eight hundred years, since it was the route funeral processions took from a synagogue (near where Tom Tower now stands) to the Jewish burial ground, now the site of the botanic garden. Oxford's medieval Jewish quarter lay along what is now St. Aldates, where this walk started. In

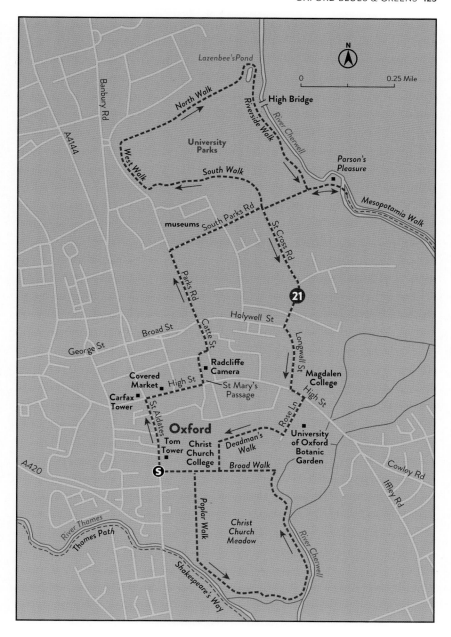

Lazenbee's Pond

North Walk

High Bridge

Banbury Rd

A4144

West Walk

University Parks

South Walk

Riverside Walk

River Cherwell

Parson's Pleasure

Mesopotamia Walk

museums

South Parks Rd

St Cross Rd

Parks Rd

21

Holywell St

Catte St

Broad St

George St

Longwall St

Magdalen College

Covered Market

High St

Radcliffe Camera

St Mary's Passage

Carfax Tower

St Aldates

High St

Rose Ln

Oxford

Tom Tower

Christ Church College

Deadman's Walk

University of Oxford Botanic Garden

A420

Broad Walk

Cowley Rd

Iffley Rd

S

Poplar Walk

River Thames

Thames Path

Christ Church Meadow

River Cherwell

Shakespeare's Way

N

0   0.25 Mile

The intellectual and ecological blend seamlessly amid Oxford's plentiful green spaces and clusters of colleges.

1290, King Edward I expelled all Jews from England, from which they remained exiled for more than 350 years.

Follow Deadman's Walk for 0.2 mile until it intersects Merton Grove, another dirt path. Go left and follow it for a few hundred feet to reach a wide dirt track, Broad Walk, at the north end of Christ Church Meadow. Go roughly 0.1 mile (toward the gate where this walk began), but turn left onto Poplar Walk, opposite Christ Church College's Venetian-style Meadow Building. Go straight, keeping the open meadow on your left, for 0.3 mile.

Reach the River Thames and bear right to walk along it. The 215-mile-long river flows southeast from here through London and onward to the North Sea. Its span through Oxford has long been known locally as the River Isis, for what reason no one really knows. (From here both the 184-mile Thames Path and 146-mile Shakespeare's Way can be accessed by heading 0.2 mile south of Christ Church Meadow along St. Aldates, crossing the River Thames on the Folly Bridge, and turning left.)

In 0.2 mile arrive at the River Cherwell's confluence with the Thames. Bear left to take the track that follows the Cherwell (not crossing it). Keeping the river on your right, follow the tree-lined trail for 0.5 mile as it curves around to meet Broad Walk. Go left on Broad Walk and continue straight for 0.4 mile to pass through the Christ Church gate, where this walk began.

EXTEND IT

From Parson's Pleasure, cross the cycle path in between the footbridge you came over and another to its left, and continue south for about 150 feet. Turn left to cross a gated wooden bridge onto a skinny island called Mesopotamia. With the River Cherwell on both sides, follow the Mesopotamia Walk for 0.5 mile to the bridge at Kings Mill Lane. Return the way you came.

EASTERN ENGLAND

London generally gets the spotlight in this region, and with good reason, as it is exquisitely alive—with humanity, mainly, but also with nature. In the late nineteenth century, novelist and historian Sir Walter Besant wrote, "I've been walking about London for the last 30 years, and I find something fresh in it every day" (and much of that time predated indoor plumbing!). Farther east is the equally epic city of Cambridge, steeped in history, dotted with parks and streams, and surrounded by rural charm. Push east from there and you'll land along the dynamic North Sea coast, thick with spirits, to revel in oft-painted seascapes.

LONDON

London (Trails 22–24) hardly needs introduction, but here goes: The capital of Great Britain is one of the largest cities in Europe. In addition to its history, museums, architecture, and theater scene, it has a remarkable number of green spaces, some rarely visited by tourists. In 2019 the National Park City Foundation named London the world's first "national park city" in recognition of its greenness and biodiversity. Nearly half the footprint of downtown London is open space, either parks (there are three thousand of them) or waterways. There are nine million people living in London, and nearly that many trees. From foxes to falcons and ferns to foxgloves, over fourteen thousand different species of plants, animals, and fungi are found in the city.

EAST ANGLIA

Also known as the "East of England," and often overlooked as a featureless swathe, East Anglia (Trails 25–29) is actually an intriguing mix of medieval market towns, rambling rivers, ancient heaths, and miles upon miles of ever-changing coastline. It's made

OPPOSITE: *Holkham (Trail 27) is sheer coastal immensity with miles of woodlands, dunes, marshes, beach, and creeks to explore.*

up of the counties of Norfolk, Suffolk, and Cambridgeshire. This is doubtless the flattest part the country, but what it lacks in height it makes up for in character.

The area remains, in many ways, as bucolic as it was when famed artist John Constable (1776–1837) painted vivid but soothing scenes of the countryside. There are wide expanses of farm and fen and wildlife-rich wetlands. Cows even roam freely in the fields surrounding Cambridge, the famed university city nestled in the midst of parks and gardens through which the ambling River Cam flows.

22 PARKS OF LONDON

This route passes through five of London's Royal Parks, each with its unique character and every one a haven for wildlife and humans alike.

Distance: 7.2 miles (one way)
Elevation Gain: 230 feet
High Point: 210 feet
Rating: ★ ★ ★ ★
Difficulty: Moderate
Year-round: Yes
Family-friendly: Yes, but use caution at road crossings; large playgrounds at

St. James's Park, Hyde Park, Kensington Gardens, and Regent's Park
Dog-friendly: Yes, leashed
Amenities: Public restrooms and concessions at parks; neighborhoods in central London have many services
Map: OS Explorer Map 173, London North
Agency: Royal Parks

GETTING THERE

GPS: 51.505118°, -0.123402°
Postcode: SW1A 2HE
Driving: Driving is highly discouraged due to traffic, parking restrictions, pricey parking lots, and congestion charges.
Public Transit: The closest London Underground (a.k.a. the Tube) stop to Whitehall

Gardens is Embankment on the Bakerloo, Northern, Circle, and District lines.
Before You Go: The tourist season slows around mid-September. Bring a light picnic blanket to enjoy the shaded lawns along the way.

ON THE TRAIL

From the gate in the northeast corner of Whitehall Gardens, head south for 0.1 mile on either of the two parallel paths. This plot is part of the Victoria Embankment Gardens, a string of green spaces atop a sewer that was installed along the north side of the River Thames from 1865–1870. At the time the gardens were finished, they were heralded as Europe's finest. (Everyone was pretty happy about the new sewer line too!) The impressive white stone building on your right, once apartments and now a hotel, was the headquarters of the secret service during World War I.

Today Whitehall Gardens continues to be a hidden oasis of flowerbeds and shrubs, as well as tall lime trees, London plane trees, and trees of heaven (imported from China in 1751).

Carefully cross Horse Guards Avenue, go straight into the next section of park, and look right beyond the fence for a set of stairs. These are a fascinating remnant of Whitehall Palace, once the largest in Europe when it spread out over a large complex of buildings with 1500 rooms, courtyards, bowling greens, and even a jousting yard. These steps were installed for Queen Mary in 1691 to lead from her residence to the river (which used to flow at the base). The palace was home to English monarchs from 1530 until it burned in 1698. The only surviving structure is the Banqueting House of 1622 that lies directly west, on the other side of the current Ministry of Defence building on your right. (Grim fact: King Charles I was beheaded out front in 1649.)

Continue straight for 0.1 mile past inviting lawns, plentiful benches, austere statues, and moving war memorials. Look left to spot the London Eye, or Millennium Wheel, across the busy river. The River Thames, the second-longest in the UK, flows for 215 miles from its origin in the Cotswold Hills to the North Sea. London is likely located here because of the river. Invading Romans sailed up it in AD 43 to settle in what they called "Londinium," which became a bustling port. The Thames water level is highly influenced by North Sea tides and, at London Bridge, the river rises 22 feet on spring tides. It is still a major supplier of city water.

Cross Richmond Terrace (which is an entrance to the huge Metropolitan Police Headquarters on your right) and go straight for about a tenth of a mile along the sidewalk in front of it. The name of the building, taken over by the force in 2016, is New Scotland Yard, though it no longer backs onto the Great Scotland Yard, from which the moniker was derived in the nineteenth century. Its enduring place in popular culture was cemented by Sir Arthur Conan Doyle's *Sherlock Holmes* series.

Upon reaching Bridge Street, look toward Westminster Bridge and the bronze sculptures of Queen Boudica (or Victory) and her two daughters, of the Iceni tribe of Celts, who led a failed uprising against the Romans. Despite not living up to her name, the Iron Age warrior queen riding a menacing war chariot is a British folk hero. Turn back to Big Ben, London's largest timepiece, and the Houses of Parliament across the way. Turn right and follow Bridge Street, which turns into Great George Street once you've crossed Whitehall, and is called Birdcage Walk at Horse Guards Road. In about a quarter mile, cross Horse Guards Road to the southeast corner of St. James's Park.

Walk a couple hundred feet beneath London plane trees to the paved path that enters the park, and turn right. In a few hundred feet, curve left to continue alongside St. James's Park Lake. Once a marshland, St. James's Park was landscaped in the mid-seventeenth century and redesigned in the early nineteenth century. It is the oldest and most manicured of the Royal Parks but, aside from its ornate flower beds, still has a bit of a wild feel in its shrubs, trees, grassland, and meadow. Both the spotted

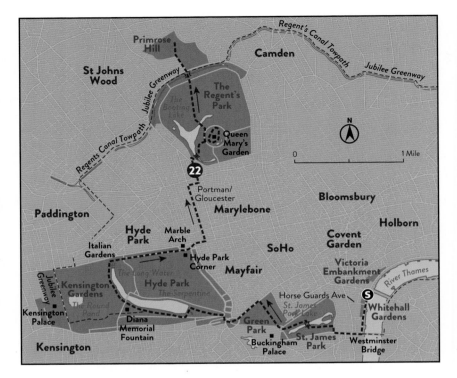

woodpecker and tawny owl breed here. Birds like the reed warbler and great crested grebe can be found along the lake and among the reedbeds. The local pelican population, which has persisted for over 350 years, is nearly as old as the park itself.

Walk 0.2 mile along the lake, beneath alder and weeping willow, then turn right to cross the bridge. To your right, Whitehall buildings and the London Eye shine in the distance. To your left is Buckingham Palace, the home of the current monarch, Queen Elizabeth II. Once over the bridge, go left to follow the path running parallel to the lake. Butterflies and bees buzz among yellow iris and purple loosestrife on the lakeshore. This park was the first of the eight Royal Parks to be opened to the public, but St. James's trees are fairly young, with few older than 150 years. Still, they are surprisingly diverse and include species like black mulberry, fig, and scarlet oak. Continue straight for about a tenth of a mile and, instead of following the path around the west side of the lake, go right and slightly uphill toward the park exit on The Mall.

Cross the road (look left for views of the large bronze and marble Victoria Memorial) and go straight ahead into Green Park. Follow the wide, paved track for 0.1 mile as it curves left. The tall trees here are mainly London plane and lime, which are fierce pollution gobblers. Rarer species, including black poplar, silver maple, oak, and hawthorn, also contribute to the microclimate that keeps the park cooler than the surrounding area on hot summer days.

When you see map placards on your right near where two narrower tracks branch off, take the left path heading northwest. (There are *a lot* of intersecting paths in Green Park. If you lose your way, just keep heading west toward Hyde Park Corner.) Go straight for 0.3 mile through acres of grassland and trees. In spring, hundreds of thousands of daffodils bloom in the park, transforming it, for at least a few weeks, into *Yellow* Park.

Upon reaching a T intersection at the edge of the park, go left, continuing for 0.3 mile along the perimeter. Pass a war memorial and bear left when the track splits. Carry on for a few hundred feet, then turn right to cross Duke of Wellington Place to the Wellington Arch. From 1826 to 1830, the majestic arch was at the entrance to Buckingham Palace. It was later moved—precisely *how* is difficult to imagine—and topped with a bronze sculpture of the angel of peace descending on a four-horsed chariot of war (an earlier statue of the first Duke of Wellington was removed long ago but the name stuck).

Go straight across the square for 0.1 mile, walk beneath the arch, bear right toward the intersection, and cross Knightsbridge at the crosswalk to meet Hyde Park Corner, with its stone arches and columns. Go straight through the gates beneath the arch toward Hyde Park. Cross the park road at the crosswalk and bear left of the map placard to enter the park.

In a couple hundred feet, bear right at the trail fork to pass through a wrought iron gate and wind past the Boy and Dolphin Fountain, through the Rose Garden, and past the Huntress Fountain. Follow the gravel path through an oasis of manicured and wildish seasonal flower plots, with benches lining the cooling fountains, for about a third of a mile. Just past the boulders on your left marking the Hyde Park Holocaust Memorial, bear right at the T intersection toward The Serpentine, a lake that bisects the park. Bear left behind the restaurant to walk along the eastern edge of the lake for 0.1 mile. Look for a great vantage point down the length of The Serpentine, which was created in the late 1720s by damming the River Westbourne.

Hyde Park, now 350 acres, was created in 1536 by Henry VIII as a hunting ground and opened to the public in 1637. It's the biggest of the Royal Parks in central London, and its mature trees, diverse shrubs, native wildflower meadows, and herbaceous plantings are important habitat for songbirds, bees, bats, and butterflies. Go straight along the south side of the lake for a little over half a mile, curving right along the lakeshore. Look for swans—a black one is seen from time to time—and other exotic-looking wildfowl. Just before you cross beneath the Serpentine Bridge, look left to the Diana Memorial Fountain, in honor of the departed Princess of Wales. The moving sculpture is a ring of Cornish marble that channels water downhill in two directions into a still basin.

Green Park is a 40-acre, triangular wedge of respite from London's urban hubbub.

Pass through the arched underpass beneath the impressive stone bridge. You are now in 275-acre Kensington Gardens, once the private gardens of Kensington Palace. Follow the shore of the lake, now called The Long Water, for 0.4 mile to the Italian Gardens, an ornamental water garden created in the 1860s. The playful fountains, classical sculptures, and carved urns are made of stone and marble.

Bear right around the gardens onto a wide track flanked by huge trees, and continue for two-thirds of a mile along the northern perimeter of Hyde Park. When the path intersects the paved bike route, bear left across it and carry on for 0.1 mile to the park's northeast entrance. You'll pass Cumberland Gate (on your left) and Speakers' Corner (on your right). Hyde Park has a lengthy history of protest, and various people still share their views at Speakers' Corner on Sunday mornings.

Go left to follow the track for 0.1 mile north-northeast toward the intersection at Marble Arch, another triumphal stone span. Cross Marble Arch to the north side of Oxford Street and go right. Follow Oxford Street for 0.1 mile to Portman Street, then go left. Continue straight on Portman Street for a little under half a mile, then go right on York Street. At the next intersection, go left onto Baker Street and follow it for about a quarter mile (note the Sherlock Holmes Museum on your left at 221B) to the Outer

Circle, the road that circumnavigates The Regent's Park. Bear right to cross the Outer Circle at the crosswalk to the Clarence Gate entrance.

At nearly 400 acres, The Regent's Park (including Primrose Hill) is a curious mix of formal gardens, tree-lined paths, sporting grounds, boating waters, a heart-pumping hill, a mosque, and a zoo. Over two hundred species of birds frequent the park—its grey herons are particularly impressive—and it has a breeding population of hedgehogs. Like Hyde Park, The Regent's Park was originally part of a hunting forest belonging to Henry VIII. It was landscaped in the early 1800s for the royal family but was opened to the public a few decades later. Regent's Park is named for the playboy prince who later became King George IV.

Once inside the park, take a right and then an immediate left to cross the Clarence Bridge. Make a left on the other side and follow the trail for 0.3 mile as it curves past the Boating Lake to meet the Inner Circle, a road circumnavigating sprawling lawns and spectacular gardens. Carefully cross the road and go straight to explore the inner sanctum of Queen Mary's Gardens, which boasts more than twelve thousand roses. There are any number of routes among the gardens; wander whichever way you like (this route makes a 0.5-mile loop), then exit the way you entered.

Cross Inner Circle road and go right to follow it 0.1 mile. At a path signed for "Long-bridge" on your left, go through the gates and continue for 0.1 mile. A few hundred feet past the bridge, bear right when the trail forks. Go straight along the path, flanked by recreation fields, for about a third of a mile. Go straight through the Monkey Gate (named for the London Zoo, to your right) and carefully cross the Outer Circle road. Follow the footpath straight ahead, in between the black, wrought iron fencing, for 0.1 mile. Cross the narrow stone bridge over the two-hundred-year-old Regent's Canal.

A few hundred feet past the canal, go right on Prince Albert Road, then make an immediate left to cross it. Go straight to enter Primrose Hill, another remnant of the former hunting grounds that was later made available to the commoners of London. Today it is a vast, open grassland with tree-lined paths crisscrossing in every direction. Go straight to follow the park perimeter uphill for 0.2 mile. When you reach a fork at a bench, bear right to continue uphill. Follow that for about a tenth of a mile as it curves toward the top of the hill. A placard on the summit quotes poet William Blake: "I have conversed with the spiritual sun. I saw him on Primrose Hill." But even on a cloudy day—spiritual or otherwise—much of central London can be seen from this viewpoint.

Retrace your steps, or venture east off the summit into the lovely Primrose Hill neighborhood via Regent's Park Road. Buses are easy to catch, and the closest tube station is Chalk Farm, just north of Primrose Hill.

EXTEND IT

Regent's Canal Towpath follows the 9.4-mile waterway from Little Venice to the River Thames. It can be accessed from where this route crosses Regent's Canal.

23 HAMPSTEAD HEATH

This route begins in one of the city's poshest neighborhoods but quickly ducks into the storied woodlands and roomy grasslands of one of its finest green spaces.

Distance: 5.6 miles
Elevation Gain: 620 feet
High Point: 375 feet
Rating: ★ ★ ★ ★
Difficulty: Easy to moderate
Year-round: Yes

Family-friendly: Yes
Dog-friendly: Yes, leashed in places
Amenities: Several public restrooms and opportunities for refreshments
Map: OS Explorer Map 173, London North
Agency: City of London

GETTING THERE

GPS: 51.556689°, -0.178329°
Postcode: NW3 1QG
Before You Go: There are many paths on the Heath, formal and informal, which means a lot of territory to explore. This route follows well-marked paths, but wandering into some of the wilder-feeling sections is greatly encouraged.

Driving: Driving is highly discouraged due to heavy traffic, parking restrictions, pricey parking lots, and congestion charges, which must be paid in advance.
Public Transit: Hampstead Station is on the Edgeware branch of the Northern line of the London Underground.

ON THE TRAIL

Exit the Hampstead tube station onto Hampstead High Street (A502). Go left (southeast) on High Street for roughly 200 feet to Flask Walk, a narrow passageway lined with shops. Turn left to take Flask Walk for a few hundred feet and, when it emerges onto a narrow road, continue straight for roughly 300 feet. Continue straight as Flask Walk leads into Well Walk, then follow it for 0.3 mile to East Heath Road. Notice No. 40 on your right, where preeminent landscape painter John Constable lived while making several studies of the Heath. The neighborhood has long been a magnet for elites, from Romantic painters and poets like Shelley, Coleridge, Byron, and Keats to fiction writers Robert Louis Stevenson, H. G. Wells, D. H. Lawrence, and C. S. Lewis. (A snowy adventure on the Heath is said to have inspired Narnia, at least according to local lore.) But those artists likely couldn't afford the current rent of Hampstead's historical homes, which are now populated with famous actors, musicians, and sports stars.

Cross East Heath Road at the crosswalk and go left. Pick up the dirt trail on your right heading into Hampstead Heath. This is Lime Avenue, named for the famous lanky trees flanking the trail. These limes don't bear citrus fruit but rather are tall, sturdy lindens with white spring blossoms and huge leaves that blanch to gold in fall.

Go straight for 0.2 mile, then make a sharp right along another wide track just before reaching a small stream. After another 0.2 mile veer left to cross in between two ponds (Hampstead No. 2 on your right and Hampstead No. 3 on your left). Dozens of ponds, fed by the River Fleet, were dug in the seventeenth and eighteenth century to supply water to the city, but are now all recreational, including several for swimming.

Continue straight past the ponds and into the trees for 0.1 mile before veering right to head east and uphill through grassland, shrubs, and wildflowers for 0.2 mile to the top of Parliament Hill. It got its current name when Parliamentary forces used the hill as a defense point during the English Civil War (1642–1651), but before then it was known as Traitor's Hill, supposedly for the 1605 Gunpowder Plot gang who waited to see Parliament blow sky high from here (thankfully, the plot was foiled). Most people visiting the Heath at some point find themselves atop this 322-foot-high hump. Even on a cloudy day the London skyline is visible, including St. Paul's Cathedral, Palace of Westminster, the Shard, and the Gerkin. It's not the highest spot in London, but it doesn't fail to impress. In his *Tour of London and the Provinces*, Daniel Defoe (who also penned *Robinson Crusoe*) wrote of the Heath: "'Tis so near heaven, that I dare not say it can be a proper situation, for any but a race of mountaineers, whose lungs have been used to a rarity'd air."

The calming high of Parliament Hill feels far removed from the restless city below.

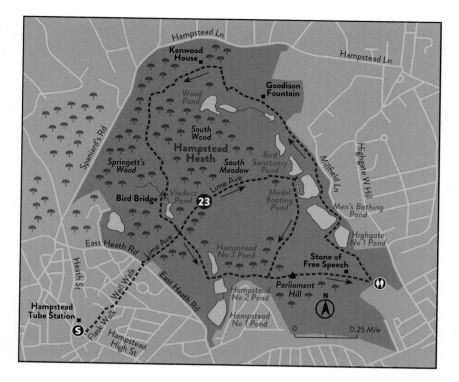

At nearly 800 acres, Hampstead Heath is one of London's largest green spaces, and a relic of the bygone countryside that used to surround London. The first written record of the Heath, as it's popularly known, is from AD 986 when the Anglo-Saxon king Æthelred the Unready ruled these parts. But there were humans here for thousands of years before that who hunted deer, elk, boars, and aurochs with prehistoric flint tools (which have been found on the Heath). The area likely looks the same now as it did then, though with less grassland and heath.

Carry on straight over Parliament Hill and continue east for 0.3 mile past the covered bandstand to the junction with the Parliament Hill Cafe. Go left at the junction and continue straight down the wide track for 0.3 mile past the Stone of Free Speech on your left and Highgate No. 1 Pond on your right. The white pillar has murky origins but is thought to have been a meeting spot to express political and religious views in the seventeenth century. Modern pagans have been known to celebrate the spring equinox there.

When the trail forks, veer right to cross in between Highgate and Men's Bathing Pond and follow the trail as it curves left. Go straight on the broad dirt path, now running parallel to a fence along Millfield Lane, and follow that for 0.6 mile as it passes through some more dense woodland and past several more ponds flickering with dragonflies. These are important habitat for frogs, toads, newts, and fish and also draw many birds, including great crested grebes, Canada geese, swans, ducks, cormorants, and herons. In summer, butterflies flash through the meadow below, and swifts, swallows, martins, and warblers also make an appearance.

In 0.1 mile pass the Goodison Fountain and continue straight through a gate toward Kenwood House. After another 0.2 mile, the trail reenters a wooded area and reaches a T intersection. Bear left, keeping Kenwood House on your right. The original structure, built in the early seventeenth century, was expanded to the present villa in the mid-eighteenth century. It's possible to visit the interior, including a world-class art collection, and landscaped gardens.

If you're looking for a rest spot, this is a great section of sloped lawn overlooking South Wood and South Meadow, followed by a shady lane lined with benches. Continue straight past Kenwood House for 0.2 mile and, when the trail forks, veer right (southwest) through a gate onto open heathland. In 0.2 mile the trail merges with another path and turns left. Follow that south for about a quarter mile, with Springett's Wood on your right and West Meadow on your left. Pass over Bird Bridge with its elegant brick arches (look for the Viaduct Bridge in the distance).

When the trail intersects a wide dirt road, go left (south) toward Viaduct Pond. Walk around the west side of the pond for 0.1 mile. (A path branching right takes you on a short detour to some historical trees including the Hollow Beech, the Wild Service Tree, and the Three Sisters.) When you reach the southern end of Viaduct Pond, go straight to follow the path 0.1 mile to intersect with Lime Avenue. If you want to cut the walk short, you can go right here and retrace your steps to the start.

Otherwise, go left onto Lime Avenue, a.k.a. the Boundary Path. This route bisects the belly of the Heath, with meadow views on your right and some dense woodland, including birch, sycamore, and oak, on your left. There are several hundred old, massive trees on Hampstead Heath, including many oaks over five hundred years old. This is a good spot for watching and listening for the many woodland species of birds that frequent the Heath, including wrens, willow warblers, great spotted woodpeckers, and several varieties of tits and finches.

Continue for 0.5 mile to the ponds and go right to pass in front of the Model Boating Pond on its west side. Carry on straight, making no turns, as the path winds south and west for 0.4 mile to intersect the path you took up Parliament Hill. Go right and retrace your steps 0.7 mile back to where you entered the Heath. Continue down Well Walk to return to Hampstead High Street.

EXTEND IT

Add an extension to Highgate Wood and Queen's Wood (featured in Trail 24), which lie roughly one mile northeast of Hampstead Heath.

24 PARKLAND WALK TO ALEXANDRA PALACE

Follow this lush, green corridor through the heart of London, exploring history and secluded woodlands, and finishing high at Alexandra Palace.

Distance: 7 miles (one way)
Elevation Gain: 650 feet
High Point: 360 feet
Rating: ★ ★ ★ ★
Difficulty: Moderate
Year-round: Yes
Family-friendly: Yes, but use caution on short portions that follow busy roads
Dog-friendly: Yes, leashed

Amenities: Public restrooms in Finsbury Park, Highgate Wood, and Alexandra Palace; eateries in Finsbury Park, Highgate, and Shepherd's Wood; scenic picnic spots at Alexandra Palace
Map: OS Explorer Map 173, London North
Agencies: Friends of the Parkland Walk, Alexandra Palace

GETTING THERE

GPS: 51.570893°, -0.096049°
Postcode: N4 1BZ
Driving: Driving is highly discouraged due to heavy traffic, parking restrictions, pricey parking lots, and congestion charges, which must be paid in advance.

Public Transit: Manor House station is accessible via the Piccadilly line of the London Underground. Finsbury Park can also be reached via several bus routes.
Before You Go: Some urban wayfinding is needed around Highgate.

ON THE TRAIL

Exit the Manor House tube stop at Green Lanes (A105) and turn right. Go through the Manor House Gate of Finsbury Park and continue straight on the wide, paved track for a few hundred feet. Veer right onto a narrower tarmac path heading northwest through the trees. Follow that for about a tenth of a mile as it winds among open lawns and pockets of trees. Just before a raised running track, make a sharp right onto a narrow path running alongside a green fence—the Capital Ring. Follow for 0.1 mile to the intersection with the tree-lined New River Path and turn left. Continue for 0.1 mile and turn right on a path leading to a bridge. The bridge spans the narrow New River, which is a double misnomer. It is neither new, nor a river. This stream is technically an aqueduct, opened in 1612, to bring London clean drinking water from the River Lea. The 20-mile long canal relies on gravity to flow around the contours of the land, dropping a mere five inches per mile. While the canal's construction was heavily contested by some London residents, the Old Aqueduct still supplies water to the city today.

Turn back from the bridge and cross the circular route to join the narrower path straight ahead. Continue for 0.2 mile as the trail climbs gently to a high point in the park. As you look around, consider the illustrious history of Finsbury. At the end of the eighteenth century, this area was being transformed from woodland to grazing fields, but the forest was apparently still a popular site for duels. At that point, dueling was illegal but somehow still "evolving" from sword to pistol use in a sideways attempt to restore one's honor. In 1857, the city bought the 115 acres that's now Finsbury Park in response to growing public demand for open space to counteract rampant urbanization. It opened in 1869 with a poplar-lined avenue circumnavigating the park, a lake, flower garden, and the so-called American Gardens. (In addition to hosting trees and shrubs from the US, Finsbury also has an American football field and a baseball diamond.) The park's impressive trees include 60-foot London planes with five-lobed leaves that suck up pollution, as well as oaks, poplars, willows, beeches, birches, cedars, horse chestnuts, and even a giant redwood.

Continue until the trail intersects the circular road again and turn left to follow the sidewalk. In 0.2 mile, just past the pond on your left and ball courts on your right, turn right to cross the road at the crosswalk and head straight for a few hundred feet to the park exit. Take the bridge over the railway tracks (trains on that line run from King's

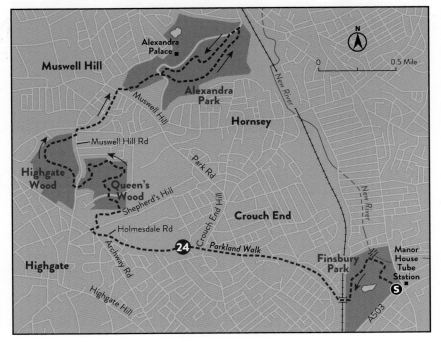

The Parkland Walk may be London's best-kept secret for escaping the city bustle.

Cross Station to Scotland), then make an immediate right onto the Parkland Walk and follow it for the next mile.

The Parkland Walk follows an old railway line that was abandoned in the 1970s. After improvements, the route opened in 1984 and was proclaimed "London's longest nature reserve," with some three hundred varieties of wildflowers including rare, medic- inal, and even edible kinds. There are also many bees and butterflies among the ivy and orchids, including the common blue, whose name belies its unique indigo irides- cence. Most of the trees along the path are less than sixty years old, since the railway didn't allow them close to the tracks. Look for natives like elder, elm, ash, aspen, and oak (there are four kinds here) as well as interlopers like sycamore, walnut, poplar, and fig (one of these rare beauties is located at the start of the path). There are also evergreens including yew, holly, and Scots pine. The greenway is important habitat for badgers, foxes, hedgehogs, and muntjac, a rare species of small deer. Finches, tits, and warblers of many varieties are common, as well as woodpeckers, song thrush, and robins (which are adorable puffballs with a red-orange breast, much smaller than their American cousins). You may even see a tawny owl roosting along the path, a hovering kestrel looking for a mouse to munch, or bats flitting around at twilight.

After 0.8 mile along the Parkland Walk, pass through a short tunnel under Crouch End Hill road. Passing a school on your left, just before the path crosses under a metal footbridge, look right for a sculpture crouched high in one of the brick alcoves extending out from the wall. This work, by London artist Marilyn Collins, depicts a legendary creature from Cornish fairy lore called a *spriggan* (pronounced "sprid-jan"). The old man with childlike features was notoriously disruptive and destructive and was blamed for all manners of mischief.

Farther on, pass between some high concrete slabs which were once passenger platforms for the railway. There's an urban legend that, from time to time, phantom trains can still be heard thundering through there. Horror writer Stephen King stayed in the area with a friend in the late 1970s. His short story "Crouch End" depicts a horrible monster living in subterranean Crouch End that feeds on people. The locals, wrote King, are "known to lose their way. Some of them lose it forever." Today the spot is thick with birch and wildflowers and popular with birds. Carry on straight ahead . . . if you dare.

Reach Crouch End Hill road and continue in the direction signed "Capital Ring" toward "Highgate Wood, 1½ miles." This is a peaceful section of woodland with sycamore, horse chestnut, and oak. Carry on for 0.8 mile until the trail ends at the Holmesdale Road tunnels. Veer left to leave the path and go right (northwest), heading uphill on Holmesdale for about 300 feet to Archway Road (A1). Go right to enter the quaint Highgate Village, Shepherd's Hill area. This lung-busting slope is why this area of London is known as the Northern Heights, and many of the names around here have either "high" or "hill" in them.

Walk 300 feet to Shepherd's Hill road, cross it, turn right, and follow it for another 300 feet. Take the dirt path on your left to descend some steps and pass narrowly in between fences (this part of the Capital Ring is not well marked), before popping out at Priory Gardens road. Cross Priory Gardens, then go right (east) to follow the tree-lined residential road for 0.1 mile to a narrow footpath on your left flanked by wooden fences. Head downhill and, in a few hundred feet, enter Queen's Wood. The wood is crisscrossed by many small trails, but this route goes straight to the center before following a counterclockwise loop to the exit on the west side of the park. Head straight (north) for 0.2 mile to the Frog Pool. In England, land that has been continuously wooded for at least four hundred years is considered "ancient" (which covers just 2.5 percent of the UK today). Queen's Wood is particularly special because it has been forested for at least the last millennia.

The woodlands weren't guarded for enjoyment, but viewed as a valuable timber crop. Centuries ago, every inch of land was worked. The timber would have been used to construct ships, buildings, and fences, and burnt as charcoal and firewood. Even oak acorns were collected as pig feed (swineherds would climb the trees to shake the branches). And before then, as evidenced in ancient pollen grains excavated here, the landscape included some heath, farmland, meadows, and pasture. Conservation of a sort began in the sixteenth century when largescale deforestation throughout the country began to ring alarms bells. In 1543, King Henry VIII signed "The Bill for the Preservation of Woods," after which a ditch and hedge bank were installed around Queen's Wood to protect it from grazing animals (signs of which can still be seen today). Despite its importance, the wood was set to be leveled to make way for housing in the second half of the nineteenth century, but the plan was scrapped following fierce public protest. It was officially named Queen's Wood to mark Queen Victoria's golden jubilee in 1887, and opened to the public in 1898.

Turn left (east) at the Frog Pond and continue for 0.2 mile to the park's edge. From there, follow the trail around the perimeter counterclockwise for 0.5 mile to reach the western exit (at the nine o'clock position). The surprisingly steep slopes were formed when glacial meltwater cut through bedrock 450,000 years ago. Today this dense mixed woodland is dominated by mature oak and hornbeam—a tough, broadleaf tree with spindly branches that can reach 100 feet high. Holly, yew, beech, Norway spruce, and other tree species also provide habitat and shelter for woodpeckers, nuthatches, cuckoos, wrens, and sparrow hawks.

Leave the wood via its west exit and cross Muswell Hill Road to enter Highgate Wood directly opposite. Upon entering Highgate Wood, follow the path as it veers left, then, when it forks, bear left. Follow this trail for 0.4 mile to a T intersection at the other side of the wood. Seventy-acre Highgate Wood is another ancient woodland, and a critical habitat for birds and bats. One rare species to look for here is the wild service tree, which is an indication of the wood's enduring age. Its leaves are similar to a maple, but it blooms in springtime with bouquets of tiny white flowers.

Go right and follow the dirt track for about a quarter mile to reach a fork. Veer left to exit the park onto Muswell Hill Road and turn left again. Continue for about 100 feet to where the sidewalk splits, then bear left of the iron fence and continue downhill and to your right to follow the trail as it crosses beneath Muswell Hill Road. Continue as the track bears left and then right to resume the Parkland Walk. Follow that without turning to reach the entrance to Alexandra Park and Palace. The 200-acre park is made up of woods and grassy knolls, a herd of fallow deer, and, of course, a palace.

Go straight and follow the raised, covered walkway as it veers first right and then left. At the fork in the trail, bear right and follow it for 0.3 mile to reach Alexandra Palace Way. Cross that and then follow the trail as it runs alongside the road for about a third of a mile to reach the lawn in front of the palace. Pause here for a picnic or to take in the views. The Ally Pally, as it's also known, is famous for its panoramic views of central London, and from its green slopes you can spot St. Paul's Cathedral, the London Eye, the BT Tower, and the Shard. Sitting high on Muswell Hill, the palace was opened in 1873 on Queen Victoria's birthday. It's always been known as the "people's palace" and, indeed, no monarchs have ever lived there. Now it hosts concerts and conventions, and there's even an ice rink and a boating lake out back.

From the palace, take a 1.2-mile clockwise loop around the lower palace grounds, then pick up a bus or train nearby.

25 GRANTCHESTER MEADOWS

An easy stroll along the tree-lined, slow-pulsing River Cam to the historical Orchard Tea Garden, ideal for a warm spring or summer day.

Distance: 4.5 miles
Elevation Gain: 250 feet
High Point: 70 feet
Rating: ★ ★ ★
Difficulty: Easy
Year-round: Yes
Family-friendly: Yes, but use caution by exposed riverside

Dog-friendly: Yes, leashed
Amenities: Restaurants and coffee shops at start and halfway point; public restrooms 0.4 mile in; benches and picnic tables along river and on Lammas Land
Map: OS Explorer Map 209, Cambridge
Agency: Cambridge City Council

GETTING THERE

GPS: 52.201573°, 0.115919°
Postcode: CB2 1RS
Driving: Leave your car at one of the many park and rides on the outskirts of the city. (Parking in central Cambridge is pricey and strictly patrolled.)
Public Transit: There are frequent trains and buses from London, and central

Cambridge is well served by buses, which can be used to reach the start.
Before You Go: Trail surfaces vary from paved to grass and dirt, which can become muddy in the rain. Steer clear of cows and their "patties."

ON THE TRAIL

Begin at the west end of Mill Lane (adjacent to a pub called The Mill), cross through the black pedestrian gate onto the brick walk, and head southwest in the direction of the green sign indicating "Riverside Walk, Grantchester 2 miles." Cross the river,

The sinuous River Cam in central Cambridge hums with life, especially on a sunny day.

pausing to overlook Mill Pond with its quintessential Cambridge backdrop of stone bridges, weeping willows, and church spires. Follow the walk as it soon veers left, and then continue straight, with the river on your left and fields on your right. From here, the River Cam flows 40 miles to the sea.

Continue straight, ignoring paths branching off to your right, as the path narrows through the fields and tree canopies of Coe Fen. At 0.3 mile take a quick spur to your left to Crusoe Bridge for views of the city's charismatic white swans and boaters on the river. Except for the dead of winter, this section of the Cam swarms with punts—flat-topped boats with squared bows that are propelled through the shallow water with a long pole wielded by a "punter" standing on the boat's bow.

In another 0.1 mile, cross the busy, paved Fen Causeway at the crosswalk. Go slightly left and then right through the black metal pedestrian gate and continue on the path through elm, chestnut, and willow. Continue for 0.2 mile along the path as it hugs the riverside and, just before reaching a pedestrian gate, bear right away from the river where the path splits. Head west-southwest along the path for a few hundred feet as it crosses through a gate and passes a couple of boathouses.

Continue straight through a thick corridor of trees and shrubs to reach a trail junction. Cross over a metal bridge, then make a sharp left to continue along a tributary and past a small parking area. The tributary soon joins the main river along the path. This is the Paradise Local Nature Reserve, a small woodland with a central marsh that floods in winter. Look and listen for bright yellow siskins, brown cream chiffchaffs (named for its call of "chiff-chaff-chiff"), and robins flitting among the alder trees. Continue along the dirt track for 0.3 mile to a wooden gate, and follow the green arrow indicating "Riverside Walk, Grantchester."

Head left onto paved Grantchester Meadows road and follow it for 0.3 mile past quaint houses that once hosted the so-called Grantchester Group, including novelists E. M. Forster and Virginia Woolf, philosopher Ludwig Wittgenstein, and economist John Maynard Keynes. (Forster, Woolf, and Keynes were also part of the Bloomsbury Set, a group of intellectuals whose liberal ideas scandalized society in the first half of the twentieth century.) The road turns to gravel and then narrows into a path with a wooden fence on your left. Continue straight for another 1.1 miles, ignoring any paths branching off to your left, along Grantchester Meadows (the actual grassy ones). You may spy a bold fox or a shy muntjac deer along the way, but you're more likely to see a lot of grazing cows. For several hundred years Cambridge University students—including, it is rumored, Charles Darwin, John Milton, Sir Isaac Newton, and William Wordsworth—would leave the confines of the city to enjoy the pastoral delights of the river and these meadows.

At the end of the meadows, continue straight onto the short, narrow public footpath leading to High Street in the village of Grantchester. You'll emerge with the lovely Church of Saint Andrew & Saint Mary Grantchester ahead of you, the oldest part of which dates from the fourteenth century. Take a left and follow the sidewalk 0.2 mile to The Orchard Tea Garden. (You can also take any of the various dirt paths to your left, which cut through a cricket field and pass around the back entrance to the tea garden lawn.) The Orchard, planted in 1868, is worth a visit (it heaves with apples in early September). Cambridge students first walked "upriver" for tea here in the late nineteenth century and were soon joined by a long list of luminaries including Woolf, Rupert Brooke, Alan Turing, Stephen Hawking, and Prince Charles. Woolf and Brooke were also known to skinny-dip in a nearby swimming hole of the River Cam known as Byron's Pool and named for poet Lord Byron (it is now a local nature reserve).

Depart High Street and head back down the footpath you came in on, then veer right down the dirt path toward the river. With the river on your right, follow the intermittent path (sometimes dirt or grass) for 1 mile. There are plenty of great lunch spots along the way, where you can sit and look for pike, carp, frogs, and grass snakes, as well as plenty of ducks and geese. Boaters, and even swimmers, are plentiful year-round. Historically, this was known as the River Granta (likely meaning "muddy" in Old English), but its name was changed to Cam, meaning "crooked," after the city was established. Some locals still refer to the upper parts of the river as the Granta.

Watch for woodpeckers and warblers in the willows (over fifty bird species have been recorded on the Cam) and, in the summer, look out for iridescent blue kingfishers whizzing along the river as they hunt butterflies and dragonflies. Overhead you may also see a kestrel looking for its next meal.

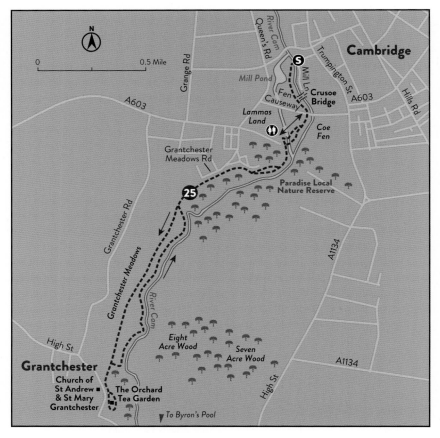

As the river and path veer left, you'll emerge again onto Grantchester Meadows (the road). Retrace your steps into and through the Paradise Local Nature Reserve, but, when you reach the silver bridge you came over initially, you can either continue back to the start or create a loop. For the loop, bear left through Lammas Land, which passes by a children's playground, a kiddie pool (a.k.a. "paddling pool"), and some open, tree-shaded areas away from the river. It's 0.4 mile until the paths converge to cross Fen Causeway. From there you can retrace the route back to the beginning, or take any of the paths winding through the pastures north toward Mill Lane.

EXTEND IT

Pair with Trail 26, which passes through some of Cambridge's amazing green spaces and along the famous college "backs."

26 CAMBRIDGE PARKS & BACKS

Explore the emerald necklace of parks that surround the city, idyllic stretches along the lazy River Cam, and magnificent architecture.

Distance: 4.3 miles
Elevation Gain: 50 feet
High Point: 30 feet
Rating: ★ ★ ★ ★
Difficulty: Easy to moderate
Year-round: Yes
Family-friendly: Yes; places to run around; spots on river to watch swans

Dog-friendly: Yes, leashed
Amenities: Restaurants and cafes; public restrooms (for a fee) at various points along the way
Map: OS Explorer Map 209, Cambridge
Agencies: Cambridge City Council, Cambridge Botanic Garden

GETTING THERE

GPS: 52.195424°, 0.122208°
Postcode: CB2 1JE
Driving: Leave your car at one of the many park and rides on the outskirts of the city. (Parking in central Cambridge is pricey and strictly patrolled.)
Public Transit: There are frequent buses and trains to Cambridge from central London and the major airports, and many different bus lines serve the city and outskirts that can be used to reach Cambridge University Botanic Garden.
Before You Go: Wayfinding is necessary to navigate the city's narrow streets, popular parks, and famous colleges. The importance of looking both ways cannot be overstated. Admission is required for entry to the Botanic Garden.

ON THE TRAIL

Turn right (north) from the main entrance of the Cambridge University Botanic Garden onto the wide, tree-lined sidewalk of Trumpington Road to head toward the city center. After 0.2 mile, make a right at Lensfield Road and walk for 0.5 mile to Hills Road. Just before the intersection, you'll pass the compact, but outstanding, Scott Polar Research Institute and Polar Museum (open to the public) on your right. On its stone face is the Latin inscription, "QUAESIVIT ARCANA POLI VIDET DEI," which translates to "He sought the secret of the pole but found the hidden face of God." In the front garden, visible from the sidewalk, is an exhilarating bronze statue of a male figure with arms outstretched, face tilted toward the heavens. It was cast by Lady Kathleen Scott, widow of Captain Robert Falcon Scott, who died returning from the South Pole in 1912. Interesting tidbit: the model for the nude was Lawrence of Arabia's younger brother, A. W. Lawrence, a Cambridge professor.

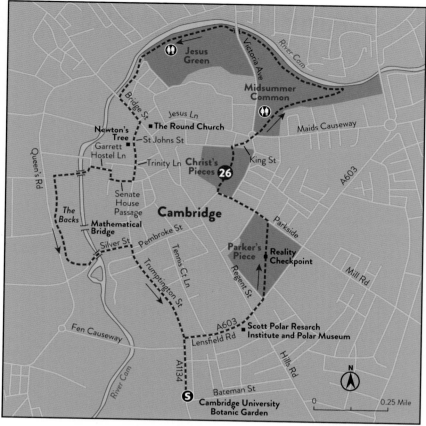

Go left to cross Lensfield Road and then straight across Regent Street and walk roughly 250 feet to enter Parker's Piece, a flat, 25-acre greenspace. Veer left onto the path that cuts diagonally, roughly 0.3 mile, across the common. At the center is the so-called Reality Checkpoint, a tall, cast-iron lamppost. Of the various theories about the origin of the name, my favorite is that it marks the boundary between the university "bubble" and the real world. A nearby plaque states that the rules governing modern soccer (what the British call football)—"emphasizing skill above force"—were established here by students in the 1860s.

Go left when the path ends at Parkside (leading into Parker Street) and walk along the sidewalk for 0.2 mile, then cross the road to make a right into Christ's Pieces. This is a traditional Victorian garden with tree-lined avenues, ornamental shrubs, extensive flower beds, and ten thousand daffodil bulbs, which burst forth on the lawns in spring.

At its center lies a memorial garden to Diana, Princess of Wales, a peaceful, bench-enclosed spot. Head straight across Christ's Pieces for 0.1 mile to the Pike's Walk exit. Continue straight for a few hundred feet to King Street and go right. The entrance to Midsummer Common is straight ahead in a few hundred feet, but you'll need to navigate around the Four Lamps Roundabout to get to it.

Once inside Midsummer Common, bear right (east) onto a trail lined with silver pendant lime trees. Make your way down toward the river, visible to the north (there are a lot of footpaths and no wrong choices). For centuries various fairs have been held on this ancient grassland (which is also still used for grazing), including the Midsummer Fair, which has been celebrated annually for over eight hundred years. Another popular event is Guy Fawkes Night, held in early November to celebrate the thwarting of a plot to blow up the House of Lords in London in 1605 (Fawkes was arrested while guarding the explosives). Huge bonfires are lit all over the country, and on Midsummer Common, there's an impressive fireworks display as well.

Once you've reached the river, roughly a third of a mile after entering the common, go left along its southern bank, which is lined with white willows and London planes. You'll see houseboats moored along the river and boathouses for most of the colleges hugging the opposite bank. After about 0.4 mile, you'll pass underneath Victoria Avenue and enter Jesus Green. In 0.2 mile you'll reach Jesus Lock, built in 1836 to make the river navigable, and the only remaining lock in the city. Take a detour here to explore the wide avenues shaded by the canopies of enormous London plane trees, before continuing along the river.

In spring, "wisteria hysteria" overtakes Cambridge when blossoms soften even the most austere buildings.

Once used for fishing and moving cargo, punting has been a popular recreational pastime on the River Cam for a century.

Exit Jesus Green and continue straight 0.3 mile as the path narrows to wooden planks alongside shops and restaurants. Make a left at Bridge Street to walk into the cobblestone heart of Cambridge. Founded in 1209, the city is dominated by its prestigious university, which houses thirty-one colleges. Its notable alumni include over 120 Nobel laureates and fourteen British prime ministers, as well as the people who first shared with the world an understanding of evolutionary biology, DNA structure, the laws of motion, stem cells, artificial intelligence, and the electron.

After about a tenth of a mile, you'll arrive at the Church of the Holy Sepulchre, a.k.a. The Round Church, built around 1130. (It was originally a chapel for wayfarers traveling on the Roman road that is now Bridge Street.) Make a right to cross the road onto St. Johns Street, which soon turns into Trinity Street. The buildings on your right are a part of St. Johns College and Trinity College—keep your eyes open for "Newton's Tree" near the college entrance on your right, which was grafted from the apple tree in Lincolnshire where Sir Isaac Newton's mother lived. The story goes that on a visit to her garden in the 1660s, Newton (then a student at Trinity College) watched an apple fall and began to theorize about gravity.

In 0.3 mile, you'll reach Senate House Passage. Pause here to look at St. Mary's Church to your left and the Kings College Chapel to your right. In recent years, a pair of peregrine falcons has been seen navigating the dizzying heights of those spires and turrets. Duck down the narrow passage on your right and follow it as it curves right into Trinity Lane. After 0.2 mile, you'll go left onto Garrett Hostel Lane, a kind of paved alley that soon leads to a bridge with stunning views over the River Cam.

Cross over the bridge and go straight for about 0.2 mile, making a left onto a dirt path right before you reach Queen's Road. Walk parallel to the road for roughly 0.4 mile in an area known as The Backs, where you can sneak a peek at the impeccably landscaped lawns and gardens of the several colleges that back onto the river. Follow the trail as it curves left around Queens' College and leads into Silver Street. ("Queens" is plural to acknowledge the founding of the college in 1448 by Margaret of Anjou and its reestablishment in 1465 by rival queen Elizabeth Woodville.)

Continue along Silver Street for a few hundred feet to again cross the River Cam. Look left to see the Mathematical Bridge on the grounds of Queens' College. First built in 1749, then rebuilt in 1866 and 1905, this wooden truss bridge is constructed entirely of straight timbers, using a series of tangents to create the arch at its center.

Reach Trumpington Street in 0.2 mile and go right to continue 0.5 mile back to the botanic garden.

27 HOLKHAM BEACH

Explore a stunning stretch of sand backed by dunes, pinewoods, and marshes—a rarity on the British landscape—in a national nature reserve.

Distance: 8 miles
Elevation Gain: 410 feet
High Point: 51 feet
Rating: ★ ★ ★ ★
Difficulty: Moderate
Year-round: Yes
Family-friendly: Yes, but note that far western section of beach is a nudist area

Dog-friendly: Yes, leashed or under close voice control
Amenities: Restrooms, cafe, and local ecology exhibit at visitor center
Map: OS Explorer Map 251, Norfolk Coast Central
Agency: Holkham National Nature Reserve

GETTING THERE

GPS: 52.964294°, 0.814338°
Postcode: NR23 1RG
Driving: From Wells-next-the-Sea, take A149 for 1.6 miles, then turn right onto Lady Anne's Drive at the brown sign marked "Holkham NNR Beach."

Public Transit: Buses run regularly to Holkham Beach from Wells-next-the-Sea.
Before You Go: Arrive before 10:00 AM in summer to park close to the start. Bring binoculars to see the impressive array of birdlife. Your feet will likely get wet on the beach.

ON THE TRAIL

From the car park, head north toward the beach. On your right is the cylindrical visitor center (called The Lookout) and a wooden signpost indicating various destinations. Turn left onto a wide dirt path toward the bird hides. In a little under half a mile, pass Salts Hole, a rare saltwater lagoon, on your left. Continue, keeping the pinewoods on your right and reed beds on your left for a little over half a mile. The grazing marsh here, where tall grasses grow in shallow water, are a haven for rare flora and fauna.

The panorama of sand and sky at Holkham Beach is a portrait of unspoiled coastal England.

Vast wetlands once covered much of East Anglia, but many areas were drained and filled for farmland and pasture, reducing habitat for various species. The remaining pockets within the 9000-acre nature reserve at Holkham are critical for birds like the bittern and marsh harrier, nearly extinct in the wild before making a comeback here. One of the most dramatic displays of birdlife at Holkham is the autumn return of raucous flocks of sixty thousand pink-footed geese.

Head left for a short diversion to a bird hide to look for otters, water voles, brown hares, lapwings, and spoonbills. Lapwings, a globally threatened species, are easily recognized by their iridescent green feathers and distinctive black head crest. Spoonbills (another threatened species that is making a comeback at Holkham) have long black legs and a lengthy spatulate bill used for fishing and making pancakes (just kidding about that second one). The birds fuss and flap above the sea lavender that settles like a blue-purple haze on the area in midsummer.

Look west toward a raised embankment, the remnants of an Iron Age fort built by local warrior tribe, the Iceni, around AD 47. Vikings sailed up a creek here during the first millennium to establish Holkham, or "ship town." It's possible that legendary Queen Boudicca of the Iceni rode her chariot through here, long red tresses catching the breeze, during the uprising against Roman invasion. Head back to the main trail and continue in the direction indicated by the wooden sign that reads "Viewpoint and

Beach." Follow a wooden boardwalk gently uphill toward the shore through a clearing in the woods.

Within about a tenth of a mile of the turnoff, you'll arrive at a lookout. Enjoy the incredible views of the North Sea and the surrounding dunes, tufted with the soft-looking marram grass and sea sandwort that are more than tough enough to withstand chilly northerly winds. Shorebirds like ringed plovers and oystercatchers shelter and lay speckled eggs amid more than a dozen varieties of dune grass and flowers, some with memorable names like pyramidal orchid, houndstongue, and lady's bedstraw. The dunes at Holkham are young, formed over the last several decades by windblown sand gathering on inland shingle ridges. Resist the urge to walk out onto the beach, as social paths seriously damage the delicate dune ecosystem. Instead, head back the way you came about 100 feet, and take a right onto a dirt path heading down into the woods.

Zigzag left and right for the next 1.4 miles through a shaded and sheltered environment with several kinds of pines—mainly maritime, Scots, and Corsican with some Monterey and Austrian varieties thrown in. Some of the trees grow straight and spindly, others stout and elbowy. They were all planted as a windbreak in the late nineteenth century at the behest of the Second Earl of Leicester.

The national nature reserve, which extends to the high water line, is still managed by the Coke family as part of their estate. That includes nearby Holkham Hall, an eighteenth-century Palladian mansion, which is also open to the public, for a fee. On a warm day, there is something exotic about the pine tree–filtered sunlight, the scent of evergreens, and the soft crunch of dried needles and pine cones underfoot.

Turn right at the wooden signpost indicating "The Beach, 325 yds," and before long you'll emerge from the pine forest with the dunes directly ahead. Of the several trails cutting through the dunes, follow the one that looks the most traveled to reach the route's high point at the crest. Watch for several varieties of butterflies in the dunes as you continue onto the impressive expanse of Holkham Beach, which stretches 11 miles east to west. Its big skies, sprawling sands, and lapping waves make Holkham the darling of commoners and royals alike. (Sandringham Estate, a favorite country retreat of Queen Elizabeth II, is about 20 miles away.) Filmmakers also covet the spot—the final scenes of *Shakespeare in Love*, when Gwyneth Paltrow's character washes ashore, were shot on Holkham Beach.

From the dunes, walk straight in the direction of the crashing waves. Where you turn right (east) depends on the tide. Wherever you turn, creeks, perhaps ankle-deep, will intersect your path as they flow to the sea, and you will have to ford them. Saltings—sandy areas normally covered by water that are mushy and tough to walk through—also appear at low tide.

Take time on the more remote western stretch of beach to engage in the Norfolk coast tradition of sea watching. Here, all aspects of nature seem to rise dramatically

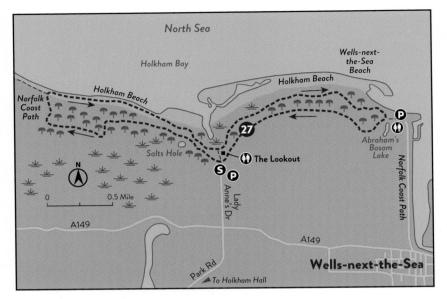

above the prevailing flatness—birds scurrying along the sand, seals bobbing in the water, even blades of grass poking out of the dunes. Watch for oystercatchers, a black-and-white wading bird with a bright red-orange beak, skittering across the shallows in search of cockles and mussels, and for mottled-brown terns, notable summer visitors to Holkham. The small, fast, noisy birds can be seen hovering and diving for fish offshore, their distinctive black-tipped yellow bills flashing in the sunlight.

Curve gently south and east for a mile as the beach wends its way around Holkham Bay. From here, you can go right and take the boardwalk back to the visitor center and car park, or you can continue along the beach for 1.8 miles, past a long stretch of colorful beach huts to arrive at Wells-next-the-Sea Beach. (The town, which now lies one mile south, used to sit nearer the shore and was one of East Anglia's busiest ports.) From there, turn right at the lifeguard station and follow the path up and over the dunes toward the Wells-next-the-Sea car park. In 0.1 mile, take another right, before the parking lot and restrooms, passing through a wooden gate and onto the wide Norfolk Coast Path (marked by an upside-down acorn). This route traverses 84 miles from Hunstanton to the west to Hopton-on-Sea to the southeast, through teeming tidal marshes, sleepy seaside villages, and wide-open beaches.

On your left is Abraham's Bosom Lake, which once emptied into the sea. In summer, watch for graceful egrets and raptors, including marsh harriers and red kites. Keeping the trees on your right and occasional pools on your left, follow the level, shaded Norfolk Coast Path for 1.7 miles back to the visitor center and car park where you began.

EXTEND IT
Cross A149 and take Park Road to Holkham Estate to explore 25,000 acres of walled gardens and large lakes with its own herd of fallow deer, as well as all five species of owls living in Britain.

28 DUNWICH BEACH & HEATH

A gloriously lonely stretch of North Sea coast with a rare expanse of lowland heath about which Henry James wrote, "I defy anyone, at desolate, exquisite Dunwich, to be disappointed in anything."

Distance: 7.3 miles
Elevation Gain: 55 feet
High Point: 55 feet
Rating: ★ ★ ★ ★
Difficulty: Moderate
Year-round: Yes
Family-friendly: Yes, but use caution atop and below fragile cliffs

Dog-friendly: Yes, leashed on Dunwich Heath trails
Amenities: Restrooms and snacks at Dunwich Beach and Dunwich Heath
Map: OS Explorer Map 231, Southwold & Bungay
Agency: National Trust

GETTING THERE

GPS: 52.278532°, 1.632460°
Postcode: IP17 3EN
Driving: From Westleton, take The Street (B1125) northeast for 0.3 mile, then go right onto Dunwich Road. After 1.5 miles, continue onto Westleton Road and drive for 0.6 mile before taking a slight right onto Monastery Hill. After 0.3 mile, merge onto

Beach Road, then take a right in 300 feet into the Dunwich Beach car park.

Before You Go: The blooming heather at Dunwich Heath is at its peak from July through September. The 4-mile stretch of beach is easiest at low tide when the sand is exposed; otherwise, it is shingle, or small rocks, which can be difficult to walk on.

ON THE TRAIL
Head to the east side of the car park and onto the berm that borders the beach. The view north is dominated by the Dingle Marshes Nature Reserve, a mix of coastal and

freshwater habitats spread out over more than 200 acres. While boats could once anchor in the estuary, the brackish lagoons, bordering the North Sea and transected by the Dunwich River, are now a refuge for ducks and wading birds.

Over the thousands of miles of coastline around Great Britain, the beaches vary from small coves to long stretches of sand or "shingle" (rock), some with seaside towns that have been popular for centuries. But Dunwich (pronounced DONE-itch) is one of the remaining spots where, instead of piers with arcade games or crowds slathered in sunblock, you'll find miles of cliff-backed shingle beach and an even bigger sky. While lacking many seaside trappings, the quiet expanse allows immense perspective. Early on in my time in England, I asked a friend, who had been stationed all over with the UK Special Forces, to name the wildest place that came to mind. "Dunwich, darling, you'll be alone there," she said. I came to realize she meant this stretch of coast offers the space to consider life's passing storms, its tides and shifting sands.

From Dunwich, the North Sea stretching out to the east looks like a tea-colored lake with gently lapping waves. But depending on the day, the air in this moody place can be raw and the sea grumbling. Writer Henry James thought the sea at Dunwich a "ruminating beast" with an "insatiable, indefatigable lip."

Walk about 200 feet over shingle to the water's edge and turn right along the sandy strip that is exposed at low tide. Head south amid the calming simplicity of cliff, rocks, sea, and sky. Depending on the season, you may spot some swimmers, though the North Sea is notoriously chilly on even the hottest days. Look for fisherfolk huddled in tents, their lines cast into the cold current. Watch for grey seals bobbing near the shore, and porpoises, which are sometimes spotted off Dunwich. (In centuries past this waterfront, with smugglers, shipwrecks, and defenses against war, was decidedly less charming, but that is for the history books.)

The farther you walk, the higher the marram grass–tufted cliffs on your right become. Keep a safe distance from their base because the soft sandstone (more specifically sand, clay, and flint-rich gravel) edges, 50-feet high in some places, erode irregularly and sometimes collapse onto the shingle beach. Though the Suffolk coast, including Dunwich, is millions of years old, it is, in fact, one of the youngest parts of Britain, and has advanced and retreated, been reborn and rearranged by wind and water, many times.

Fishing and shipping made the city of Dunwich one of the largest and most affluent in medieval England, but it was a faulty foundation on which to build an empire. Storm-fueled erosion undermined its high, sandy cliffs and ultimately consumed the vast majority of the city. (See more on this in Trail 29: Greyfriars Wood & Monastery Ruins.) If you'd been walking along this spot of coastline in the year 1300, you would have been strolling down narrow streets crammed with homes, shops, and churches. Can you imagine the bustle of the port city, the chatter of merchants in the marketplace, and the singing of sailors on the quay, unaware of what peril was to come? After spending time near the

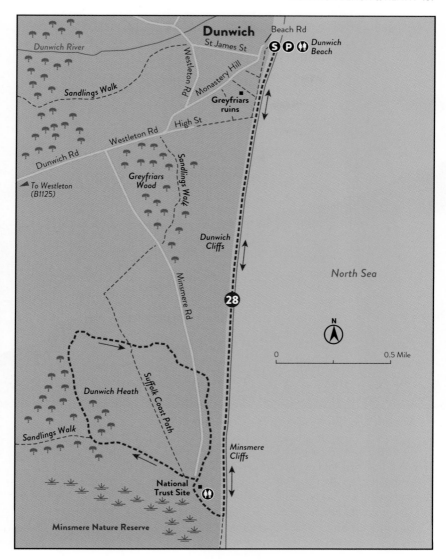

lost city in the 1830s, renowned Scottish geologist Sir Charles Lyell equated the unstoppable tides at Dunwich to a volcano spewing ash and magma. "It is scarcely necessary to observe, that the control which man can obtain over the igneous agents is less even than that which he may exert over the aqueous," he wrote.

History, mystery, and splendid isolation greet visitors to Dunwich Beach.

Two miles farther along the beach, arrive at a break in the cliffs with a big, colorful National Trust sign that reads, "Welcome to Dunwich Heath." Follow the path straight uphill (ignoring one that branches left) for about 0.1 mile before it curves right and ends at a complex of low buildings and parking lots. Head a few hundred feet to your left, away from the structures, to a fingerpost near the restrooms that reads, "Walks start here."

Nearby is a posted map showing the trails sorted by color. This route follows the 2-mile pink loop, which circumnavigates the main area of heathland. (The 3-mile orange trail transects the heath and is particularly beautiful when the heather is blooming.) Follow signs in the direction of "The Heath." Dunwich Heath is 250 acres of mixed lowland heath—one of the UK's rarest habitats. Lowland heath like this was once omnipresent along the Suffolk coast but has declined nationally over 90 percent in the past 120 years due to intensive grazing by sheep, cattle, and goats, as well as building construction. This part of the route follows the Sandlings Walk, which spans 58 miles from Ipswich to Southwold, on the Suffolk coast. It covers a variety of terrain, with large expanses of forest, heathland, and coastal walking.

Follow the pink arrows by the impressive hump of heath covered in cross leaved heather, bell heather, ling heather, and two kinds of gorse. The heather explodes in pink and purple in the summer months and gives off a woody, mossy scent. The gorse blooms in beaming yellow nearly year-round—and smells vaguely of coconut. Many types of birds, insects, and animals depend on this specialized habitat. Bees as big as pinballs, legs laden with pollen, bob around the sea of heather, sampling nectar. Little redstarts with grey-black wings and bright orange tails flit among the shrubs. Once on the heath I saw a peacock butterfly, so named for the multicolored eyespots on their wings.

On the west side of the track, watch for red deer taking shelter amid huge old oaks, silver birch, and pine. Foxes, badgers, rabbits, weasels, bats, and several rodent varieties also make their home here, as well as birds like the Dartford warbler, stone curlews, woodlark, and nightjar. Lizards and snakes can also be seen, including adders, Britain's only poisonous snake.

The pink loop ends at the National Trust buildings—including historical coast guard structures—where you began. From here, retrace your steps back to the water, watching for gulls and terns swooping and gliding busily. If the tide has come in, you'll have lost some of the sandy strip, which means a tougher walk back on the rocks. Listen for the relaxing, fizzing sound the water makes as it flows over the crust of shingle.

Before you end this walk, turn back one last time to take in the scenery, and to consider the sunken city, which have beguiled so many writers, scientists, and artists. Eminent British painter J. M. W. Turner was a frequent visitor to the East Anglian coast. The artist was also a keen walker, sometimes logging 25 to 30 miles per day. Many of his depictions of Suffolk, which vividly capture the power and moods of sky and sea, focus on the doomed village. One extraordinary painting took its perspective from near where you're standing. In *Dunwich, Suffolk* (1830), Turner placed what remained of the All Saints Church, the last of which finally fell into the sea in 1919—high on the crumbling cliff with mariners below, struggling against the waves to launch a wooden skiff. Nature, 1; humanity, 0.

EXTEND IT

Adjacent to (south of) Dunwich Heath are miles of additional trails at Minsmere, a 2500-acre Royal Society for the Protection of Birds nature reserve. Its reed bed, heath, grassland, forest, and shingle habitats are "billed" as one of the best bird-watching sites in the UK.

29 GREYFRIARS WOOD & MONASTERY RUINS

Discover a surprisingly lush stretch of forest, remnants of a twelfth-century monastery, and the story of "Britain's Atlantis."

Distance: 5 miles
Elevation Gain: 75 feet
High Point: 75 feet
Rating: ★ ★ ★
Difficulty: Easy to moderate
Year-round: Yes
Dog-friendly: Yes, leashed

Family-friendly: Yes, but use caution atop and below fragile cliffs
Amenities: Restrooms and cafes at car park and Dunwich Heath
Map: OS Explorer Map 231, Southwold & Bungay
Agency: Dunwich Greyfriars

GETTING THERE

GPS: 52.278532°, 1.632460°
Postcode: IP17 3EN
Driving: From Westleton, take The Street (B1125) northeast for 0.3 mile, then go right onto Dunwich Road. After 1.5 miles, continue onto Westleton Road and drive for 0.6 mile before taking a slight right onto Monastery Hill. After 0.3 mile, merge onto Beach Road, then take a right in 300 feet into the Dunwich Beach car park.

Before You Go: On a warm day, follow the suggested direction to tackle the uphill portion of this loop (which can be joined with Trail 28) first, finishing with a walk along the sea.

ON THE TRAIL

Exit the car park the way you arrived, but pause to look at a sign, near the restrooms, with an artist's rendering of what the area looked like centuries ago—a fascinating glimpse into the ingenuity and fragility of humanity, and the power of nature. Continue past the sign onto Beach Road and follow it for 0.1 mile. Look for the trailhead on your left (where a small green sign says "Footpath"). Ascend a few steps into a corridor of trees with gnarled branches forming a canopy of green overhead.

After a few hundred feet, take a short spur off the main trail to your left. Reach the cliff's edge to (carefully) take in spectacular views up and down the coast. The beginning of this route traverses some of the 50-mile Suffolk Coast Path, which runs from Lowestoft in the north to Felixstowe in the south, across heath and marsh and along cliffs, sea walls, and rivers. Rejoin the main trail and continue for about 300 feet to a shady enclave on your left between the trail and the cliff's edge—the site of the so-called Last Grave. This weathered but otherwise ordinary-looking tombstone marks where Jacob Forster was buried in 1796, hinting at the meteoric rise and disastrous fall of Dunwich and its people.

Today Dunwich is a blink-and-you'll-miss-it fishing village (although with some lovely Georgian and Victorian structures) roughly 90 miles northeast of London. But it was once the capital of East Anglia and a booming port that the Saxons are believed to have settled in the early fifth century. It was perfectly positioned near abundant herring shoals to take advantage of the growing North Sea fishing industry. By the eleventh century, Dunwich had three churches and roughly four thousand people (making it one of the largest towns in England), situated around a sheltered harbor where the Dunwich River flowed into the North Sea.

In the High Middle Ages, Dunwich expanded across a range of low, seaside hills, becoming a safe harbor for the royal navy and a customs cash cow, and one of the most important and richest ports around. Salt, stone, grain, and wool departed, and silk, spices, furs, and wine arrived. By the middle of the thirteenth century, the gated

The flint and stone ruins of the Greyfriars Monastery now haunt the Suffolk Coast.

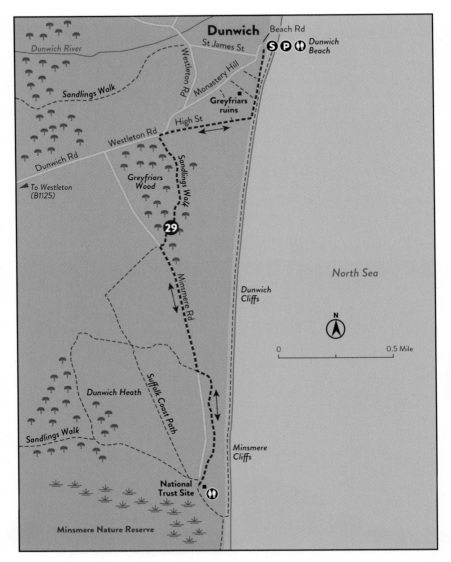

city was one mile across, the same size as or bigger than London at the time, with eight churches and several thousand parishioners, two monasteries, two hospitals (one specifically for lepers), and a guildhall. Interestingly, there was also a mint where money was made by hand at the order of the king, as well as a preceptor of the Knights

Templar, a monastery of the military order used to recruit and train knights and to raise crusade funds.

Coastal erosion in the area had been well documented as far back as the famous Domesday Book of 1086, a huge land survey and Britain's earliest public record. And then the storms came. On New Year's Day 1286, wind and rain lashed the city and it was whomped by a monster storm surge. Locals fought to save Dunwich, but another fierce storm came the next year, and so on over the following decades and centuries. Entire neighborhoods were swallowed up, and whole houses of worship tipped into the relentless tides. One storm essentially rerouted the Dunwich River 2.5 miles to the north, and the old port filled with silt and sand. Choked and flooded, the port-less town was all but abandoned. The remains of lives lived and lost now lie under water a mile offshore. Dunwich is sometimes called "Britain's Atlantis," and local lore says that when storms churn the water, church bells can still be heard tolling from beneath the waves.

The Last Grave is the final remnant of the churchyard of the medieval All Saints Church. The view east from here centuries ago would have been of a bustling city. The church itself sat roughly 130 feet from this spot, until it fell off the cliff over a century ago. The churchyard and its departed inhabitants have met a similar fate; old bones still emerge from the cliffs from time to time, and with every storm, the cliff edge creeps a little closer to Jacob Forster. Before it succumbed to the sea, the last remaining tower buttress of All Saints was moved to St. James Church in the center of modern-day Dunwich, where it can still be seen.

From the grave follow the trail along a rock wall as it curves right. In a few hundred feet you'll reach the ruins of Greyfriars, Dunwich's medieval monastery. Make a right into the site at the information panels, then continue a few hundred feet farther through the grass to what's left of the friary. Walk among the remaining stone and flint walls, two stories high in some spots, with the impressive arches of several doors and windows still evident—Greyfriars is among the best preserved medieval monasteries in England. Historians believe the friary was founded in the twelfth century and originally located farther east, perhaps on the site of a former Roman camp or settlement. Erosion must have forced the friars inland to this site, which was built in the fourteenth century. The Franciscans served the sick and poor, and for that reason were quite popular. In its heyday, the monastery was a sizable complex made up of several large buildings and a church surrounding an interior courtyard, or cloisters. Most of what's left is believed to be the former kitchen and refectory, essentially the friars' cafeteria. It's possible to imagine them huddled around tables in their simple brown robes, the smell of bread baking. A bit farther west, two impressive stone archways mark the perimeter of the site.

Rejoin the trail and walk straight for 0.1 mile before turning sharply right. Walk straight for another 0.4 mile, ignoring several carved wooden "public footpath" signs branching off in various directions, as the trail dips down, widens, and then runs

The mainly mature, native forest of Greyfriars Wood forms a thick, leafy canopy in summer.

alongside High Street. At a fingerpost with a green "footpath" sign (which also says "Sandlings Walk"), turn left down a narrow paved road.

Within a few hundred feet, the trail curves left and then straightens out, entering Greyfriars Wood. On a clear day, the sun mottles the forest floor with warm pools of light through the tops of oak, ash, yew, beech, chestnut, sycamore, holly, and more. Trees in Greyfriars Wood were once revered for their spirits, with many rituals and celebrations centered around them (tree worshiping was later banned in the ninth century).

Elder trees, which can also be admired along this walk, held a particular mysticism for ancient people, despite the fact that they aren't the most beautiful or useful for building. Yet Druids associated elders with the Earth Mother and believed the goddess could be channeled through them. They considered the elder's small, white flowers and deep purple berries a gift and were inspired by its power to regenerate in adverse conditions. Even after tree worship was banned, the elder was used for medicinal purposes and to ward off evil. (*Harry Potter* fans may remember that the Elder Wand was the most powerful and coveted specimen of its kind.) Today, elderberry tarts and elderflower cordial are still popular in Great Britain.

Within 0.2 mile of the High Street turnoff, cross through a gate and continue as the dirt track narrows in between dense shrubs and bracken. Wind through the woods for 0.4 mile to where the trail intersects Minsmere Road, the access road to Dunwich Heath. Cross it and continue in the direction of a green "footpath" sign. Almost immediately you will reach a junction where a National Trust sign marks the start of "Dunwich Heath" and "Mount Pleasant Farm." Go left, in the direction of the orange and purple arrows.

Continue straight for 0.5 mile, first through an exposed section abutting the former farm—which is being restored to heath and grassland—and then back into the trees.

Look for many species of birds, including woodpeckers, sparrow hawks, and tawny owls. Watch for the tiny goldcrest—the UK's smallest bird—flitting from tree to tree with its distinctive yellow crest feathers and high-pitched chirp. Birders take note: the Dunwich cliffs are part of a major migration route between northern Europe and Africa, and many rare species have been seen here.

When the trail again intersects Minsmere Road, cross over and pick it up directly across the street. Before long you'll leave the trees behind to emerge onto Dunwich Heath, which bursts with blue-purple heather and yellow gorse. Follow the sandy track for 0.5 mile, enjoying big views of the North Sea to the east and the rolling heathland to the west.

At the National Trust's Dunwich Heath complex ahead, there's a visitor center, restrooms, cafe, shop, and picnic tables. If you can resist the urge to explore the heath (covered in Trail 28), return the way you came, through the sheltering shade of the woods, or head north along the beach (also covered in Trail 28).

EXTEND IT

Once you arrive at Dunwich Heath, take one of the loop trails marked by grey, orange, pink, or purple to add 1–3 fascinating miles to your walk.

SOUTHERN ENGLAND

Southwest England is spectacularly diverse in topography, history, and scenery. There are, of course, tons of coastal routes, but the high moors and rocky tors draw walkers inland with equal measure. The weather is highly changeable on this peninsula, which juts out between the Celtic Sea to the north and English Channel to the south. Best to prepare for sun, wind, and "mizzle," a common local expression for a mix of fine rain and saturating fog or mist. Any walker spending at least a few days in the southwest will experience it.

CORNWALL
Cornwall (Trails 30–32), or "Kernow" in Cornish, is roughly 300 miles from London, but its slower pace makes it feel even farther. The topography encompasses 250 miles of coast, with surfing waves and wild dunes, to rugged moorland, postcard-worthy harbors, and countless sandy beaches. Its sheltered bays and river estuaries tell tales of smugglers and shipwrecks, and the foggy moors and ancient woodlands are full of spirits and pixies. After a long walk, or during a rain break, have a Cornish cream tea or a pasty, an empanada-like English specialty.

DEVON
East of Cornwall lies Devon (Trails 33–35), a county including nearly all of Dartmoor National Park and one third of Exmoor National Park (the remainder lies in Somerset). Exmoor, on the north coast, has an open and remote feel with heather-clad hills and massive pastures yielding to swift streams and deep, wooded vales where Exmoor ponies and red deer may be seen. Its shoreline features high cliffs, plentiful beaches, and charming fishing villages.

OPPOSITE: *Spectacular rock outcrops at Carnewas (Trail 32), rumored to be the stepping stones of giants, dwarf mere mortals.*

Dartmoor, in the south, is a wild upland area of tor-topped moors that look like tumbled-down granite castles. It is, in fact, the largest expanse of moorland in southern Britain (significant, since the moors have greatly eroded elsewhere), full of legends, purple heather, prehistoric burial mounds, and ancient stone bridges. It is a sparsely populated, fickle-weather spot that beguiles at every level. The queen of mystery writers, Agatha Christie, favored the moors and, when she was not writing, would walk alone in the spooky expanses, crafting characters and twisting plots.

DORSET & THE JURASSIC COAST
Perhaps all that needs to be said is that half of Dorset county (Trails 36–37) has been designated an Area of Outstanding Natural Beauty, and three-quarters of its shore is included in the fascinating Jurassic Coast World Heritage Site. The area's mellow valleys, steep limestone ridges, and dynamic coastline have drawn humans for over ten thousand years. Dorset faces the English Channel, with cliffs, coves, and beaches aplenty. Some of its iconic geological features include Hooken Cliffs, Lulworth Cove, and Durdle Door. It was also the home of Mary Anning, a pioneering paleontologist who found and classified dinosaur fossils in the early 1800s, and is still famous for its fossil-finding potential.

30 THE LIZARD

Starting from the iconic Lizard Lighthouse, this walk explores the history of peril and innovation in maritime navigation along a spectacular stretch of Cornish coastline.

Distance: 4.2 miles
Elevation Gain: 1230 feet
High Point: 210 feet
Rating: ★ ★ ★ ★ ★
Difficulty: Easy to moderate
Year-round: Yes
Dog-friendly: Yes

Family-friendly: Yes, but use caution on steep drop-offs along coast path
Amenities: Restrooms and refreshments at car park
Map: OS Explorer Map 103, The Lizard
Agency: National Trust

GETTING THERE

GPS: 49.961136°, -5.204240°
Postcode: TR12 7NT
Driving: From the village of Lizard, head south on Lighthouse Road for 0.5 mile to Lizard Point National Trust car park on your left.

Before You Go: Check hours for Lizard Lighthouse Centre, which (for a fee) has great exhibits and a tour. The rolling nature of the Cornwall coast can make distances deceiving.

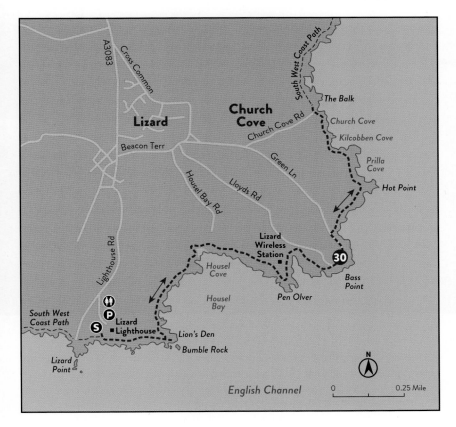

ON THE TRAIL

Head south from the car park toward the coast for 0.1 mile until the trail intersects the South West Coast Path. Go left and, keeping the water on your right, continue toward the lighthouse. The Lizard Light Station was established in 1619 by a rich landowner, John Killigrew, to guide boats through an important shipping channel, and the twin towers you see today were built in 1752. The beacons in those early days were huge coal fires that had to be stoked through the night, until they were replaced by oil lamps and reflectors in 1812. When the poet Alfred, Lord Tennyson visited the Lizard in the mid-nineteenth century, he called the Lizard lights "the southern eyes of Britain."

The lighthouse, which was finally electrified in 1878, is still critical for navigating one of the world's busiest shipping lanes. Even during fog, when the light can't be seen, boats can hear the foghorn. If you visit in thick weather, be prepared to protect your

Even the large Lizard Lighthouse seems small on the colossal Cornish coast.

ears (every 30 seconds!) from the bone-rattling bellow. Today only the 60-foot-high eastern tower houses a light—a single rotating arc lamp whose beam can be seen 25 miles out at sea. While modern day GPS has taken a lot of treachery out of sea navigation, ships without it still rely heavily on lighthouses like this one.

Rounding the lighthouse point, take a quick (but somewhat steep) detour to your right, down to the cliff's edge for views of Lizard Point to the west and across the wide mouth of the Housel Bay to the northeast. The big sea stack just offshore is Bumble Rock, and the huge depression just short of the cliff is called Lion's Den. This depression is actually a crater that formed around 1850 when a sea cave roof collapsed, a reminder of the changeability of this rugged coastline.

Rejoin the coast path and continue east for 0.3 mile along Housel Bay. Follow the trail down the steep stairs and then head right, to Housel Bay Beach, a small, sandy cove exposed at low tide. After exploring this secluded spot (if you like), which requires scrambling over rocks, follow the wider track for 0.2 mile to ascend again to the clifftop, past the Housel Bay Hotel, on the other side of the cove.

Pause at the bench at the top to enjoy lovely views of the Lizard Lighthouse, Bumble Rock, the Lion's Den, and Housel Bay Beach, as well as an array of colors, from the aquamarine sea and robin's-egg sky to glowing green grasses and wildflowers in orange, yellow, white, and pink. On a sunny day, with swimmers and surfers bobbing on the waves, this part of Cornwall could be confused with the Caribbean.

Continue following the coast path for 0.2 mile around the next headland of Pen Olver. For a brief but worthwhile detour, go through the gates on your left to the Lizard Wireless Station. These two well-maintained buildings were the workshop of Guglielmo Marconi, an Irish Italian pioneer of wireless telegraphy, and house some original and replica instruments in a small radio museum.

Prominent scientists of the late nineteenth century scoffed at the idea of long-distance communication "through the air." But in early 1901, twenty-six-year-old Marconi proved them wrong when he fielded a radio transmission from the Isle of Wight, nearly 200 miles away—the first of its kind. Later that year he received the first wireless signal across the Atlantic Ocean, from Poldhu (roughly 6 miles north-west of Lizard) to Newfoundland, Canada, 2200 miles away. The message was a simple dot-dot-dot—Morse code for the letter s. Some science historians doubt the signal, which used medium-wave frequency during daylight hours, could transmit that far. They believe that what Marconi heard was simply atmospheric noise. Regardless, the feat won him worldwide fame, and his experiments laid the groundwork for future radio innovation. (While Marconi is generally known as the "father of the radio," it was Nikola Tesla who filed the earliest radio patents, years before Marconi.)

From the wireless station, walk 0.2 mile past a large, white building, Lloyds Signal Station, erected in 1872 at Bass Point. Ships coming and going from the English Channel would send and receive visual signals here via semaphore—a system of flags, lights, or pole arms moved at different angles to indicate letters or numbers. A person using a telescope could see and interpret the messages, which were then forwarded to ship owners via telegraph land lines. It was the only practical way of communicating with passing ships, until wireless telegraphy came along.

Carry on along the coastal path for 0.5 mile to round Hot Point and arrive at Kilcobben Cove. There you'll see the curved roof of the Lizard Lifeboat Station, set in an indentation along the coastline. As beautiful as this area is, the savage reefs offshore have claimed many ships and lives over the centuries. The station opened in 2012 and is vital to the nearby community of Church Cove, and to the seafarers in the hundreds of boats passing by Lizard Point each day. It's a strategic location that also presents some logistical challenges for crews who have to run down (and then back up!) over two hundred steps every time a rescue boat is launched.

Continue for about a tenth of a mile to Church Cove (the hamlet and inlet). This pretty little bay is a popular spot from which to launch small watercraft and to snorkel in the clear blue-green water. The grassy cliffside shoulders of The Balk hunched over the cove are a good spot to have a picnic and watch for peregrines, ravens, and buzzards (a.k.a. hawks) along the cliffs and for shearwaters, gannets, and guillemots soaring over the waves. From Church Cove, retrace your steps back to the lighthouse.

EXTEND IT

West of the lighthouse, continue straight for 0.3 mile to visit Lizard Point, the southern-most spot in mainland Britain. Like the rest of the above route, this added leg lies along the epic South West Coast Path, a 630-mile long route around England's southwest peninsula.

31 KYNANCE COVE TO LIZARD POINT

Cornish poet John Harris called the spectacular tidal beach and dramatic cliff scenery of Kynance Cove "one of the wildest and weirdest spots frolicsome Nature ever produced in an elfish mood"—a powerful sentiment from a guy sent to work at age twelve extracting copper and tin from one of the many mines that were once the area's lifeblood.

Distance: 4.8 miles
Elevation Gain: 1130 feet
High Point: 210 feet
Rating: ★ ★ ★ ★
Difficulty: Moderate
Family-friendly: Yes, but use caution on open cliffside along coast path

Dog-friendly: Yes, but there are seasonal restrictions at Kynance Cove
Year-round: Yes
Amenities: Restrooms and snacks at the start
Map: OS Explorer Map 103, The Lizard
Agency: National Trust

GETTING THERE

GPS: 49.975142°, -5.225150°
Postcode: TR12 7PJ
Driving: From the village of Lizard, go north on A3083 for 0.5 mile, then left onto an unnamed road (well signed) toward Kynance Cove. Continue for 1 mile to the National Trust car park.

Before You Go: There are two routes to Kynance Cove—0.6 mile over the heath at high tide, or 0.3 mile along the white sand beach at low tide (do not attempt to swim the shore route when the tide is in). The rolling nature of the Cornwall coast can make distances deceiving.

ON THE TRAIL

From the west side of the car park, follow signs to take the wide, gravel path about a tenth of a mile west toward Kynance Cove and the South West Coast Path. Keeping the water on your left, follow the coast path another 0.1 mile to the stairs above Kynance Cove, where you'll see rock stacks, turquoise water, grass-covered cliffs, and sandy beaches—if the tide is low. Descend the stairs to cross the beach. At low

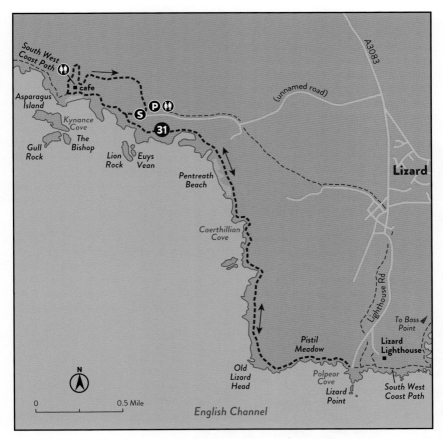

tide on the west side of the cove, they'll be a tombolo, or sandy isthmus, between the mainland and Asparagus Island (yes, native wild asparagus grows on the island, as it does on the cliffs throughout the Lizard Peninsula). Explore several caves with colorful names like the Parlour and the Ladies Bathing Pool, remnants from the Victorian era when Kynance Cove was a popular tourist spot. After poet Alfred, Lord Tennyson saw the spot in 1848 he wrote, "Glorious grass-green monsters of waves. Into caves of Asparagus Island. Sat watching wave-rainbows. Glorious ranks of waves and billows." Beyond Asparagus Island are the jagged humps of Gull Rock and The Bishop.

Take a good look at the rocks here, which are mostly the typical blocky grey granite and folded black slate of the Cornish coastline. But you'll notice the cliffs near Kynance are also red, white, and dark green, evidence of rock that lay miles underground three

The rising tide rushes into sandy Kynance Cove with its sea caves and rock pools aplenty.

hundred million years ago, until a violent collision of continental plates drove it all to the surface. Polished by the crashing of countless waves, this serpentinite rock looks sleek and shiny, like the skin of a reptile. (This is not, regrettably, why this is called the Lizard Peninsula. The name likely comes from the Cornish words for "high" and "place.")

Ascend the stairs from the beach and join the path to the left of the cafe. Take the wide dirt track as it zigzags for 0.6 mile across the heath back to the car park (this is the high tide route). Rising about 200 feet in elevation, this section offers some excellent views of the cove and islands. Keep an eye out for Cornish heath, a flower which thrives only in the acidic soil of serpentine rock. Also abundant are the bright pink bell-like heather flowers that bloom in summer and fall.

Again from the west side of the car park, head east on the coastal path toward Lizard Point. In about a half mile the trail passes above a long sandy stretch of Pentreath Beach that's popular with surfers (a steep scramble is the only way down to the beach). At low tide, the last remnants of the 1912 wreck of the steam trawler *Maud* are visible.

Follow the coast for 0.2 mile to Caerthillian Cove, a hotspot for birders looking for England's rarest breeding bird—the Cornish chough. This red-legged member of the crow family is noted for its long curved red beak. Legend has it that King Arthur's soul was carried from this world by a chough, and the bird proudly appears on Cornwall's coat of arms. The Cornish chough was fairly common until the double whammy of trophy hunting and habitat degradation seemed to doom it to extinction. But after being absent from Cornwall for thirty years, choughs started staging a comeback in 2001 on the Lizard Peninsula.

The coastal grassland at Caerthillian is also the ideal habitat for many wildflower varieties, and is overrun with violet, pink, and white buds, including sea thrift, sea campion, and squill, in most seasons. Offshore, you may see dolphins, grey seals, and basking sharks. The latter cruise the coast of Cornwall in the spring and summer, munching offshore plankton blooms and crustaceans. Look for the 30-foot dorsal and tail fins of these gentle giants cutting through the waves.

From Caerthillian Cove continue on the path around Old Lizard Head for 1 mile. This rolling section gains and loses a few hundred feet in elevation above a stretch of coastline riddled with rocky shoals. Cornwall is famous for its shipwrecks, and the Lizard in particular has claimed many lives and vessels. When the Danish boat *Ospra* went down in 1832, locals made off, as they often did, with some goods that washed ashore (they also went to great lengths to rescue the sailors). The salvaged cargo included Cuban coffee, which no doubt brightened their long winter days. Operating from 1859 to 1961, the lifeboat station at Polpeor Cove near Lizard Point saved 562 lives from 136 wrecks.

Descend some stairs and cross a footbridge to arrive at Pistil Meadow, owned by the National Trust. This tranquil copse of tamarisk is rumored to be the final resting place of nearly two hundred people who drowned when the *Royal Anne Galley*, a navy frigate, sank after running aground on some rocks in 1721. There were only a handful of survivors.

From Pistil Meadow, go up the steps and onward to the small cluster of buildings at the most southerly spot on Lizard Point and the southernmost spot on the mainland of Britain. It's a great spot to enjoy the stunning coastal scenery, and maybe an ice cream, while watching for interesting birds and marine life. But it hasn't always been such a peaceful place. It was here in July 1588 that the Spanish Armada was first spotted. The flapping sails of 130 ships cruising by at close range, intent on invading England and overthrowing Queen Elizabeth I, must have been quite remarkable to see. Over the ensuing centuries, alliances seemed to shift as often as the changeable Cornish winds, and these waters saw battles between Dutch, Spanish, French, and British fleets.

Retrace your steps along the coast back to the start. If you want to shave off some mileage, a popular loop takes Lighthouse Road north from Lizard Point for 0.5 mile to Lizard village. From there, the off-road Lizard Coastal Walk heads west to the Kynance Cove car park.

EXTEND IT
Continue past Lizard Point to Bass Point (see Trail 30) along the 630-mile long South West Coast Path.

32 BEDRUTHAN STEPS TO PORTHCOTHAN

Some North Cornish coast bests lie here, including rocky headlands, massive sea stacks, small coves, swimming beaches, cliffside castle remnants, and cathedral-like caves.

Distance: 7.7 miles
Elevation Gain: 1350 feet
High Point: 290 feet
Rating: ★ ★ ★ ★
Difficulty: Moderate
Year-round: Yes
Family-friendly: Yes, but coast path has steep sections and sheer cliffs

Dog-friendly: Yes, though some beaches have seasonal bans
Amenities: Restrooms, gift shop, and tea room at the start
Map: OS Explorer Map 106, Newquay & Padstow
Agency: National Trust

GETTING THERE

GPS: 50.481414°, -5.031997°
Postcode: PL27 7UW
Driving: From Mawgan Porth, go north on B3276 for roughly 2 miles to the turnoff on your left for the Carnewas at Bedruthan Steps National Trust car park.

Before You Go: The beach at Bedruthan Steps cannot be accessed at high tide. Caution should be taken on clifftops and beaches; even quiet-looking coves can be subject to fast-moving tides.

ON THE TRAIL

Head west from the car park toward the shore for 0.1 mile. When the trail intersects the South West Coast Path, go right (north), enjoying wide and striking views. Continue for 0.2 mile down the cobblestone path to the lookout above Bedruthan Beach. Take the narrow stairway 120 steps to the beach—if you time it right with low tide, you can explore the sandy expanse (swimming is not recommended here because of the strength of the currents). Otherwise, stop at the viewpoint that is eye-level with the sea stacks for a truer appreciation of their enormity.

The slate islands are said to be stepping stones for the mythological giant Bedruthan to keep his feet dry at high tide. Or that may be a legend concocted by savvy local hoteliers hoping to lure holidaymakers from nearby Newquay at the end of the nineteenth century. This area was also briefly mined for iron ore, lead, antimony, and a silver and copper mix. To better access Bedruthan Beach, workers scratched away at the cliffs to carve stairs. Five of the isles have names—Carnewas, Pendarves, Redcove, Samaritan, and Queen Bess. The latter is the northernmost pyramidal island, which, at the correct angle, looks like a woman in a flowing dress (at least from the neck down, since the head broke off in the 1980s). The Samaritan reportedly earned its name in 1846, when a vessel called *Good Samaritan* laden with satins and silks wrecked against its rocks and was giddily salvaged by locals. When times again got tough, a dark saying emerged: "It is time for a 'Good Samaritan' to come."

Continue north along the coastal path as it turns into a wide grassy track along the clifftop. Curve inland on a narrower dirt track to enter the National Trust's Park Head area. Stay on the trail, as the fields to your right host ground-nesting skylarks and corn buntings in spring and summer. Scores of unusual plant species thrive in this harsh mix of wind and sea, like rock sea lavender, which, with its tiny purplish blooms, looks a lot like heather. Tree mallow and betony also draw bees and butterflies, as do the tiny, blue star flowers of spring squill.

Veer left about a half mile after the Bedruthan Steps to follow the contour of the coast. There are excellent views of Diggory's Island just offshore and back toward the Bedruthan Steps and beyond. Several natural arches can be seen, as can the earth-work remnants of Redcliff Castle. On this capricious stretch of coast—a sunny day can easily turn sullen—an array of colors are omnipresent: orange-red sand, black-platinum rocks, cobalt-lavender sky, turquoise-sapphire sea, olive-emerald grass, and too many

The north Cornwall coastline is most iconic overlooking the rock stacks of Carnewas at Bedruthan.

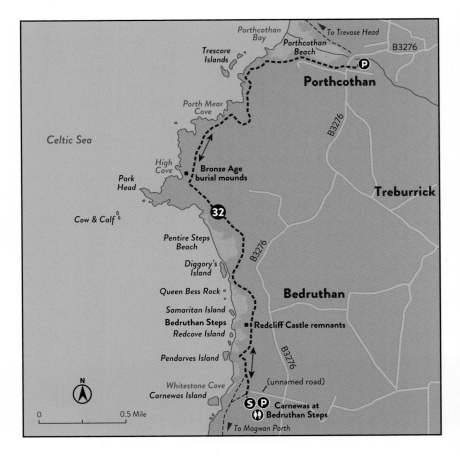

wildflower hues to catalog. Though it faces the Celtic Sea, this part of Cornwall feels the full fury of the Atlantic, and while this area is a sparkling jewel when the sun is out, it is even more intriguing when it's being lashed by the gales of an angry storm.

Walk north past Diggory's Island to a viewpoint above the Pentire Steps Beach, a near perfect semicircle of sand beneath crumbling cliffs. Follow the coast path for 0.7 mile as it veers west along the rhino horn of Park Head. If you want to explore, leave the trail and walk west roughly 0.2 mile to the tip of the headland (take extreme care in wind or fog on the narrow peninsula). There was once a fort enclosing a castle here, and some banks and ditches remain.

Just beyond Park Head is High Cove. Near the trail are several Bronze Age burial mounds. Walk on for 0.6 mile to reach rocky, sheltered Porth Mear Cove, with the

Trescore Islands resting just offshore. Note the folded slates and sandstone—which are forever shifting and eroding at the whim of winds, waves, and rain—and bright mounds of pink sea thrift growing improbably on the rocks.

Follow the coast for another mile to arrive at the narrow mouth of Porthcothan Bay. (Fans of the TV program *Poldark* may recognize this stretch of coast as the scene of much clifftop galloping, and Porthcothan Bay beach as a stand-in for Nampara Cove.) Porthcothan is a popular spot for swimming, with easy access at its east end. From Porthcothan, retrace your steps back to Bedruthan.

EXTEND IT

Continue north along the coast path for another 4 miles to Trevose Head, a prominent headland with a working lighthouse.

33 TOUR OF TORS

This circuit across the moors includes a magical woodland and some of Dartmoor's famous tors, a rare concentration of massive granite outcrops. While a clear day is always welcome, it's when the moors are enshrouded in clouds that legends emerge from the fog.

Distance: 5.2 miles
Elevation Gain: 1200 feet
High Point: 1420 feet
Rating: ★ ★ ★ ★
Difficulty: Moderate to challenging
Year-round: Yes

Family-friendly: Yes
Dog-friendly: Yes, leashed near grazing animals
Amenities: None
Map: OS Explorer Map OL28, Dartmoor
Agency: Dartmoor National Park

GETTING THERE

GPS: 50.571866°, -3.769261°
Postcode: TQ13 9XS
Driving: From Haytor Vale, go southwest on B3387 for 1.5 miles to reach the Saddle Tor South car park on your right.

Before You Go: The number of trails crisscrossing the moors can make even this established route tricky to follow. Dartmoor's fickle weather can also complicate navigation.

ON THE TRAIL

Leave the car park on the sole trail, which quickly branches into three tracks. Follow the center one straight and gently uphill toward Saddle Tor (1400 feet), the dome-shaped rock at the top of the rise. Granite, the bedrock of these moors, has been laid bare in the tors by thousands of years of freezing, thawing, and erosion. The three main minerals

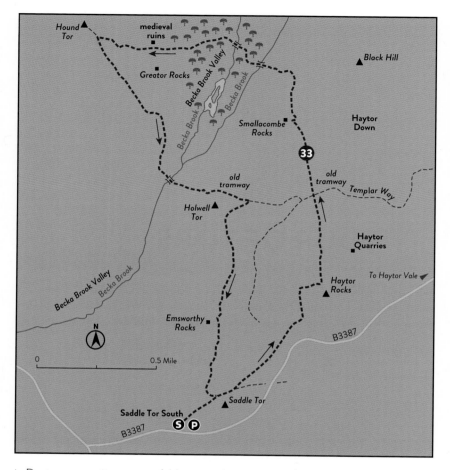

in Dartmoor granite—quartz, feldspar, and mica—mean the rock can look grey, white, or even pinkish, depending on the light. The rocks that have broken away and tumbled down the slopes are called "clitter" and "clatter."

After 0.2 mile, the trail skirts to the left of Saddle Tor. Continue straight for 0.5 mile along the wide track, ignoring the many trails branching off. Haytor Rocks (1500 feet), which look a bit like a crouching sphinx, are straight ahead. Where the trail forks, bear left toward the "face" of the sphinx and walk about a quarter mile around the base of the rock mound. There are a lot of legends attached to Haytor Rocks, but perhaps the most well known is of a young woman who leapt from the top to avoid marrying a much older squire. As she was falling, her dress billowed out like a parachute and she floated to the ground, a feat which apparently emboldened her to run away with her true, age-appropriate love.

Of the dozen or more tracks heading off the fern-covered slopes of Haytor Rocks, pick the one heading downhill to the north. Follow it for 0.4 mile through low, dense gorse thickets to reach the disused Haytor Granite Tramway. (If you get off course here and end up at the Haytor Quarries, a set of small lakes, don't worry. From there, walk northwest until you reach the old tramway and turn left.) The tramway was made of granite to haul granite from a quarry to a canal several miles away. Go straight across the rocky tramway and head uphill toward Smallacombe Rocks, which you can glimpse the outline of even in thick fog. In 0.4 mile from the tram track, continue straight when the trail branches off in several directions to pass to the right of Smallacombe Rocks. Keep an eye out for hawks gliding over the moors, which bloom with forget-me-nots and heather, depending on the season.

Head straight and downhill for 0.2 mile to pass a young oak, conspicuous on the otherwise treeless landscape. In another 0.2 mile, bear left where the trail forks. The views across the fields and farms are vast and lovely. Even on a day dim and heavy with steely clouds, one ray of sun illuminating the lush, green fields gives the landscape a fairyland appearance. Walk for 0.2 mile down through acres of bracken to reach the woodland of the Becka Brook valley.

Continue into the woodland for 0.1 mile to cross Becka Brook on an impressive granite slab footbridge. This is known as a clapper bridge, an ancient construction style common on the Devon moors (*clapper* is Latin for a "pile of stones"). The woodland is dense and enchanting, with sessile oak and downy birch extending their arms over moss-covered boulders. Continue through and then out of the woods, crossing Becka Brook a second time and passing through several gates, for 0.2 mile.

Bear right at the fork to follow the trail lined with a thick blanket of ferns along the base of Greator Rocks, a massive fractured wall of granite used for scrambling and bouldering. Within a few hundred feet of the last gate, the trail passes what remains of the medieval village of Hundatora, now Hound Tor. This handful of thirteenth-century structures includes several stone longhouses that sheltered farming families, and a handful of stone barns once used for drying grain. (The homes were long so that humans could live on one end and animals on the other.) Nestled in between two rocky piles—Hound Tor (1360 feet) and the Greator Rocks—this village would have had a spectacular view across the hills and valleys of eastern Devon. People had been living here for centuries when, in the Middle Ages, milder weather and population growth encouraged more folks to cultivate the higher moors. The Domesday Book, a kind of census report that came out in 1086, reported six households, seven cows, twenty-eight sheep, and eighteen goats in this village, all ruled by a guy named Lord Reginald. But those builders and farmers wouldn't stay long—some combination of weather, famine, and plague drove them to abandon the site sometime between the mid-fourteenth and

The spellbinding tor-land and moorland of Dartmoor have an otherworldly air.

early fifteenth centuries. At its height, the Black Death wiped out roughly one-third of Devon's population.

From the former settlement, continue straight for about a third of a mile to the base of Hound Tor. The tor is full of tales (and tails, apparently), as legend has it that, while out on a hunt, a group of dogs and their master were turned to stone after disturbing a vengeful coven. That story supposedly inspired Arthur Conan Doyle's *The Hound of the Baskervilles*. Even on a mostly clear day, one half expects to hear the long, low howl of a hound somewhere distant. A few different trails lead to the top of Hound Tor, but this route turns left (south) down the wide grassy track of Houndtor Down. Continue southeast, this time keeping Greator Rocks on your left. In 0.3 mile, cross through a gate and follow the fingerpost in the direction of Haytor Down. Continue downhill along this track for almost half a mile, ignoring any paths that diverge. Pass through a gate and cross Becka Brook again on a different clapper bridge amid silvery birch, wildflowers, and mossy green boulders.

In 0.2 mile, bear left onto the defunct tramway, keeping the base of Holwell Tor to your right. Follow the tramway for roughly 0.2 mile, then go right at the trail fork. In a few hundred feet, when the trail reaches another fork, go right again. In 0.6 mile, pass Emsworthy Rocks on your right. Continue for 0.4 mile toward Saddle Tor to intersect the trail you took at the beginning of the route. Turn right and continue for 0.2 mile back to the car park.

EXTEND IT
Follow the short but steep trail to the summit of Hound Tor.

34 TEIGN GORGE & FINGLE WOODS

From Castle Drogo, this walk drops quickly into the Teign Gorge for an out-and-back stretch along the river and through the ancient forest of Fingle Woods that can be as short or long as you like.

Distance: 9.5 miles
Elevation Gain: 1300 feet
High Point: 840 feet
Rating: ★ ★ ★ ★
Difficulty: Moderate
Year-round: Yes
Family-friendly: Yes

Dog-friendly: Yes, leashed
Amenities: Restrooms and refreshments at start and Fingle Bridge Inn; restrooms at border of Fingle Woods
Map: OS Explorer Map OL28, Dartmoor
Agencies: Dartmoor National Park, National Trust

GETTING THERE

GPS: 50.697522°, -3.805639°
Postcode: EX6 6PB
Driving: From Drewsteignton, go west toward Castle Drogo (follow the brown National Trust signs) for 0.5 mile, bearing left to stay on the main route. In 0.2 mile,

turn left at the entrance and continue for 0.4 mile to the car park on your right.
Before You Go: This has been billed as the most famous walk on Dartmoor, so arrive early for parking.

ON THE TRAIL

Exit the car park the way you came in and turn left. Follow the dirt path alongside the road for under a tenth of a mile, then turn right at the signpost marking "Estate Walks to Fingle Bridge, Gorge and River." Continue for 0.1 mile along a shady, wooded stretch, then turn sharply right and descend some stairs to arrive at a T intersection.

Go left onto Hunters Path toward Fingle Bridge (head right to complete the loop in the opposite direction), and follow that east, along the north side of the gorge. Pass by several short stretches of crooked oaks and beeches over the next 0.4 mile, watching for a gap in the trees on your right with a phenomenal view, up and down the gorge. Also pass Sharp Tor on your right, formed by two bulky crags of metamorphic rock (unusual in this area of igneous granite). Glance back as well for a nice view of Castle Drogo on its promontory several hundred feet above the River Teign. The castle was constructed between 1911 and 1930 in a pseudo-Tudor style, and is the last castle built in England. (It is open for tours and has magnificent formal gardens.)

In summer and early fall, this trail is lined with thickets of golden gorse and blackberry brambles in pinkish white bloom, along with a dizzying variety of wildflowers. The rocky soul of Devon is also visible here in the blooming violet heather adorning the granite crags. In another 0.2 mile, when the trail comes to a junction, continue straight (east). Go 0.4 mile to where the path splits again, and bear right, signed toward "Fingle Bridge." Descend 400 feet over 0.5 mile through a serene stretch of oak woodlands to the River Teign.

At the bottom of the gorge, arrive at an intersection with a tarmac road at a parking area. Go right and follow the road for 0.1 mile past the inn to reach Fingle Bridge spanning the River Teign. This span was built in the thirteenth century to move timber and grain products across the gorge via packhorse. The beautiful engineering and materials, including rectangular ashlar stones, hint at the bridge's historical importance.

Ancient woods crowd the river in Teign Valley, an area frequented by humans for thousands of years.

Cross the bridge and go left at the T intersection. (You'll return to this spot later.) In several hundred feet on your left are the remnants of a corn mill from the eighteenth century. This is the River Teign Walk, which closely follows the scenic river through Fingle Woods—an 825-acre revelation in any season. On a summer day it's shady and cool by the river, where meadows and small beaches are excellent for a picnic, or even a swim. In spring the riverbanks and woodland paths are lined with wild daffodils and bluebells. (Warning: legend has it that you will be taken away by pixies to a fairyland if you step into a ring of those beauties.) In fall, elder, ash, beech, rowan, and oak glow yellow and orange, and juniper, yew, hawthorn, and holly burst with berries. In winter, the ground may be shrouded in snow while the frosty trees reflected in the river look like ice sculptures.

This area has been frequented by humans for at least the last three thousand years. Since the Iron Age, the ancient woodland has suffered logging and, later, the introduction of invasive species. But restoration efforts over the past decade—one of the largest projects of its kind in the country—have meant a comeback for thousands of species of plants and animals. Visitors from the US Pacific Northwest might recognize the dominant conifer here—Douglas fir. It was introduced to the UK in the early nineteenth century as a source of timber by Scottish botanist David Douglas. As a foreigner, it's now being culled in significant numbers to give the natives a fighting chance. Look for where they have been thinned to see clumps of heather humming with bees. But the firs have also become an important place for many species to rest, nest, and feed—from the dormouse at the bottom to the ravens at the top—making restoration a complex undertaking. Though it is non-native, some firs will be left to stand alongside the native broadleaves as an integral part of Fingle's mixed woodland. Birders will delight in searching out the thirty-six species of breeding birds that have been recorded in these woods, from huge, agile kestrels and hawks hovering over the valley to tiny, dazzling kingfishers unmistakable in turquoise and orange, zipping along the surface of the river and dipping in to catch small fish. Watch for butterflies as well as signs of otters trolling for salmon and sea and brown trout.

Follow the River Teign for roughly 2.7 miles to Clifford Bridge. One of South Devon's main rivers, it's remarkably diverse over the 31 miles it runs from the boggy open moorlands of Dartmoor to the mudflats near Teignmouth before flowing into the English Channel. Along this stretch are several weirs, low dams built to regulate the flow of the river and to trap fish. Clifford Bridge is an arched, granite expanse constructed in the seventeenth century and widened a couple hundred years later.

From Clifford Bridge, retrace your steps to Fingle Bridge. Instead of crossing back over the bridge, continue straight ahead on the wide dirt track. Take a look behind you at the impressive expanse of the Fingle Bridge and, on the hill backing the Fingle Bridge Inn, the site of Prestonbury Castle, some 400 feet above the river, one of several ancient hillforts in the area. This beautiful, shady stretch is known as the Fisherman's Path, and you'll follow it along the south bank of the River Teign for the next 1.6 miles.

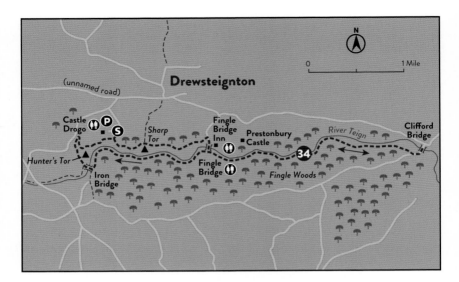

Above the lull of the current, listen for the sound of industrious woodpeckers hammering away to build their homes. Enjoy pretty views of the river as you gently climb, passing a large weir and a small hydroelectric plant, before running alongside a drystone wall known as the Deer Park wall.

At a gap in the wall, go over a rock stile in the direction of Castle Drogo. Cross the Iron Bridge, a narrow suspension footbridge over the river, go up the stairs, and bear left slightly to cross the Dartmoor Way (a long-distance trail) and continue straight. You're now on the Two Moors Way, also known as Devon's Coast to Coast, which spans 100 miles from the north coast of Exmoor National Park to the southern edge of Dartmoor National Park. This stretch alternates between dirt and paved sections for 0.4 mile as you climb out of the gorge in the shade of oak, larch, and horse chestnut. Turn right at the turnoff for "Hunters Path–Castle Drogo" and pass through the wooden gate between two large beech trees.

When the trail reaches a T intersection in 0.3 mile, bear right to stay on the Two Moors Way. Continue for 0.4 mile along the flanks of Hunter's Tor until you reach the junction from the start of the hike. Go left and retrace your steps 0.2 mile back to the car park.

EXTEND IT

A few hundred feet after crossing the Iron Bridge, go right on a trail to climb steeply up 200 feet to the top of Hunter's Tor, with great views of the surrounding terrain. This actually shortens the route by a little under half a mile, but requires sure-footedness and lung power.

35 VALLEY OF ROCKS

Explore one of the most intriguing and spectacular spots on the Exmoor coastline via a short section of the South West Coast Path that's long on views, geology, and folklore.

Distance: 2.5 miles
Elevation Gain: 800 feet
High Point: 440 feet
Rating: ★ ★ ★
Difficulty: Easy to moderate
Year-round: Yes
Dog-friendly: Yes, leashed

Family-friendly: Yes, though there are sheer drop-offs at Castle Rock and on the sometimes narrow coastal path
Amenities: Restrooms and picnic area at the start
Map: OS Explorer Map OL9, Exmoor
Agency: Exmoor National Park

GETTING THERE

GPS: 51.231895°, -3.847619°
Postcode: EX35 6JH
Before You Go: The exposed waterfront is sometimes windy and rainy. The sunsets seen from Castle Rock can be spectacular.

Driving: From the center of Lynton, follow Lee Road west as it turns into Longmead. In 0.5 mile, the Valley of Rocks car park is on your left.

ON THE TRAIL

Leave the car park the way you came in and make an immediate right to walk along the sidewalk. In about 300 feet, cross the road at a gate and pick up the paved trail heading uphill to the northwest. Continue straight on the main track for 0.2 mile to climb above the pastures, curving right to reach a T intersection. "Valley of Rocks" will start to make sense as the trail squeezes through a gap of serrated rock with the churning sea ahead.

Go left (west) onto the South West Coast Path (also, confusingly, called North Walk here) for 0.4 mile over somewhat vertigo-producing terrain. Pass beneath Chimney Rock in 0.1 mile and, in another 0.2 mile, Rugged Jack, a block-headed tor with a chiseled-jaw profile apparent from a particular angle. There's a nice set of benches nestled into the cliffside that offer a bit of shelter and a view out across the Bristol Channel toward the Celtic Sea.

When the trail veers slightly inland, bear right off the main track to climb a steep, rugged path about a tenth of a mile up roughly 150 feet in elevation to the top of Castle Rock. The arresting summit of jagged rock, coated with lichen and interspersed with abundant wildflowers, stoically faces a restless sea and ceaseless wind. To the west are views of Wringcliff Bay and, to the east, Hollerday Hill.

The Valley of Rocks is now dry, but it wasn't always this way. A river carved this serpentine valley, but where it went and why is a mystery. One theory is that the cliffs

Along the epic South West Coast Path in the Valley of Rocks, there are showstopping views of the North Devon coast.

eroded to such an extent that the course of the river shifted; another is that during the last ice age, a temporary river carved a new channel, the one we see today.

Return the way you came and continue west along the grassy track toward Wringcliff Beach (with Castle Rock on your right). In 0.1 mile, where the trail splits past the roundabout, leave the coast path and bear right toward the shore along a minor track. Reach an overlook above Wringcliff Bay in 0.2 mile, watching for a herd of Exmoor ponies and feral goats on either side of the trail.

First recorded here at least one thousand years ago, the goats died out in the mid-1960s. A small population of the nimble cliff walkers were reintroduced in the 1970s and have since flourished—and, according to land management schemes, the goats' grazing improves plant biodiversity in the area. Like most unusual features around here, a tall tale explains the goats' presence: nearby Castle Rock was once home to the devil. He was enraged by the good cheer and dancing of the local Druids and turned some into stone, and others into goats.

Gone are the smugglers from the eighteenth century who used bays like Wringcliff to hide ships that were trafficking in cheap goods. At the time the British government levied high customs duties (up to 30 percent) on imports, including popular items like tea, cloth, and booze. Smuggling became big business, and large, well-organized gangs formed to feed locals' appetite for reduced-priced items. What's now a scenic coast path would've been a major thoroughfare for contraband-laden donkeys hoofing it up the steep cliff paths.

Continue 0.1 mile down steep switchbacks to a small, secluded cove with a sand-and-shingle beach. At high tide there may not be much land, but it's still a dramatic spot to admire the geology of the area. The bygone river cut through what's called the Lynton Beds, made up of sandstone and slate and, therefore, highly fossiliferous (which may be the most fun word in the English language to say).

During the last ice age, glaciers extended as far south as the north Devon coast and brought a cycle of freezing and thawing that shattered the stone into slabs, boulders, and scree. The rock scrabble below the steep slopes of Wringcliff are a good place for fossil hunting. If you find a fossil in loose rock, it's yours to keep (it's illegal to dig or

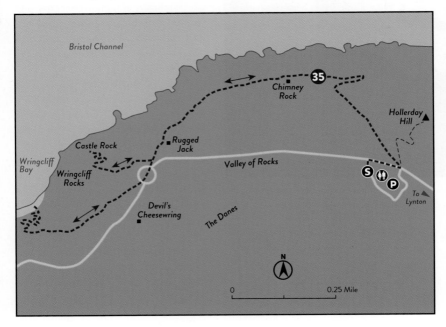

A secluded cove on Wringcliff Bay along the rugged Valley of Rocks coastline of North Devon

hammer) or, better yet, leave it behind for someone else to discover.

The Valley of Rocks has inspired many writers and painters over the centuries, particularly the Romantics fleeing the urban pollution of Victorian Britain. Many found this fascinating vale somewhat eerie and equated the rocks to bones and skeletons. Samuel Taylor Coleridge and William Wordsworth visited the area together in 1797 and agreed to co-write a story set in the valley, called "The Wanderings of Cain," but apparently it was never completed. Coleridge nonetheless captured our tendency to search for something familiar or comforting in alien landscapes. "The pointed and shattered summits of the ridges of the rocks made a rude mimicry of human concerns, and seemed to prophecy mutely of things that then were not; steeples, and battlements, and ships with naked masts," he wrote.

Leave Wringcliff Bay and retrace your steps back to the car park. From this angle you can make out the profile of the White Lady conjured by the cracks in Castle Rock. Also look for the Devil's Cheesewring on the opposite side of the valley, in an area called The Danes, an evocative group of rocks that looks intentionally stacked.

EXTEND IT

Add the summit of Hollerday Hill (800 feet) on the way back to the car park. Just before reaching the road you crossed to access the trail, take the fainter path to your left. Pass crags and woodland for roughly 0.6 mile, climbing 400 feet, to wonderful views of the surrounding area.

36 BRANSCOMBE & HOOKEN CLIFFS

This stretch of the Jurassic Coast showcases the drama of its white cliffs, striking pinnacles, Eden-like forest, and wide beaches, where fossil-hunting is compulsory.

Distance: 4.8 miles
Elevation Gain: 1100 feet
High Point: 450 feet
Rating: ★ ★ ★ ★
Difficulty: Moderate
Year-round: Yes
Dog-friendly: Yes, leashed near livestock

Family-friendly: Yes, but take caution near steep drop-offs on coast trail
Amenities: Restrooms and tea room at start; restrooms and cafe at Branscombe Beach
Map: OS Explorer Map 116, Lime Regis & Bridport
Agency: National Trust

GETTING THERE

GPS: 50.692563°, -3.137634°
Postcode: EX12 3DB
Driving: From Sidford, take A3052 for 4.5 miles, then take a slight right onto Locksey's Lane. Continue for 1.6 miles to a T intersection, then go right and follow an unnamed road for a few hundred feet to

the National Trust Branscombe car park on your right.
Before You Go: Parking is limited. The South West Coast Path is challenging due to its steep inclines and declines. There are great spots for skipping rocks and picnicking at Branscombe Beach.

ON THE TRAIL

Cross the road from the car park (the 450-year-old operational forge next to it is well worth a visit) and pick up the narrow gravel trail next to the stone wall. Pass the Old Bakery and, in a few hundred feet, cross a cement footbridge over a creek on a trail lined with apple trees. In another 300 feet or so, cross the creek again on a curvy wooden footbridge. Go through the gate straight ahead and up the hill, following a grassy track for a few hundred feet to a set of gates bookending a small footbridge. Cross the bridge and continue along the top of a field toward a cluster of stone structures. Descend for about a tenth of a mile to a gate.

Take a right immediately after the gate (following the wooden fingerpost signed "Link to Coast Path"). Go up the stairs and through another gate. At the next small footbridge, pass stone buildings and a water wheel to your left. This is Manor Mill, which ground grain for flour and animal feed in this once-bustling village. There's some evidence that there has been some type of mill here since medieval times, when one of three area streams was diverted to form the lea and which still powers the mill today.

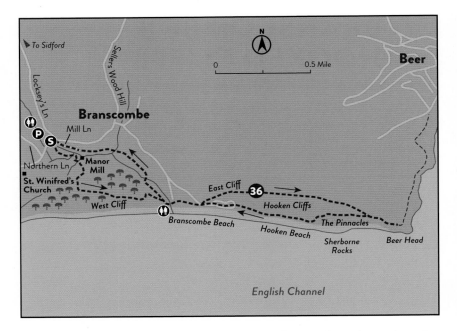

Branscombe also had a grist mill like this one, as well as one for timber and another for gypsum (used to improve soil and for plaster of Paris, popular in the Victorian era). The Manor Mill was operational from the eighteenth century until World War II and still gives working demonstrations.

From the mill, continue uphill toward the top of West Cliff, ascending about 200 feet in elevation over the next 0.2 mile. Bear left at a fingerpost with a yellow arrow and oak leaves (the symbol of the National Trust). Continue straight and, in 200 feet or so, cross a wooden stile. Ascend a long set of stairs for a few hundred feet to another stile and a T intersection.

Go left to join the South West Coast Path (marked by an upside-down acorn) heading east. On your left are nice views of Branscombe village tucked into the fold of Branscombe Valley, whose wide bottom was scoured out during the last ice age by meltwater floods. The village actually sits at the junction of three valleys or "combes" (from the Old English *cumb*, which has Celtic origins). It's likely been inhabited for four thousand to five thousand years and probably began as a fishing hub. Later on, locals focused on two curiously divergent products—lace and flints (used in guns as an ignition mechanism). Today Branscombe centers on livestock and tourists, both of which are plentiful. Its thatched-roofed stone cottages charm with blooming vines and hanging baskets, and St. Winifred's Church dates from the twelfth century.

Follow the path straight into a densely wooded area. Breaks in the bracken and brambles allow for views of the English Channel and soaring sea birds, green pastures, and the Hooken Cliffs to the east. (Take caution where the trail comes very close to the cliff edge, because it is a sheer drop of a few hundred feet to the sand.) Look for birds of prey, including peregrine falcons and buzzards, as well as dolphins.

After about 0.6 mile begin to descend, passing hardy but cheerful wildflowers, toward the beach. Go down a set of stairs through a coppice and cross through a gate into a field. Follow the grass track across the field and, in another 0.2 mile, pass through a gate at a cafe facing the beach, Branscombe Mouth. (Beware of the Sea Shanty cafe, which peddles addictive, salty cheese fries.)

Go through the gate and cross in front of the grassy lawn and wide, pebble beach facing Lyme Bay. The 13.5-ton anchor you see is what's left of a cargo ship that was caught in a windstorm in 2007. Its crew of two dozen were rescued and the vessel was beached with over two thousand containers still on it. It's possible to swim here, but the

The chalk pinnacles and wooded folds of the Hooken Cliffs on the Jurassic Coast are a UNESCO World Heritage Site.

water can be turbid with occasional plankton blooms. Offshore there are wrecks and reefs that attract divers.

Cross the cement-slab footbridge spanning a stream and bear right through the gate marking the entrance to East Cliff. Follow the signed "public footpath" toward Hooken Cliffs and Beer village (the "coast path" is used on the return route). Go straight for 1 mile through several gates and over a few stiles, ascending over 400 feet in elevation to the hilltop.

While resting at one of the hill's well-positioned benches, look back at the spectacular Jurassic Coast west of Branscombe. The area gets its name—in part—from the geology it reveals. Over its roughly 100 miles of coastline is rock from the Triassic, Jurassic, and Cretaceous periods. Their chronology runs from west to east, oldest to youngest, with the oldest rock at Exmouth dating from 250 million years ago. Different layers of rock took shape here—red mudstone, beige sandstone, and white chalk—as the earth's crust stretched and contracted, sea levels rose and fell, tropical forests came and went, and dinosaurs lived and died. The abundant, well-preserved fossils emerging from the cliffs played an important part in the development of the field of paleontology, and the Dorset and East Devon coast is now a UNESCO natural World Heritage site, recognized for its importance in the study of earth sciences.

Continue along the hedgerows lining the fields and, as the trail levels out, you'll get your first views of the glowing white Hooken Cliffs and the Pinnacles from above. Pass by the gate leading to the coast path on your right and carry on for 500 feet or so onto the spit of land marking Beer Head. To the east are expansive views of the village of Beer and the cliffs and hills surrounding it.

Return to the gate for the coastal path and turn onto it to head steeply downhill. Soon you'll descend into an unexpected wildland, the result of a huge landslide. One March evening in 1790, a huge fissure developed in the land above the cliffs. The split freed a large section of rock that slid toward the sea on a bed of undermined land. About fifteen million tons of chalk and sandstone ultimately fell away—the distinctive white pinnacles are the remaining shards of those cliffs. Soon after the soil settled, plant life started to take root. Over time it's developed into a kind of oasis that draws butterflies and birds—even some peregrines have taken up residence here.

Over the next 0.5 mile, keep bearing left to head downhill toward the beach. From the shore, follow the wide shingle beach 0.5 mile west, back to Branscombe Beach. The blocks of chalk that have broken away from the cliffside here are a good place to look for fossils. (Be wary of falling rocks near the base of the cliff.) Also peek into some of the many rock pools for crabs and sea anemones.

Once past the beach shacks on your right, head inland. Bear left around the cafe and pick up the wide, well-maintained trail alongside a towering conifer, heading northwest toward Branscombe village. In 0.2 mile cross the stream on a wooden footbridge and, when the trail forks twice in a few hundred feet, bear left both times. In about a quarter mile cross another footbridge and bear left. Continue straight (west) for another 0.2 mile and pass through a gate onto a narrow tarmac road (Mill Lane). Follow that for about a tenth of a mile to where it emerges near the car park. Go left and walk for a few hundred feet to return to where you started.

EXTEND IT

Continue from Beer Head for roughly 2.5 miles along the coast path, past the village of Beer, to the mouth of the River Axe and the Axe Estuary, a link between inland wetlands and the open ocean with abundant wildlife.

37 LULWORTH COVE & DURDLE DOOR

Explore some of Dorset's iconic landmarks along a mostly undeveloped stretch of Jurassic coastline of clear water, white cliffs, and sweeping arches.

Distance: 3.5 miles
Elevation Gain: 990 feet
High Point: 410 feet
Rating: ★ ★ ★ ★ ★
Difficulty: Easy to moderate
Year-round: Yes
Dog-friendly: Yes

Family-friendly: Yes, but take caution around cliffs as the ground shifts
Amenities: Restrooms at visitor center; restaurants and cafes near visitor center
Map: OS Explorer Map OL15, Purbeck & South Dorset
Agency: Jurassic Coast Trust

GETTING THERE

GPS: 50.619930°, -2.253432°
Postcode: BH20 5RS
Driving: From the Castle Inn in West Lulworth, go south on Main Road for 0.6 mile to the Lulworth Cove car park and visitor center on your right.
Before You Go: The beaches are busy in summer. The west end of St. Oswald's Beach

is cut off at high tide, and the eastern path up to Lulworth is steep. An alternate route runs from Durdle Door to Lulworth Cove along the clifftop above St. Oswald's Beach.
Public Transit: Buses from Wool, Dorchester, and Weymouth run to Lulworth Cove from May through September.

ON THE TRAIL

Head west from the car park, uphill and away from Lulworth Cove. Go through the gate and follow the wide stone path up the hillside. As you ascend, the hills swell in shades of

The sheer chalk cliffs of the Dorset coast are full of curiosities like Bat's Hole arch in the distance.

olive and gold as the turquoise sea comes into view. When the trail splits in 0.4 mile, take the middle track to follow the South West Coast Path heading west, and continue for 0.3 mile to where the trail turns sharply left (south) toward the shore.

Continue for another 0.3 mile to pass above Man O'War Beach, a cove naturally sheltered by surrounding rocks, and down to an overlook offering the first look at Durdle Door. The natural limestone arch is a rarity in this area, as most of the porous rock has eroded away. Someday this arch too will succumb to the relentless sea, but take heart, it's been called Durdle (derived from Old English *thirl* meaning "to pierce") for at least the last thousand years, so it's likely not going anywhere soon.

Continue west for 0.3 mile, enjoying some of the best views of Durdle Door, to arrive at an area humorously named Scratchy Bottom, a coastal valley where farmland meets cliff. (Despite being a strong contender, Scratchy Bottom does not take the prize for most unfortunate place name in Britain. That honor goes to nearby Shitterton, which lies about 11 miles north of Lulworth Cove.) Look west for tremendous views of Swyre Head (320 feet) and, beyond that, Bat's Head. Their sheer cliffs consistently shed rock onto the pinkish-orange sand below. When enough of this debris is scooped up by the waves and suspended in the water, the sea takes on a greenish-blue tint. Below Bat's Head, look for Butter Rock, a stand-alone chalk sea stack, and Bat's Hole, an intriguing little arch (if the Bat Cave is nearby, it does not appear on any maps). Offshore is a line of small rock islets called, from east to west, the Bull, the Blind Cow, the Cow, and the Calf, names harkening back to the ancient agrarian history of the area.

Return to the stairs above Durdle Door and take them down to the beach. On a hot day, the 200-foot arch looks like the trunk of a huge elephant—or maybe a long-necked dinosaur—dipping in for a drink. Look closely for some large holes in the arch, the fossilized remains of several cycad trees alive during the late Jurassic period (roughly 145

million years ago). Most of the rock around Durdle Door is from the comparatively recent Cretaceous period, which ended with the dinosaurs dying out about sixty-six million years back. This shoreline has appeared in numerous films and in the work of many artists, writers, and musicians. Irish writer and playwright John O'Keefe wrote in 1792, "They persuaded me to keep on, and at last stranded me on the pebbles, exactly opposite the magnificent arch of Durdle-rock Door. Here I stood and contemplated with astonishment and pleasure this stupendous piece of Nature's work."

Go up the stairs north of Durdle Door onto the isthmus that separates the two coves. Take the less steep of the two paths down into Man O'War Cove and walk around its near perfect arc, pausing to look back at the side view of Durdle Door. Over time the tides have been wearing away limestones, siltstones, and sandstones on either side of the isthmus. On this side, the faults and folds of the now-visible rocks and fossils reveal a stunning snapshot of the Mesozoic era—continental plates shifting, climate changing, evolution going gangbusters. Offshore, look for the limestone Man O'War Rocks and, backing the cove and beach, Hambury Tout (440 feet).

Continue along the reddish sands to St. Oswald's Bay Beach. Admire the caves in the cliffside from afar, as this is a dynamic landscape with occasional rockfalls. This beach is part of the Dorset Area of Outstanding Natural Beauty, a hub of biodiversity and home to over 80 percent of all Britain's mammal species, 70 percent of its butterfly

This famous limestone arch first appeared on Ordinance Survey maps in 1811 but has been a work in progress for 140 million years.

species, and 48 percent of its bird species, including cormorants, jackdaws, ravens, rooks, and, if you're lucky, a kestrel or peregrine falcon. While their riches are mainly scenic nowadays, the coves and beaches near Lulworth also have an illustrious smuggling history. Even after customs officials were installed on-site in the eighteenth century, smuggled goods continued to flood local markets and sometimes made it as far as London (cocoa beans for "drinking chocolate" were popular contraband for urban elites of the early 1700s). While smuggling cocoa, brandy, or lace may sound frivolous, the livelihoods of the smugglers and the tax men were at stake.

The beach reaches the base of Dungy Head 0.7 mile from Man O'War Cove. While it is possible to follow the very rocky beach around the headland at low tide, the following route can be used at high tide. Find the trail cutting up the hill to your left (east) through tall grasses. Follow the steep track 0.2 mile to the end of Bitwell Drive, a narrow paved road. Continue along Bitwell Drive for 0.2 mile, then turn right to rejoin the signed coast path toward Lulworth Cove.

After 0.2 mile the trail passes in front of Stair Hole—a beautiful spot made up of three miniature coves carved out of soft rock. They are almost completely protected by a series of arches and caves excavated out of the rock by the crashing waves. If the surf is up, keep an eye out for water shooting through a blowhole near the top center. This is what the area around Man O' War Cove likely looked like ten thousand years ago.

Directly to the east of Stair Hole you'll reach the west side of famed Lulworth Cove, whose appearance changes every day as more and more rock is cut away by the tides. Follow the trail down to the pebble beach to get a closer look at the placid green-blue water dotted with sailboats. Lulworth is still a working fishing cove, but it is also popular for swimming, snorkeling, and diving. Follow the track back up to where the path splits and veer right to reach Main Road in 0.1 mile. Turn left and follow the road 0.1 mile back to the car park.

EXTEND IT

For a panorama of the Dorset coast, add the summit of Hambury Tout. From the car park, take the trail to the right of the South West Coast Path for 0.3 mile up roughly 350 feet of elevation gain. Walk past the summit, marked by a "bell barrow" burial mound from 1500–1100 BC, to intersect a trail heading south to meet the coast path.

WALES (CYMRU)

Though relatively compact, each square mile of Wales has enchantment to rival its bigger neighbors. Nearly the whole country seems steeped in folklore with a staggering diversity of inland and coastal terrain (from hump-backed Wales to humpback whales!) as well as deep lakes, tall peaks, and rugged coastline that make one restless for adventure. The Welsh themselves are warm, welcoming folks with a tongue-twisting (or basically impossible for non-native speakers to pronounce correctly) language, a rich culture, and a keen sense of humor. Some of the funniest sayings are used to describe heavy rain. If you hear someone say, "It's raining old women and sticks," get out your galoshes.

SNOWDONIA NATIONAL PARK
North Wales is dominated by 800-square-mile Snowdonia National Park (Trails 38–40), a mountainous region encompassing the highest ground in Wales and England. It's a striking landscape of bowl-shaped valleys and jagged peaks, born of bygone volcanoes later worn away by ice. Heaps of enduring legends mean that Snowdonia is as mythical as it looks, with walks of all levels.

BRECON BEACONS NATIONAL PARK
Named for the east-west band of mountains at its core, Brecon Beacons National Park (Trails 41–42), also called Parc Cenedlaethol Bannau Brycheiniog, has four ranges in all. Those to the west are generally more remote, while those to the east are more heavily visited. The park covers roughly 520 square miles of sweeping, barren-looking highlands with wide ridges and flat-topped peaks beloved by walkers, and rolling moorlands and valley pastures beloved by sheep and ponies. It also harbors some rare wildlife and impressive waterfalls.

PEMBROKESHIRE COAST NATIONAL PARK
In the far southwest corner of Wales, Pembrokeshire Coast National Park (Trails 43–45) encompasses some of the most dramatic coastal scenery in Great Britain.

OPPOSITE: *A view from Pen y Fan, the highest peak in South Wales, to Cribyn in the Brecon Beacons*

Its (relatively) mild climate makes the sheer cliffs, quiet coves, golden beaches, rock arches, and remote islands that much more alluring.

38 CWM IDWAL

This relatively short (though heart-pumping) loop in Wales's first national nature reserve roams past rare plants, clear waters, and jaw-dropping scenery steeped in folklore and history.

Distance: 3.5 miles
Elevation Gain: 940 feet
High Point: 1737 feet
Rating: ★ ★ ★ ★ ★
Difficulty: Moderate to challenging
Year-round: Yes
Dog-friendly: Yes, leashed

Family-friendly: Yes, but with a steep climb and sheer drop-offs
Amenities: Restrooms, cafe, and parking at Idwal Cottage
Map: OS Explorer Map OL17, Snowdon
Agency: Snowdonia National Park

GETTING THERE

GPS: 53.123403°, -4.019085°
Postcode: LL57 3LZ
Driving: From Capel Curig, take the A5 west for 5 miles to the YHA (Youth Hostels Association) Idwal Cottage, which has a parking lot on your left.

Public Transit: The bus stop for YHA Idwal Cottage is Pen y Benglog.
Before You Go: Rocks by streams, waterfalls, and the lake can be slippery. The weather can change rapidly and low clouds and mist can make the higher elevations difficult to navigate.

ON THE TRAIL

Pick up the trail to the east of the YHA Idwal Cottage (heading in the direction of the arrow on a slate sign nailed to a tree reading "Llyn Idwal Path"). Gently climb a path of large, flat rocks, soon passing a wooden schema carved with the glaciated peaks of the Glyderau, which are directly ahead—Tryfan (3009 feet), Glyder Fach (3261 feet), and Glyder Fawr (3283 feet). Glyder may derive from the Welsh word *gludair*, meaning "heap," because their tops appear to be piled with a jumble of jagged rocks, while *tryfan* means "sharp head or summit."

Pass through an impressive wrought iron gate depicting the area's rugged topography—rock walls, lakes, and cataracts—and take a wooden footbridge over the Afon Idwal, a river tumbling waterfall-like over dark boulders with bright pink foxglove blooming on its banks. Continue uphill along the rocky trail for about a tenth of a mile to a fork, and veer right to stay on the paving stones. Watch for bees bobbing lazily among the purplish, bell-shaped buds of heather flanking the trail.

At this point you have gained a bit of elevation; the landscape is striking, with grassy, boulder-strewn undulations and the grey-purple walls of the Glyderau massif. As you walk deeper into enchanting Cwm Idwal, watch for Carneddau ponies, a wild and hardy breed that struggle to survive in the cold, wind, and precipitation of their namesake mountains to the north. King Henry VIII ordered their destruction four hundred years ago because he thought they were too small to carry a knight in full armor. Some survived the slaughter, and about two hundred freely roam all of Snowdonia today, without a knight in sight. Other creatures in residence include fallow deer, brown hares, foxes, badgers, and the secretive pine marten.

At 0.4 mile from the trail fork, arrive at the shores of Llyn ("Lake") Idwal. The still water reflects the rough-hewn visages of the glacial cirque as it curves around the end of the cwm (meaning "valley"), like a parentheses at the end of a sentence. Those cliffs, carved by ice long ago, look like ancient faces creased with a record of past expressions. Idwal may have been named to honor the multiple Welsh princes with that name over time, but there is a popular, and more intriguing, origin story that has endured for centuries. Prince Owain Gwynedd, who reigned from AD 1137 to 1169, had a son, Idwal, whom he put in the care of Nefydd Hardd. Legend has it that Idwal was a mighty giant—which may have meant he was heroic (in terms of his military prowess and valor) or perhaps he was literally of large stature. Whichever it was, fear or jealousy led Nefydd's son to drown Idwal in the lake. Some say wailing can be heard in the cwm during storms. Idwal was allegedly buried near the lake, and believers contend that no birds will fly over the haunted waters.

Patient birders, however, might see a defiant buzzard, peregrine falcon, or skylark in the area. Skylarks are known for their intense song-flights, which can last an hour and take them up nearly 1000 feet before they plunge back to earth. They are now a protected species in the UK because their numbers have declined rapidly due to habitat loss. In "To a Skylark," English Romantic poet Percy Bysshe Shelley wrote: "What objects are the fountains / Of thy happy strain? / What fields, or waves, or mountains? / What shapes of sky or plain? / What love of thine own kind? / What ignorance of pain?"

Take a right when you reach the lake to again cross the Afon Idwal, this time over a bridge made of slate slabs. From there, follow the trail left and cross through a metal gate, keeping to the western shore of Llyn Idwal for 0.1 mile. Ignore the right branch when the trail forks and head left onto a narrow, rocky beach—a tempting stop for a picnic lunch. Watch the light breeze rippling over the lake and the gauzy clouds clinging to the mountain tops some 2000 feet above.

Walk the beach for 0.1 mile before passing through a gate in a rock wall, then continue along the trail as it skirts the lake and crosses over another stream, the Afon

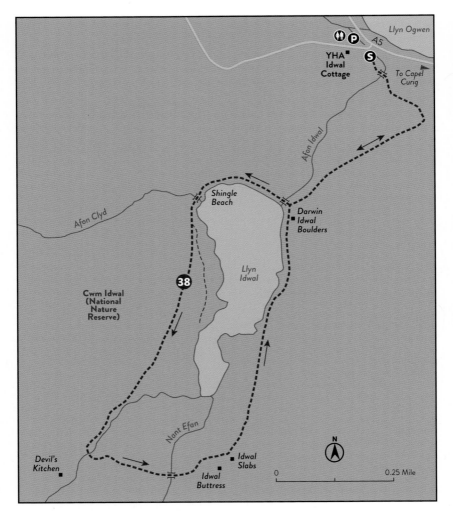

Clyd. Soon you'll leave the water's edge and begin to climb through heather-clad hummocks. In 0.4 mile from the last gate, reach another fork in the trail. The left branch continues to circumnavigate the lake, but head straight on the right branch, where the real ascent into the rock amphitheater begins.

Continue up a steep slope and a lot of rock stairs for 0.5 mile as the trail bears left and levels out. At the next junction take the loop trail to your left, heading straight onto a flat, grass-covered rock outcropping overlooking the hanging valley, another perfect rest spot with huge views, including of Llyn Idwal—0.5 mile long by 0.2 mile wide—sprawling out far below. The bony nub of Pen Yr Ole Wen (1542 feet) and the western edge of Llyn Ogwen are also visible when the sky is clear.

Cwm Idwal is sometimes called a "hanging garden" or a "botanist's paradise," and the outcropping is indeed lush with grasses, wildflowers, ferns, moss, and lichen, with many moths and butterflies flickering around. This upland environment is as far south as Great Britain's remaining Arctic-Alpine flora persists. The rocky ledges of Cwm Idwal are a haven for rare and fragile plants like the Snowdon lily and Welsh poppy. Watch for merlin here, the UK's smallest (and arguably coolest) bird of prey, climbing and diving powerfully in loops. Bigger than robins but smaller than crows, they are fierce hunters. According to Juliana Berners's *The Book of Hawking, Hunting, and Blasing of Arms*, published in 1486, the merlin was designated specifically for female falconers.

From here you can continue climbing up Cwm Idwal toward the peaks of Y Garn and Glyder Fawr, or stick to the trail, as this route does, to head downhill toward the eastern shore of Llyn Idwal, a lovely loop with a gentler slope and fewer stairs. In about a quarter mile, pass beneath the so-called Devil's Kitchen, also called Twll Du (meaning "Black Hole") in Welsh. Look to your right for a dark cleft splitting the rock of Clogwyn y Geifr ("Goat Cliff") between Y Garn and Glyder Fawr. Misty plumes, once thought to be steam, can sometimes be seen rising from the chimney-like crack. That meant the devil was cooking, some believed. Others thought the Druids fashioned lightning there, to deflect the Roman invasion around AD 57. In reality, wet air cools and condenses against the rock and rises.

It's below Clogwyn y Geifr that the violent origins of this landscape become most evident. Four hundred million years ago, North Wales was beneath an ocean, where volcanoes were erupting, laying down new rock. Then two land masses collided, causing the Snowdonia massif to rise and fold into a range that once rivaled the Himalayas. Millions of more years of wind and water wore them down—the large boulders on your right were peeled from the cliffs above by ice retreating roughly ten thousand to thirteen thousand years ago.

Cross a few small scree fields to arrive at a slate bridge with guardrails, spanning Nant Efan over a deep chasm in the rocks. A waterfall careens down from several hundred feet above and follows the rock gash beneath the bridge on its course to the lake below. From the bridge, continue for 0.2 mile to join the trail circumnavigating the lake, scanning for rock climbers on the famous Idwal Slabs, a prominent rock formation sloped at a 50-degree angle to your right. The Welsh call these rocks Rhiwiau Caws, which means "Cheese Hills," the reason for which was not obvious to me. Many mountaineers, including Sir Edmund Hillary and Charles Evans (his Welsh teammate), have trained here.

From the junction, walk 0.5 mile to the next intersection (crossing one gate on the way). Turn right to rejoin the trail you took to the lake on the way in, passing the Darwin

In the hanging valley of Cwm Idwal, its namesake lake shines like a big blue question mark in a land full of mystery.

Idwal Boulders—a set of prominent glacial erratics to your right. Charles Darwin, the English naturalist, biologist, and geologist, first visited the area in 1831. He was interested in the age of the earth and the debates about when and how it was formed. In the erratics on the shores of Llyn Idwal, he found fossils of prehistoric sea creatures—now 1200 feet above sea level—and later recognized that they must have been uplifted over time. When Darwin returned home from Snowdonia, an invitation to join the crew of the *Beagle* as a naturalist was waiting for him. Despite his father's disapproval, the twenty-two-year-old Darwin left for a five-year circumnavigation of the globe—which turned out to be key to his development of the "theory of evolution by natural selection."

When Darwin returned to North Wales in 1842, he realized that the glorious amphitheater of Cwm Idwal was not the result of a biblical flood, as he'd first posited, but a glaciated landscape—"the plainly scored rocks, the perched boulders, the lateral and terminal moraines. Yet these phenomena are so conspicuous that . . . a house burnt down by fire did not tell its story more plainly than did this valley," he later wrote.

From those inspirational rocks of ages, walk 0.5 mile back to the start.

EXTEND IT
Cross the road from the YHA Idwal Cottage and complete the 3-mile loop around Llyn Ogwen. Legend says that Bedwyr Bedrynant, a knight of King Arthur, cast the famous sword Excalibur into Llyn Ogwen, where it's said to remain to this day.

39 LEGENDS OF BEDDGELERT

Two of Wales's most renowned and captivating tales originate from around Beddgelert, where burbling rivers, shade trees, vast meadows, rock features, and intriguing architecture create a feeling of glorious isolation.

Distance: 1.5 miles
Elevation Gain: 70 feet
High Point: 177 feet
Rating: ★ ★ ★ ★
Difficulty: Easy
Year-round: Yes
Family-friendly: Yes; easy walking with legends to share

Dog-friendly: Yes, leashed
Amenities: Paid public restrooms near river (near first gate); many cafes, restaurants, and hotels in Beddgelert, including (I contend) the best ice cream shop in Wales
Map: OS Explorer Map OL17, Snowdon
Agency: Snowdonia National Park

GETTING THERE
GPS: 53.011502°, -4.104787°
Postcode: LL55 4YD
Driving: The Snowdonia National Park Visitor Centre at Beddgelert sits on the A4085, 17 miles from Betws y Coed, and on the A498, 13 miles from Caernarfon.

Public Transit: Beddgelert is served by buses from Betws y Coed and Caernarfon.
Before You Go: There are two public car parks in the village, but they tend to fill up quickly (especially in summer). The visitor center is open daily most of the year but only from Friday to Sunday during the winter.

ON THE TRAIL
Facing the front of Snowdonia National Park Visitor Centre, go right and continue 0.1 mile along A498 to the much-photographed double-arch stone bridge in the center of the village. Don't cross the bridge, but instead continue straight along a narrow road (in the direction indicated by a brown sign with an arrow pointing the way to "Gelert's Grave"). The river, Afon Colwyn, is on your left, while on your right are several impressive structures built from dark rock mined locally. Reach a footbridge in roughly

300 feet and go right, keeping the water, now the Afon Glaslyn, on your left. Almost immediately, pass through an elaborate iron gate with the outline of an animal's paw at its center (you will soon learn why).

Enter a huge, gently sloped meadow dotted with broadleaf trees and backed by green-grey hills. About 150 feet to your right is the Church of St. Mary, an attractive stone structure with steeply pitched roofs, long stained-glass windows, and a bell tower. In the sixth century an early Christian community sprung up here, and several centuries later an Augustinian priory was founded. The order was expanded in the Middle Ages with the support of Welsh nobles, including the powerful Prince Llewelyn the Great. The current church, which has been restored over the centuries, incorporates medieval remnants from the thirteenth century (services are still held here). Behind the church, to the southwest, are several sun-dappled peaks, including the dominant Moel Hebog (2565 feet).

Carry on along the river for 0.2 mile, then take a trail branching off to your right at another sign pointing to "Gelert's Grave." Walk for a few hundred feet under the generous canopies of English oaks before the path veers left into open meadow and passes through an opening in a stone wall. Straight ahead, in about 250 feet, you'll arrive at a small fenced-in area. Beneath two small trees is a large stone slab flanked by two knobby rocks. Look for carved stone plaques that explain the legend of the faithful hound, Gelert.

The story goes that, in the thirteenth century, Prince Llewellyn left his infant son under the protection of his dog, Gelert, while he went out hunting. When the prince returned, the dog and nursery were covered in blood and the child was nowhere in sight. Thinking his canine companion had killed the boy, Llewelyn slayed the dog with his sword. A moment later the prince heard his baby cry, and he found him unharmed beneath the overturned crib—alongside the body of a huge wolf, which Gelert had killed. Llewellyn was devastated by his awful error and apparently never smiled again. He buried the hound on this spot and named the area Beddgelert, or Gelert's grave.

In truth, this story was most likely the marketing ploy of a savvy innkeeper who moved to the area in the late eighteenth century. David Prichard, then-manager of what's now the Royal Goat Hotel, is suspected of coming up with the tear-jerking tale, or at least its finer details. The fable's origins stretch back thousands of years, and versions of the story have been told in different parts of the world. It's more likely that the village was named for Saint Gelert, a hermit and healer who lived in the area in the seventh century, and who may have been martyred and buried here. Regardless of the tale's origins, thousands of people per year make a pilgrimage to this site, some even leaving flowers. Surrounded by a towering ring of peaks insulating the quiet valley from the outside world, it is easy to get caught up in imagining, and in thinking about passion, judgement, friendship, and life and death. After mentioning the dog in his 1862 book, *Wild Wales*, English writer George Henry Borrow wrote, "Such is the legend which, whether true or fictitious, is singularly beautiful and affecting."

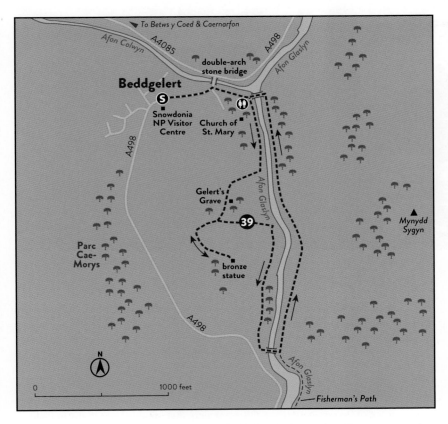

To Betws y Coed & Caernarfon

Afon Colwyn

A4085

A498

Afon Glaslyn

double-arch
stone bridge

Beddgelert

Ⓢ

Snowdonia
NP Visitor
Centre

⑪

A498

Church of
St. Mary

Afon Glaslyn

Gelert's
Grave

39

▲
Mynydd
Sygyn

Parc
Cae-
Morys

A498

bronze
statue

N

0   1000 feet

Afon Glaslyn

Fisherman's Path

But the British hadn't been enchanted by Wales for long when Borrow wrote that line. Up until the late eighteenth century, they thought of North Wales as savage and untamed. Then one of the most famous travel writers of his day, Thomas Pennant, wrote his eight-volume *A Tour in Wales*, after exploring the area between 1773 and 1776. Pennant portrayed this part of Wales as wild, even exotic, and wholly different from England's refinement. He encouraged the British to feel entranced by, and tethered to, Wales, and to travel there—which they did, including many artistic and literary luminaries.

The Welsh legends fascinated the Romantics in particular. Landscape painters (and frenemies) Thomas Girtin and J. M. W. Turner (born just months apart in London in 1775) both painted captivating scenes in and around Beddgelert with legendary mastery of light and shadow. Poet William Wordsworth also visited Beddgelert in 1791, when he was twenty-one, completing a dawn ascent of Yr Wyddfa, or Snowdon.

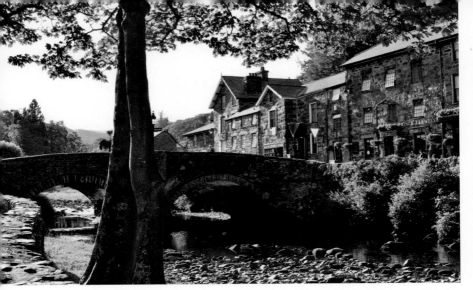

The gleaming village of Beddgelert sits in a quiet valley at the confluence of the Rivers Colywn and Glaslyn.

But it seems Pennant hadn't completely convinced the English of Welsh civility. In 1840, James Hews Bransby wrote in his *Descriptive and Historical Sketch of Beddgelert and Its Neighborhood*: "People have deceived themselves that Wales is inhabited only by 'Souls made of fire, and children of the sun' . . . Though the occupations of the people in this wild district are rude and simple, the people themselves are not ignorant, or fierce, or unfeeling."

Carry on following the path behind the grave for roughly 150 feet, in the direction of the remnants of an old stone house. Step through the doorway to find a life-sized bronze statue of Gelert peering out of the opening, then double back to the trail along the river. Keep the river on your left for the next 0.4 mile, passing through two gates along the way.

Keep to the path as it crosses a gated bridge. Stop there for views north over the wildflower-lined Afon Glaslyn to the rocky bulges of Craig Wen (1798 feet) and Yr Aran (2451 feet). "Truly, the valley of Gelert is a wondrous valley—rivalling for grandeur and beauty any vale either in the Alps or Pyrenees," wrote Borrow. The 16-mile-long river is important habitat for salmon and sea trout. From Beddgelert the river flows south for several miles to the Bae Ceredigion but, before that, it passes through Pont Croesor, the first known breeding site for osprey in Wales. They arrived in 2004 and still return to breed in growing numbers, though catching a glimpse of them is rare.

Go left at the end of the bridge onto the track alongside the river (or go right to continue on the Fisherman's Path). Start working your way back to the village over the next 0.5 mile, passing through two gates on the way. Before long you will return to the footbridge you passed at the beginning of the walk, opposite a small green area surrounded by cottages. From here take in views of the confluence of the Afon Glaslyn and Afon Colwyn, and beyond, to the top of the tree-covered hillock of Dinas Emrys 2 miles east.

The second celebrated legend tied to this area is rooted in Dinas Emrys, where two dragons were said to dwell. In the fifth century, Celtic King Vortigern wanted to build a castle on the hill, but the royal masons' tools kept disappearing and the walls they built kept crumbling. A sorcerer told the king that to end the vandalism the construction site must be sprinkled with the blood of a half human, half magical child. That child, Caer Myrddin (better known as Merlin), was found nearby. Vortigern was preparing to sacrifice the child when Merlin told him that two dragons, one red and one white, were living beneath the hill and its underground lake, and were angered by the construction. Clever Merlin said the castle could only be built when one of the dragons had been sent packing. Vortigern's workers dug quickly into Dinas Emrys and drained the lake, driving the dragons to battle. The white dragon eventually fled and the red dragon returned to its lair. The castle was built and the red dragon landed on the Welsh flag, where it is still celebrated. When the site was excavated in the 1940s, ruins from Vortigern's time were unearthed, as well as a subterranean lake. (But still no sign of the dragons.)

From the bridge, follow your footsteps back to the visitor center.

EXTEND IT
Continue past where this hike turns around for another 6 miles along the Fisherman's Path, passing through a lush copse, spectacular gorge, and historical valley (Cwm Bychan), and around a placid lake (Llyn Dinas).

40 SNOWDON (YR WYDDFA)

A straightforward but challenging walk up Yr Wyddfa (commonly known by its English name, Snowdon), Wales's highest mountain, in Snowdonia National Park.

Distance: 8 miles
Elevation Gain: 3070 feet
High Point: 3560 feet
Rating: ★ ★ ★ ★
Difficulty: Challenging

Year-round: No
Family-friendly: Yes, but can be a foggy or wet slog in exposed terrain
Dog-friendly: Yes, leashed

Amenities: Restrooms at car park; restrooms and cafe at Hafod Eryri, the summit house

Map: OS Explorer Map OL17, Snowdon
Agency: Snowdonia National Park

GETTING THERE

GPS: 53.073509°, -4.144431°
Postcode: LL54 7YS
Driving: Drive north on A4085 from Beddgelert for 5 miles, then turn left into the National Park Authority car park (opposite the Snowdon Ranger Station and YHA Snowdon Ranger).

Public Transit: Buses run from central Beddgelert to the trailhead next to the YHA Snowdon Ranger.
Before You Go: This is a very popular peak, and parking is limited. Given its annual precipitation rate of 200 inches, you will likely get wet. Do not be fooled by a clear start.

ON THE TRAIL

With the lake, Llyn Cwellyn, behind you, carefully cross the road from the car park and bear slightly right to the trailhead. Turn left up the trail, in the direction indicated by the green sign and "Snowdon Ranger Path" stone marker. In 200 feet, follow the path, turning sharply left to run alongside the railroad tracks. Reach a T intersection in another 200 feet, and turn sharply right to go through the gate and over the tracks. Head straight for 0.1 mile, past some tall pines and stone farm buildings, then veer right through another gate to follow the wide, graveled Ranger Path. The track is believed to be the original of six classic routes now snaking their way to the summit. It was first used to haul copper from the Britannia Mine on the mountain's eastern slope (near Llyn Llydaw). But the path's current name refers to a self-appointed ranger, John Morton, who led clients up Yr Wyddfa in the early nineteenth century, and also ran an inn and pub, now home to the youth hostel at the start.

Ascend roughly 600 feet up switchbacks over the next 0.9 mile. Much of the terrain of North Wales is dominated by countless ridges snaking across the landscape like exposed, rocky tree roots. Lakes and valleys, villages and streams, remain essentially hidden, until you've climbed high enough for the alpine topography to reveal some of its secrets. Even in foul weather, there should be good views west to Llyn Cwellyn and the rock- and tree-clad slopes behind it. The 120-foot-deep, 215-acre glacial moraine lake is one of the few in Wales with a population of Arctic char.

Peer down into the valley and consider the tale of the young shepherd from a nearby village who fell in love with a fairy living in the lake. The two wed, but on the condition that if the shepherd ever touched her skin with iron, she would return to the lake. After many years of happy marriage, the shepherd accidently brushed his wife's cheek with the iron bit of a bridle he was putting on a horse—and she vanished.

Continue straight along the wide path across the grassy hillside cut through by plentiful streams, lined with ancient stone walls, and riotous with pink lupine and other wildflowers. Snowdon is a national nature reserve, and the flanks of Yr Wyddfa are speckled with rare but hardy Arctic-Alpine plants like the shy but cheerful Snowdon lily, which blooms light yellow from late May to early July.

Cross a few gates, always leaving them as you find them, and ignore a track climbing steeply to your left and another descending steeply to your right. Pass above another large lake, Llyn Ffynnon-y-gwas ("servant's well"), which is rumored to have a good stock of wild brown trout.

Descending the Ranger Path, one of the six officials trails to the summit of Yr Wyddfa, a pyramidal peak first climbed in 1639

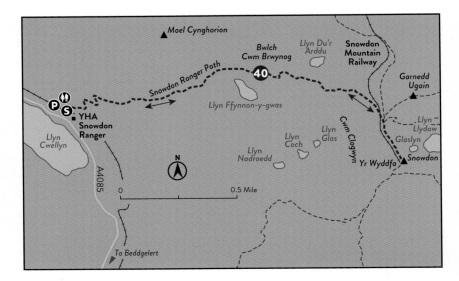

From here glimpse the impressive bulk of Yr Wyddfa. The mountain is the highest peak on the British Isles outside of the Scottish Highlands, and holds a firm place in the history of UK mountaineering: the first British team to summit Everest, including Sir Edmund Hillary, trained on Yr Wyddfa in the early 1950s.

Just beyond the lake, switchback up roughly 1500 feet over the next 1.3 miles as the terrain transitions from sheep-grazed slopes to craggy outcrops coated in lichen, remnants of Yr Wyddfa's volcanic origins. Look for erratics, ice age boulders carried away by glaciers and abandoned to their current angle of repose.

To your right (southwest) are the cliff-like sides of Cwm Clogwyn, curved like a giant's amphitheater. It is one of several cirques, or ice-carved valleys and their corresponding ridges, which give the mountain its stark and unusual shape. From overhead, its high ground looks like a starfish.

Snowdon derives from Saxon for "snow hill," but its Welsh name, Yr Wyddfa, has a much more colorful origin. It translates to a "tumulus," or tomb, and legend holds that it is the grave of an ogre who assassinated kings and wove their beards into a coat. It was none other than King Arthur himself who climbed Yr Wyddfa and slayed the giant.

Continue climbing through rocky terrain to traverse the slopes of Moel Cynghorian, then Bwlch Cwm Brwynog. The track steepens further, at times over steps and loose rock, as you continue up Yr Wyddfa's west-northwest ridge. Once atop the ridge, the gradient mellows out as the trail meets the Snowdon Mountain Railway tracks. If you haven't already seen the railway cars in the distance, you may get a close-up here. (It can be quite dramatic to simply hear the whistle through a thick fog.) The narrow-gauge rack-and-pinion railway—the only one in the UK—opened in 1896 and continues to shuttle people from Llanberis to the peak.

Carefully cross the tracks, continuing south and uphill to a large stone marker where the Ranger Path, Llanberis Path, Pyg Track, and the trail from Garnedd Ugain (Wales's second-highest summit) all converge. Follow the Llanberis Path for 0.4 mile, heading up the steps to the summit, where a pillar and toposcope mark the direction of dozens of locations near and far.

From atop Yr Wyddfa, millions of years of geological and human history lie at your feet. To the north and west are thirteen other summits over 3000 feet, forming a complex ice-scoured landscape of cliffs, lakes, ridges, arêtes, and plateaus. In his 1862 guide to *Wild Wales*, George Borrow wrote, "There we stood on the Wyddfa, in a cold bracing atmosphere, though the day was almost stiflingly hot in the regions from which we had ascended . . . enjoying a scene inexpressibly grand, comprehending a considerable part of the mainland of Wales. . . . Peaks and pinnacles and huge moels stood up here and there, about us and below us, partly in glorious light, partly in deep shade."

If the clouds close in on your summit day, take heart that even poet William Wordsworth reached the top of Yr Wyddfa in a "dripping fog." In his autobiographical work, "The Prelude," he wrote that at his feet, "Rested a silent sea of hoary mist. / A hundred hills their dusky backs upheaved / All over this still ocean."

As clouds are fickle things, especially in these parts, be sure to pause and look back from time to time as you retrace your steps along the Snowdon Ranger Path.

EXTEND IT

Include the pyramidal peak of Garnedd Ugain, also called Crib y Ddysgl. Return to where the trails converge at the railway tracks, and take the northeasterly path roughly 0.3 mile to the 3494-foot summit of Wales's second-highest peak. Along with Yr Wyddfa, Garnedd Ugain is part of the 7-mile circuit called the Snowdon Horseshoe, a classic ridge walk linking four principal summits. Since the route covers some knife-edge terrain, only the sure-footed with a head for heights should attempt it.

41 THREE PEAKS OF THE BRECON BEACONS

This popular horseshoe circuit summits three of the most beloved peaks in Brecon Beacons National Park—Corn Du (2864 feet), Pen y Fan (2907 feet), and Cribyn (2608 feet).

Distance: 11.4 miles
Elevation Gain: 2800 feet
High Point: 2907 feet
Rating: ★ ★ ★ ★ ★
Difficulty: Challenging
Year-round: No
Dog-friendly: Yes, leashed

Family-friendly: Yes, but with steep climbs in exposed terrain and possible boggy sections
Amenities: Picnic tables at car park
Map: OS Explorer Map OL12, Brecon Beacons National Park, Western Area
Agency: Brecon Beacons National Park

GETTING THERE

GPS: 51.836973°, -3.380726°
Postcode: CF48 2UT
Driving: From Pontsticill, go northeast on C0151 for 3.7 miles to reach the Owl's Grove, Taf Fechan Forest car park on your right.

Public Transit: The Brecon Mountain Railway runs from Pant to Torpantau Station, where a short trail links to this route.
Before You Go: Steeper sections can be slippery in wet weather, and conditions are highly changeable and can be extreme.

ON THE TRAIL

Turn right (north) out of the car park and follow the road for 0.6 mile uphill (gaining 250 feet of elevation) through the Taf Fechan Forest to reach a smaller car park on your left. Taf Fechan Forest, in the glacial valley of the same name, is roughly 100 acres of grassland and ancient broadleaf woodland with a river cutting a narrow gorge through limestone. It's a small but mighty mosaic of beech, birch, alder, willow, and abundant wildflowers that attracts many butterflies and birds. Look, or listen, for tawny owls and great spotted woodpeckers, wild thyme and common spotted orchids.

Cross through the small car park to pick up a gravel track beyond a gate. Wind around a hill capped with conifers, ignoring a trail branching off to your left in 0.1 mile. In another 0.4 mile, when the trail branches, bear left (northwest) to follow the "Taff Trail." Continue uphill for the next 0.6 mile, crossing through several gates with views of the long ridges and high peaks this route traverses. When you reach a fork with a maintenance road heading to your right, bear left to follow the narrower track (you will rejoin the trail here at the end of the loop).

In 0.4 mile, you'll reach the southern end of the Neuadd Reservoir complex. Bear left (west) to skirt the restricted area and cross a bridge over the Taf Fechan. This river originates at the base of Pen y Fan and joins the Taf Fawr to form the River Taff, which flows south through Cardiff. In 0.1 mile, the trail turns right (north). Continue for another 0.1 mile, then follow the trail as it veers left and heads west again. Climb steeply up rock steps, gaining roughly 650 feet over the next 0.5 mile, toward the Craig Fan Ddu ridge.

The trail levels out somewhat before reaching a T intersection, where you'll go right to continue northwest along the ridge. Over the next 2 miles, and 850 feet of ascent, skirt the summits of Cefn Cul (2430 feet), Rhiw yr Ysgyfarnog (2450 feet), and

Craig Gwaun-Taf (2710 feet). Unless there are low clouds, this stretch has vast views of the peaks ahead—Corn Du, Pen y Fan, and Cribyn—arranged in a high arc with sides dropping away steeply into the Neuadd Valley. Countless streams cut through sandstone and mudstone laid down at least sixty million years ago. The broad, green slopes and flat-topped mountains look gentle, but there are plenty of rocky crags and steep drop-offs.

Several trails join or leave the main track as you continue 0.4 mile straight toward the top of Corn Du (pronounced "Corn Dee"), the second-highest peak in the Brecon Beacons, via Bwlch Duwynt (meaning "Windy Pass"). The mountain's name means "black horn" in Welsh, likely due to its cone-like tip. Find the cairn at the summit marking a Bronze Age burial chamber, a popular feature of peaks in the area. On a clear

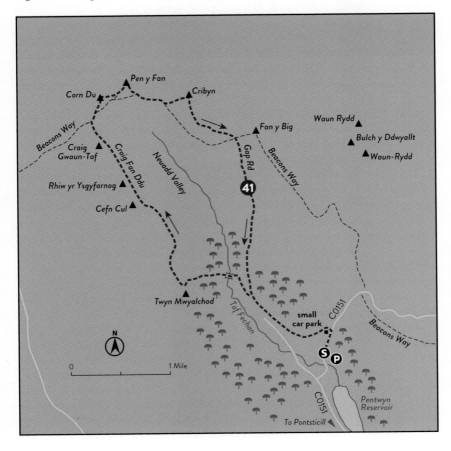

The sandstone peaks of Corn Du (left) and Pen y Fan (right) in the central Brecon Beacons drop precipitously to sweeping glacial valleys.

day, look 10 miles west to the distinctive cliffsides of the Carmarthen Fans (more popularly known as "the Fans," or "Bannau Sir Gaer" in Welsh) in the Y Mynydd Du (Black Mountain) range of the national park. Roughly 0.3 mile to the northeast is Y Gryn—the top of Pen y Fan—and your next stop.

From Corn Du, drop down into the saddle and follow the well-worn path for about a third of a mile to the summit of Pen y Fan (pronounced "Pen a Van" and meaning "the top peak"), southern Britain's highest mountain. There is another cairn and burial chamber here which, when excavated in the early 1990s, unearthed a spearhead and a bronze brooch. Look to the northwest for a view across the precipitous slopes and down into the Cwm Llwch valley, where there is a picturesque glacial tarn of the same name (with a legendary but invisible island inhabited by pixies). To the south are uninterrupted views of the Neuadd Valley, with its glacier-sculpted slopes and pocket forests, and north, beyond the town of Brecon, even Cadair Idris (2930 feet) can be seen, 60 miles away at the southern end of Snowdonia.

From Pen y Fan, follow the trail southeast downhill for 0.5 mile across Craig Cwm Sere, the ridge connecting the two peaks. Toward the end of the steep descent, take the track bearing left and uphill (again!) for 0.3 mile, up 300 feet in elevation, to the top of Cribyn. Pause to look back at the profile of Pen y Fan, its mood shifting with the light as the near-vertical northeastern face drops dramatically to the Cwm Sere Valley. There's another smaller cairn marking the summit of Cribyn, a less popular, and therefore usually quieter, peak. This one feels even more precipitous than its siblings, thanks to the glacial erosion that cut its steep north and east faces. Keep an eye out for some of the many soaring birds of prey frequenting the area, including red kites, peregrine falcons, and buzzards (or hawks).

From the top of Cribyn, continue downhill 0.8 mile to the junction of several trails. Take the widest, the Gap Road, heading south. This track was the first in the area that horse-drawn carriages could use to cross these mountains. The 99-mile Beacons Way intersects the Gap Road as it cuts across some of the best of the national park, including highlands, moorlands, and valleys.

Follow the Gap Road for 2 miles, through heather and pine, back to the trail you started on. From there, retrace your steps roughly 1.8 miles back to the car park, looking back along the way for new views of the three iconic peaks.

EXTEND IT

Add a fourth peak—Fan y Big (2356 feet)—to the walk. After descending 0.8 mile from Cribyn, take the short, steep track 0.3 mile, and up 300 feet in elevation, to the summit, then retrace your steps to rejoin the route.

42 FOUR WATERFALLS OF THE BRECON BEACONS

This route in Bro'r Sgydau, or "Waterfall Country," visits four falls hidden in the folds of an ancient forest.

Distance: 5 miles
Elevation Gain: 850 feet
High Point: 1100 feet
Rating: ★ ★ ★ ★
Difficulty: Moderate
Year-round: Yes
Dog-friendly: Yes, leashed

Family-friendly: Yes, but some short, narrow sections with drop-offs to river, and light rock scrambling
Amenities: None
Map: OS Explorer Map OL13, Brecon Beacons National Park, Eastern Area
Agency: Brecon Beacons National Park

GETTING THERE

GPS: 51.800152°, -3.544892°
Postcode: CF44 9JF
Driving: From Penderyn, take A4059 north for 1 mile, then bear left on the narrow road signed to Ystradfellte. In roughly 1.6 miles, turn left at the signs for "Waterfalls" and

"Gwaun Hepste." In 0.2 mile, you'll reach the Gwaun Hepste–Four Falls Trail car park.
Before You Go: The large car park fills up quickly. Rock surfaces and exposed tree roots, particularly near the waterfalls, can be very slippery. The rivers are cold and swift.

Rainfall draining the southern slopes of the Brecon Beacons plunges over a sandstone ledge at Sgŵd y Eira.

ON THE TRAIL

Head south from the trailhead, following a large brown sign with a red footprint marked "Four Falls Trail," on a forestry road. When the trail splits in 0.7 mile, bear right onto the narrower track in the direction of the red arrow. This is part of the Fforest Fawr (the spelling with two f's means "Great Forest"), known for its steep, tree-lined gorges cut by gushing water. In 2005, it was designated a UNESCO geopark for its "geological heritage of international significance."

Continue through the woods for 0.4 mile to a junction with trails branching off in several directions. Go straight toward Sgŵd Clun-Gwyn ("Fall of the White Meadow"), the first waterfall on this route, for 0.2 mile. At the sign indicating the falls, continue for several hundred feet down to the 30-foot-high Sgŵd Clun-Gwyn tumbling over two balconies of rock. The river is Afon Mellte, which carves its way decisively through waterfall country. It borrows its name from the Welsh word for "lightning" because of how quickly its waters rise and fall after rain.

Instead of returning to the main trail, pick up the one heading south along the river. Wind through the woods and skirt rocky outcroppings before rising above the Afon

Mellte for great views of the unusual, rocky riverbed. Geological faulting, consistent weathering, and the force of water over time are responsible for the area's unique look, where eroded mudstone reveals tougher, underlying sandstone. Reach the second falls, Sgŵd Isaf Clun-Gwyn ("Lower Fall of the White Meadow"), in about a half mile. It's a four-level waterfall that gradually drops nearly 100 feet over its several steps. This cataract tends to be a bit less populated, which makes it a good spot to look for the various woodland and song birds that frequent this deep forest.

Continue along the river, including over some boardwalks in boggy spots, for 0.3 mile. This rugged stretch is best known for its cascades, but equally captivating is its primordial feel, with ancient sessile oak and ash clinging to cliffsides and overhanging rushing waters—as well as over two hundred kinds of ferns, mosses, and liverworts. Reach the third falls, Sgŵd y Pannwr ("Fall of the Fuller"; *fuller* meaning "someone who cleans and thickens wool during cloth-making"), which flows elegantly over elongated shelves in a calmer section of the river, giving the area an oasis-like feel.

With Sgŵd y Pannwr at your back, take the trail that veers to your right (instead of straight, which is how you arrived at the falls). Climb the stairs and continue uphill out of the valley, ascending roughly 250 feet in elevation over 0.3 mile. The trail levels out

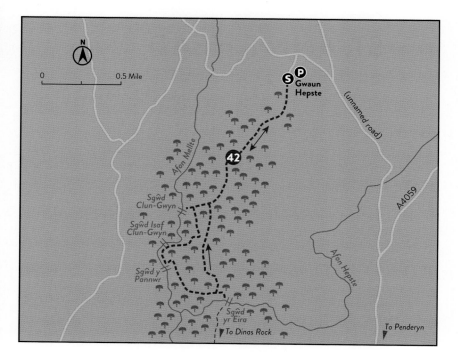

as it reaches a junction. Go right to join the main track toward Sgŵd yr Eira. In 0.2 mile, reach a turnoff on your right for the fourth waterfall.

Head down the steps into the gorge for 0.2 mile. At the bottom, follow the track left for a few hundred feet along the river for views of the sheer veil of Sgŵd yr Eira ("Fall of Snow"). These waters are the Afon Hepste, a tributary of the Afon Mellte, which plunges roughly 50 feet over an impressive gritstone cliff. (To explore past where this route ends, follow the rough trail behind the falls.)

Climb back up the steps to the main trail. Go right and follow the wide track for 0.1 mile to a junction. Go left and follow the trail as it curves west, and then north, for 0.6 mile. Upon reaching the junction you crossed at the beginning of the hike, go right to retrace your steps uphill for 1.2 miles back to the trailhead, glimpsing the surrounding hills as you emerge from the woodland.

EXTEND IT
Add Dinas Rock, at the edge of the village of Pontneddfechan, by crossing behind Sgŵd yr Eira, and following the trail southwest for 2 miles to reach the imposing limestone cliff and its impressive nearby waterfall, Sgydau Sychryd.

43 ST. ANN'S HEAD

This loop on the Dale Peninsula in southern Pembrokeshire follows the scenic coast path around St. Ann's Head. It is dramatic, rocky coastline with quiet coves, green pastures, a lighthouse, a castle, and several sheltered bays.

Distance: 7 miles
Elevation Gain: 860 feet
High Point: 170 feet
Rating: ★ ★ ★
Difficulty: Moderate
Year-round: Yes
Family-friendly: No; walking is mostly along open cliffside

Dog-friendly: Yes, leashed, though prohibited on some beaches in summer
Amenities: Several cafes and pubs in Dale; closest public restrooms are the square behind The Griffin
Map: OS Explorer Map OL36, South Pembrokeshire
Agency: Pembrokeshire Coast National Park

GETTING THERE

GPS: 51.709452°, -5.170011°
Postcode: SA62 3RB
Driving: From Milford Haven, go west on Dale Road (B4327) for 8.5 miles to Dale Beach car park on your right.

Before You Go: Elevation changes can make even a short distance on the coast path deceptively difficult.

Red rock cliffs back Westdale Beach, accessible from the Pembrokeshire Coast Path via a steep path.

ON THE TRAIL

Exit the car park and cross the road toward the sand and shingle beach. Turn right and, keeping the water on your left, bear left at the fork 250 feet ahead to skirt the edge of the village. Dale has a lengthy seafaring history—fishing and shipbuilding—and in the sixteenth century was an important port (and smugglers' hideout). Follow the one-way road for 0.8 mile, first along the sea wall as it curves around the Griffin Inn, then past a short stretch of houses as it climbs gently through a shady, forested area.

Roughly 0.1 mile past the Field Studies Centre, the landscape expands with fields on your right and sea views on your left. The sense of openness is immense. Looking left (east) is the Milford Haven Waterway and port. This natural channel is unusually deep, and it's been used for centuries by Vikings, medieval traders, World War II convoys, and present-day containers filled with thirty million tons of cargo annually. The settlement on the Milford waterfront has an interesting link to the US. It was established in the late eighteenth century as a whaling community by Quakers from Nantucket (off the coast of Massachusetts near Boston) who fled American soil during the Revolutionary War.

Look for a gate on your right marked by a wooden fingerpost with an upside-down acorn (the symbol used for national trails in Wales and England). Pass through it and continue on the unpaved Pembrokeshire Coast Path. Walk along the edge of the field for 0.3 mile to enter a lush, forested area. Descend slightly and cross a wooden footbridge with a rocky cove on your left. Climb the stairs out of the wooded area, occasionally glancing back to the picturesque cove of Castlebeach Bay and at some of the red sandstone cliffs that characterize the region.

Go through a gate at the top of the stairs, beneath the compact branches of a sessile oak bent inland by unrelenting coastal winds. Follow the edge of the field for 1 mile, passing through several gates and ascending about 200 feet. Head straight as you pass above a cove and intersect a trail on your left, which descends down to a sheltered, sandy beach at Watwick Bay. Continue to hug the coast, passing through patches of gorse and hedgerows of blackberry. The next headland takes you by West Blockhouse Point, with navigation towers and former coastal defense structures (now vacation rentals).

Continue for 1 mile, descending to meet a cove at Mill Bay, a popular swimming spot with a notable history. Henry Tudor was born at Pembroke Castle roughly 11 miles east of Mill Bay. He spent most of his life in exile in France, but in his late twenties, he staged a dramatic comeback. In 1485 he landed at Mill Bay with dozens of ships and thousands of troops intent on overthrowing King Richard III and reclaiming the throne. After their secret landing, they marched north, gathering supporters as they went. King Richard brought twelve thousand heavily armed soldiers on horseback to Pembrokeshire, and they clashed bloodily with Henry's men. Despite outnumbering Henry's forces, Richard was defeated. Henry walked on to London and took up the throne as Henry VII, head of the Tudor dynasty.

From the rocky cove, continue around St. Ann's Head for 0.6 mile, passing through several gates and across open pasture. If St. Ann's Head lives up to its reputation as the sunniest spot in Wales, you'll have great views east across the mouth of the inlet, to the Angle Peninsula. At the gate leading to a narrow gravel track, go right onto the path toward the lighthouse and cottages. There has been a lighthouse on this spot since 1714, but the current 43-foot-high St. Ann's Head Lighthouse was finished in 1844. It is the only working mainland light in Pembrokeshire and still guides ships through rocky shoals into Milford Haven.

The gravel track turns into a narrow paved road, which you'll follow for 0.2 mile past a black tower (the old lighthouse, now another vacation rental). Continue straight along a fence to reach a gate on your left. Cross through and onto the red dirt track. Follow the cliffside along this more remote section of coastline, where centuries of storms and tides have carved rugged rock pinnacles. As the path comes particularly close to the clifftop on a small promontory, look down to find out why it's called Vomit Point. Porpoises, dolphins, and grey seals can often be seen offshore in the cool waters of the Celtic Sea along this stretch.

In 0.6 mile, arrive at the point directly above Frenchman's Bay, a great gouge in the peninsula where the path again runs close to the cliff edge. The rock here tells the story of millions of years of compression, folding, and faulting, as tectonic plates collided

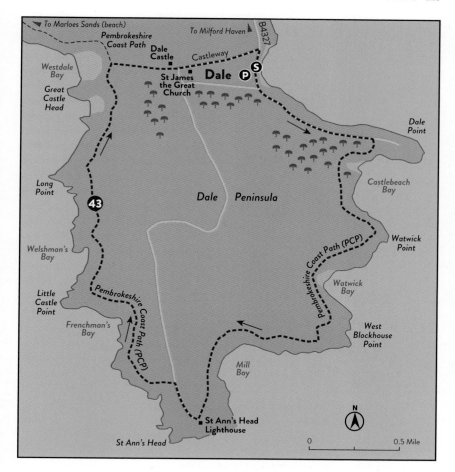

To Marloes Sands (beach)

To Milford Haven

B4327

Pembrokeshire
Coast Path

Dale
Castle

Castleway

St James
the Great
Church

Dale

P S

Westdale
Bay

Great
Castle
Head

Dale
Point

Long
Point

Dale   Peninsula

Castlebeach
Bay

43

Watwick
Point

Welshman's
Bay

Pembrokeshire Coast Path (PCP)

Little
Castle
Point

Pembrokeshire Coast Path (PCP)

Watwick
Bay

Frenchman's
Bay

West
Blockhouse
Point

Mill
Bay

N

St Ann's Head
Lighthouse

St Ann's Head

0   0.5 Mile

and inland seas receded. To the west, 3–4 miles offshore, is Skokholm Island, founded as Britain's first bird observatory in 1933, which is also part of the national park. It's now critical habitat for all kinds of birdlife including guillemots, razorbills, Manx shearwaters, fulmars, and puffins. Watch for occasional peregrine falcons, storm petrels, and buzzards crossing from the island, and numerous ravens and choughs. Choughs are the rarest member of the crow family, but distinctive with red bills, legs, and feet. They are aerial acrobats that nest in the high coastal cliffs.

Walk along the north side of Frenchman's Bay for about a quarter mile to reach Little Castle Point, the site of an Iron Age fort, beyond which is an impressive red-black fin of rock jutting out into the water. In another 0.5 mile, cross through a gate and pass

Solid swells and strong currents draw experienced surfers to Westdale Bay on the Dale Peninsula.

above Welshman's Bay. From there, follow the trail for 0.8 mile as it cuts inland for a brief stretch past wild patches of pink sea thrift before reaching Great Castle Head, the site of another Iron Age fort, on a promontory overlooking Westdale Bay. Little remains of the original footprint of the two-thousand-year-old fort (due to landslides), but during a site excavation, shards of prehistoric pottery were found, as well as Roman pottery and fragments dating back to the thirteenth century, when it's believed the site was "remodeled."

From Great Castle Head, look east across the narrow neck of the peninsula to the Milford Haven Waterway—and the way back toward the village of Dale. Continue along the trail as it descends steps toward the sandy beach at Westdale Bay. Where the trail levels out, pass through a gate on your right to leave the Pembrokeshire Coast Path and head east across the pasture toward Dale Castle, 0.3 mile away. The medieval castle, extensively renovated and extended over the centuries, remains a private residence.

The path ends just past the castle, leading onto paved Castle Way. Continue straight to follow the narrow lane past St. James the Great, Dale church with its austere, medieval-era tower. As a fisherman, St. James would have been particularly close to the hearts and livelihoods of centuries of Dale residents, and likely still is. Continue past private homes and the Dale Meadows for 0.4 mile. When you arrive at the waterfront, go right and follow the B4327 back to the car park.

EXTEND IT

From Westdale Bay, continue along the Pembrokeshire Coast Path for 1.5 miles to Marloes Sands—a remote and stunning mile-long beach backed by shale and sandstone cliffs. In total, the PCP is a challenging 186-mile route (with 35,000 feet of ascent and descent) that follows the wild undulations of western Wales.

44 STACKPOLE HEAD, BARAFUNDLE BAY & BOSHERTON LAKES

This walk encompasses some of coastal Pembrokeshire's bests—dramatic cliffs, sandy beaches, sweeping dunes, freshwater lakes, dense woodlands, and a lot of wildlife watching.

Distance: 6 miles
Elevation Gain: 600 feet
High Point: 100 feet
Rating: ★ ★ ★ ★
Difficulty: Easy to moderate
Year-round: Yes
Family-friendly: Yes, but with sections of open water and cliffs

Dog-friendly: Yes
Amenities: Restrooms, picnic tables, and refreshments at start and Bosherton
Map: OS Explorer Map OL36, South Pembrokeshire
Agencies: Pembrokeshire Coast National Park, National Trust

GETTING THERE

GPS: 51.625063°, -4.902817°
Postcode: SA71 5LS
Driving: From Trewent, head southeast on an unnamed road for 1.1 miles. Turn left toward "Stackpole Quay and Barafundle,"
and continue for 0.7 mile to the Stackpole Quay National Trust car park.
Before You Go: Barafundle Bay is hugely popular in the summer and the parking fills up fast.

ON THE TRAIL

Walk to the information boards and picnic tables at the east end of the car park, and bear right around them onto the narrow dirt path. Pass the stone structure with restrooms and continue straight for about 500 feet to reach the cove and Stackpole Quay. The eighteenth-century masonry quay was built to export limestone from a nearby quarry and to import luxury goods for Stackpole Court, a once-palatial nearby estate. Today Stackpole Quay protects one of Pembrokeshire's smallest harbors, which is also a popular launch point for kayakers and divers.

Turn right onto the Pembrokeshire Coast Path, heading south. Climb the long flight of stairs to pass through a gate at the top, and walk across the open field on the well-worn path toward Barafundle Bay. As you climb slightly, enjoy spectacular views. Behind you are red sandstone cliffs laid down as sediment on a riverbed four hundred million years ago, while in front are limestone cliffs formed beneath the sea fifty million years later by the accumulation and compression of tiny creatures.

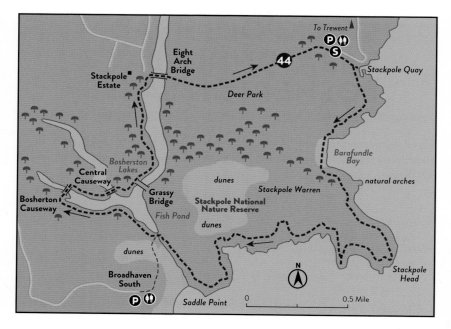

Follow the coast path for 0.5 mile to the clifftop above Barafundle Bay, considered by many to have one of the most beautiful beaches in the world. Look across the mouth of the bay to the large natural arch, called Lattice Windows, that juts out into the water from the peninsula. Such arches, and the stacks they create when they eventually collapse, are dramatic evidence of the effect of the waves on the porous limestone.

Go through the manmade arch at the top of the beach and take the path down to the sand. Cross the 0.2 mile-wide beach, however you choose, to reach the forest patch on the opposite side, where the coast path resumes. Follow it for 0.7 mile past spindly trees, through a gate, up into the dunes, and onto the peninsula plateau. Stackpole Warren, the grassland on your right, is covered with wildflowers in the warmer months. The site is believed to have been a ceremonial gathering place during the Bronze Age, roughly five thousand years ago. Other evidence in the area of human activity from that era includes standing stones and burial chambers. The current name of "Warren" refers to its time as a rabbit farm in the Middle Ages.

Continue on to round the promontory of Stackpole Head. Watch for seabirds that breed on cliff ledges, like guillemots with black-and-white plumage and scarlet-red feet. At just three weeks old, before they can even fly, chicks jump from the nest into the turquoise waters, where their fathers keep an eye on them until they can fend for themselves. This stretch is also popular with climbers, who clamber up and rappel down the cliff faces.

Continue along the cliffside for 1.1 miles to reach a trail junction. Bear left to stick to the coast, following the path along another peninsula around to Saddle Point. From there, look back to see several huge caves carved into the cliffside at Raming Hole, as well as bottlenose dolphins, porpoises, grey seals, and, occasionally, basking sharks in the deeper water.

From Saddle Point, follow the path for another 0.6 mile, with emerging views of the sand beach at Broadhaven South. Go through a gate and along a stone wall to continue up over the dunes, studded with sea holly and sea kale, to where the beach meets the Bosherton Lakes outlet. (There are many social trails through the dunes, and it doesn't matter much which one you take; just keep heading northwest

Near-vertical limestone cliffs of Stackpole Head cut an austere profile on the Pembrokeshire Coast.

toward the back of the beach.) Broadhaven is a popular swimming spot, despite some strong currents. The cliffs here are peppered with caves, and there are rock pinnacles offshore.

At the wooden fingerpost, go over the stone slabs that span the spillway. Follow the narrow path toward Bosherton for 0.7 mile along the fish pond and the so-called Western Arm of the lakes. This is one of three slender fingers of the 100-acre man-made Bosherton Lakes, also known as the Lily Ponds, which are now managed by the National Trust as part of the Stackpole Estate. They are filled via freshwater springs that are fed by a natural underground reservoir. Below the surface, look for stickle-backs, perch, pike, tench, and eels. The eel population makes the area popular for otters, which you can spy poking their sleek heads above the water. At the surface, look for breeding pairs of moorhen, little grebe, heron, and kingfisher.

Bear right at the junction (the left path leads to restrooms in 300 feet) and keep right to stick close to the water. Go over the Bosherton Causeway, a narrow stone footpath with a wooden railing, and when it ends, go right to follow the north shore of the Western Arm for 0.3 mile. At the junction, bear right to climb onto the limestone bluff overlooking the ponds, where the lilies bloom resplendently from June to September. It's a favorite spot for dozens of species of butterflies and dragonflies.

Carry on straight for another 0.1 mile to cross the Central Causeway, another narrow stone footbridge. Follow the path around to your right, ignoring Grassy Bridge (which is actually a dam) on your right, to follow the path for 0.7 mile along the Eastern Arm of the lakes toward Eight Arch Bridge. Pass through a fantastical stretch of forest dominated by massive beeches and sweet chestnuts, as well as oak, ash, and sycamore. Ferns blanket the forest floor year-round and, in warmer months, they mingle with wild garlic, bluebells, and primrose. This abundance draws wrens, goldcrests, and chiffchaffs (and a lot of bats), as well as larger bird species including buzzards, sparrowhawks, and tawny owls.

These woods, lakes, and bridges are part of a careful and ambitious landscaping project begun on the Stackpole Estate in the late eighteenth century. The once grand home, Stackpole Court, is long gone, but the natural areas remain as the still-beating heart of that multigenerational effort.

Cross the impressive stone Eight Arch Bridge, built in 1797 to allow the estate access to Stackpole Quay. Continue straight and uphill along the wide dirt track for 1 mile through what used to be a deer park. Go through a gate to continue toward a wooded area, then through two additional gates to enter the car park on its west end.

EXTEND IT

Go straight past Eight Arch Bridge for roughly 0.5 mile to explore the grounds of Stackpole Court, including two gardens, two bridges, and some historical structures.

45 ST. DAVIDS & TREGINNIS PENINSULA

Beginning in St. Davids, this walk follows the Pembrokeshire Coast Path along the steep cliffs, spectacular headlands, and sleepy coves of the Treginnis Peninsula, to the lifeboat station at St. Justinian.

Distance: 11 miles
Elevation Gain: 1200 feet
High Point: 210 feet
Rating: ★ ★ ★ ★ ★
Difficulty: Moderate to challenging
Family-friendly: No, due to long stretches of open cliffside
Dog-friendly: Yes, leashed where livestock is present

Year-round: Yes
Amenities: Restaurants and cafes in St. Davids; refreshment kiosk at Porth Clais Harbour
Map: OS Explorer Map OL36, South Pembrokeshire
Agencies: Pembrokeshire Coast National Park, National Trust

GETTING THERE

GPS: 51.881585°, -5.272114°
Postcode: SA62 6RJ
Driving: From the center of St. Davids, take Goat Street west for 0.2 mile and go right on Catherine Street. Continue for 0.1 mile, then go left onto Pit Street. The Merrivale car park will be on your left in roughly 0.1 mile.

Before You Go: This is an exposed cliffside walk and, while most of it is well marked, the return requires some brief wayfinding.

ON THE TRAIL

Leave the car park and go right (southeast) on Pit Street as it crosses the River Alun. In a little over 0.1 mile, go right onto Goat Street. Continue straight toward St. Non's Chapel for 0.6 mile, past stone houses, stone walls, and open fields, until you reach the end of the road at the sea. When you see the sign for St. Non's Retreat Centre, continue past a small car park and take a right onto a narrow, graveled path heading downhill.

In a few hundred feet, arrive at the holy well and chapel ruins of St. Non, named for a nun who gave birth there in AD 475, to a baby who later became St. David, the patron saint of Wales. The chapel, which was built later (some evidence suggests between the seventh and ninth centuries), may be one of the oldest Christian structures in Wales. According to legend, when she was roughly twenty-five, St. Non labored alone during a violent thunderstorm. The grotto, which is covered by a stone arch and a small shrine,

So-called Seal Cove on Treginnis Peninsula is great for spotting Atlantic grey and harbor seals.

reputedly sprang to life during that time. It is believed to have healing properties, which made it a popular destination for pilgrims in medieval times.

With the chapel ruins on your right, walk straight across the grass for a few hundred feet toward a wooden gate at the far corner. Cross through the gate and over the stone stile and follow the path as it veers right and merges with the Pembrokeshire Coast Path. Continue straight (west) along the coast path with stunning views of the aquamarine waters of St. Non's Bay and the dramatic, jagged cliffside on your left. The path zigzags along the shore for 0.7 mile before turning north to run alongside Porth Clais Harbour. Once past the National Trust sign for Porth Clais, continue another 0.2 mile to where the trail divides, and veer left to continue to the end of the harbor on a narrow path. The harbor was built in the twelfth century and soon became an active trading port dealing in coal, limestone, timber, and grain. The Romans are believed to have built the old harbor wall. Today it's popular with small boats and kayaks, and for catching crabs.

When the narrow path meets a wider one, go left over the bridge and pick up the coastal path on the opposite side of the boat launch. With the harbor on your left, climb gently uphill through gorse and bracken and continue through several gates to enjoy some of the best views on this hike. In spring, this stretch of coast bursts with spring squill, scarlet pimpernel, and even heath spotted-orchid. In summer and early fall, it's brilliant with golden gorse and purple heather. The rugged string of islands offshore include Carreg Frân and Carreg yr Esgob.

After 1.2 miles, the trail turns north to round Porthlysgi Bay, an area famous for shipwrecks in centuries past. Continue for 0.6 mile around the stunning sheltered cove, dipping briefly onto the shingle beach, before resuming the footpath up the steps at the wooden fingerpost. This is a good spot to admire some of the oldest rock in Wales, much of which was formed by volcanoes roughly six hundred million years ago.

When the path levels out, cross through a gate marking the entrance to "Lower Treginnis," a spectacular rocky headland. To the west, Ramsey Island lies just a half mile offshore. Its twin peaks are bygone volcanoes. To the north and east are miles of historical farms and rocky *carns* (literally "pile" in Welsh), or igneous outcroppings. Follow the coastal path around the head, ignoring any paths leading inland.

In about 1.25 miles, watch for the remnants of an old copper mine on the slope between the trail and the water. Head uphill alongside a fenced-in area above the

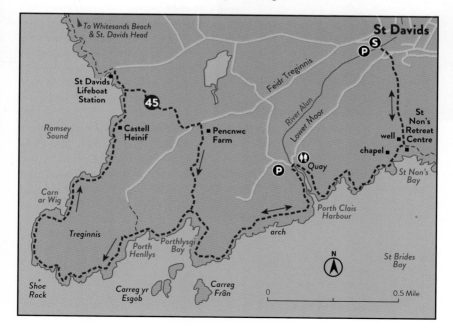

Gorse and heather blanket the Pembrokeshire Coast in a lavish seasonal display.

grey-black cliffs of an impressive cove, Carn ar Wig. Just beyond the cove is a flat, grassy spot—great for a picnic and for spotting seals and local birdlife, including gulls, gannets, guillemots, and razorbills.

Walk on from the so-called seal cove and look for the curved roofs and steep ramps of St. Davids Lifeboat Station (at St. Justinian), roughly 1.4 miles ahead. Along the way, pass a grass-and-rock promontory on your right called Castell Heinif, the ruins of an Iron Age fort. The lifeboat station has a shop and runs tours, if you hit it at the right time, and there are also summer ferries to Ramsey Island that leave from here. The waters of Ramsey Sound can be violent with epic waves and gale-force winds. Since 1867, lifeboats have been launched from the station to aid those in peril at sea and on cliffs and rocky isles. Its crews have rescued several hundred people and received fourteen medals for gallantry.

From the lifeboat station, retrace your steps back 0.2 mile to a wooden kissing gate on your left signed "National Trust: Treheinif." Pass through the gate to enter coastal grazing pastures and farmland. The field edges here are intentionally unkempt to encourage wild grasses and flowers, which in turn attract pollinators and small birds, like pretty little finches, wings winking in the sunlight.

Keeping the field to your right, continue for 0.1 mile over a small hill and through two more gates. At the latter gate, turn right to follow the direction indicated by the pink route arrows on the National Trust sign. Zigzag for 0.5 mile across several more fields and gates, heading southeast as indicated, again, by the pink arrows.

Emerge onto a narrow paved road (Feidr Treginnis) at Pencnwc Farm. Go left (east) for roughly 300 feet to reach a stile (with another pink arrow) on your right. Cross over and walk straight across the field to cross another stile in 500 feet. Continue south, toward the water, for 0.5 mile to reach the coastal path at Porthlysgi Bay. Go left and retrace your steps back along the coast to St. Davids.

EXTEND IT

Continue on the coast path past St. Justinian to wide Whitesands Beach in 2 miles, and then onto St. Davids Head, a spectacular headland, in another 3.4 miles.

SCOTTISH LOWLANDS

Scotland shares a soft border with the rest of Great Britain, but it has a language, culture, and landscape all its own. Its fight for independence began in 1297 and, although the Scots technically joined the United Kingdom in 1707, they still defend their unique ways. Whether on a "wee" walk or something much longer, you'll follow in the footsteps of bold invaders and proud clansmen alike. For walkers, the Scottish Lowlands are often over-shadowed by their loftier neighbor to the north, the highlands. But there is great diversity of terrain to discover in and around hilly Edinburgh—including the quiet, yet stunning, Pentland Hills—and along East Lothian's many miles of charismatic coastline.

EDINBURGH
Situated in the Lothians, an area sandwiched between the Firth of Forth's southern shore and the Lammermuir Hills, Scotland's capital (Trails 46–47) is a walkers' city. Edinburgh has huge parks, quiet churchyards, hidden gardens, rocky pinnacles, and rambling waterfronts, as well as a long, shaded riverwalk begging for exploration.

PENTLAND HILLS
Pentland Hills Regional Park (Trails 48–49) lies just several miles south of Edinburgh, but it's a world away, really, with roughly 25,000 acres and 60 miles of trails. Its dark rock hills were formed when ash and lava spewed out of ancient volcanoes, then were rounded by glaciers during the last ice age. Today it offers a peaceful day's ambling among heather moorland, farmland, reservoirs, and, of course, plenty of hills.

EAST LOTHIAN
Pressed up against Edinburgh to the east, East Lothian (Trails 50–54) juts out into the Firth of Forth with sandy beaches, teeming marshes, towering dunes, castle ruins, and

OPPOSITE: *The peaceful North Sea coast of East Lothian was once the epicenter of many historic battles.*

fascinating geology. It is also a rich ecological haven and the scenic birthplace of the great John Muir.

46 HOLYROOD PARK LOOP

Edinburgh is a city of hills, and this walk conquers the top one—Arthur's Seat (824 feet), with panoramic views of iconic city landmarks, splendid coastline, and beyond.

Distance: 3.2 miles
Elevation Gain: 1100 feet
High Point: 823 feet
Rating: ★ ★ ★ ★
Difficulty: Moderate
Year-round: Yes

Family-friendly: Yes, though some exposed and steep sections
Dog-friendly: Yes, under voice control
Amenities: Restrooms and cafe at the start
Map: OS Explorer Map 350, Edinburgh
Agency: Historic Environment Scotland

GETTING THERE

GPS: 55.952790°, -3.172280°
Postcode: EH8 8DX
Driving: The scarcity and high cost of parking are legendary and, along with congestion, should be major deterrents to driving.
Public Transit: The closest bus stops to the Palace of Holyroodhouse are Abbeyhill

Crescent and Scottish Parliament.
Before You Go: This hike can be made difficult by poor visibility, high winds, or wet weather, which can make the rocks slippery. In the spring, the park bursts with yellow gorse; in summer, with purple heather.

ON THE TRAIL

This walk has a stately start—the impressive, sixteenth-century Palace of Holyroodhouse (also called Holyrood Palace), the official Scottish residence of the British monarch. Take a left out of the courtyard onto Horse Wynd and follow the sidewalk for 0.2 mile to a roundabout, bearing left onto Queen's Drive. Already you'll have big views of the natural rocky ramparts of the Salisbury Crags directly ahead.

At the roundabout, cross Queen's Drive and go left onto Volunteer's Walk, a wide, red, paved path. When it turns to dirt and forks in a few hundred feet, ignore a sign leading right onto Radical Road and follow the trail uphill. In the sunshine (if you're lucky enough to experience some), the grassy hillsides and rocky outcroppings gleam as if polished.

In 0.3 mile take the short, steep spur trail left to the ruins of Saint Anthony's Chapel, which sit on a rock formation above St. Margaret's Loch. Not much remains of the chapel except the North Wall, but judging by its impressive arches, vaulting, and thick stone walls, it must have been striking in its day. While details of its history are sketchy, the earliest known reference is a 1426 document granting funds for repair from the pope, indicating it may have been built earlier, perhaps in the fourteenth century. It likely fell into disrepair after the Reformation began in 1560, but is still described in one eighteenth-century book as "a beautiful Gothick [*sic*] building, well suited to the rugged sublimity of the rock."

Leaving the ruins, return to the main trail and begin the real climb up Arthur's Seat. This stretch of trail, called Dry Dam, passes through and above a shallow glen lined with dark green scrub and light green grasslands. While it's now a 650-acre public space, Holyrood Park is a rare modern example of an unimproved grassland (no livestock grazing is allowed). Signs of thousands of years of use and settlement can be

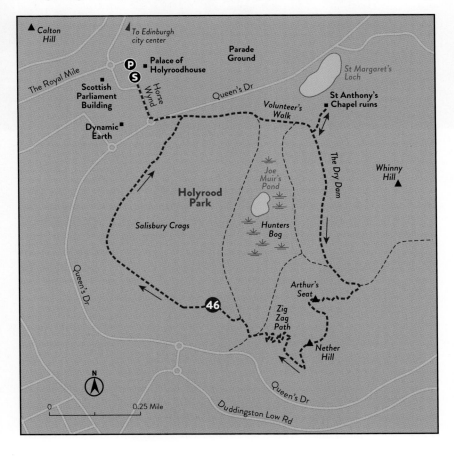

The Firth of Forth lies beyond the summit of Arthur's Seat, which writer Robert Louis Stevenson called "a mountain in virtue of its bold design."

found here, including the remnants of agricultural terraces, quarry sites, defensive walls and forts, and hunting tools. But Holyrood is, in some ways, little changed since its enclosure as a royal park in the sixteenth century and, thanks to active promotion and protection of biodiversity, it is again a haven for wildlife like hares, newts, and falcons.

The modern world recedes quickly on this island of open countryside at the core of Scotland's capital city, and its rich histories and many mysteries emerge. One involves a group of schoolboys hunting for rabbit near here in 1836. They made a strange discovery in a small cleft concealed by stone slabs on the northeast slopes of Arthur's Seat—seventeen miniature coffins. All of the wooden boxes, just four inches long, were skillfully carved from a single piece of wood. Within each was an intricately carved figure in custom-made clothing. In the centuries since they were found, theories swirled about their origin and purpose—witchcraft, devil worship, honorific burial, and lucky talismans were just a few. Ultimately it was determined that the coffins were linked to the biggest news story of the day—the so-called body snatchers William Hare and William Blake. Edinburgh was at the center of medical advances in the 1830s, and the two Bills had been supplying its booming human dissection market, where cadavers were in short supply. Hare and Blake did not steal bodies from graves, as some did, but murdered people and sold the victims postmortem. The most likely theory is that the person who crafted the tiny coffins and then hid them on Arthur's Seat wanted to, in some way, properly lay those bodies to rest. Eight of the surviving coffins have been on display in the National Museum for Scotland for over a century.

Climb 0.4 mile, ascending nearly 400 feet in elevation, to make a sharp right turn along some chain links, which are useful handrails if the rocky trail is slick. From there continue 0.1 mile past tall grass speckled with white and yellow flowers, as well as clusters of purple heather, to the top of Arthur's Seat. The last push to the peak, which requires some light rock scrambling, is littered with social trails. Do your best to stay on the most well-worn track—both for safety and to prevent additional erosion.

On a clear day, the panorama from the orange-black rock summit is immense. To the north and east are Whinny Hill (580 feet), the Firth of Forth, and the North Berwick coast; to the south are the lower expanses of the park and the Pentland Hills beyond; and, to the west, the medieval roofscape of Edinburgh's Old Town, the Royal Mile, and Edinburgh Castle. Edinburgh is a post-glacial landscape, and 824-foot-high Arthur's Seat is the plug of an extinct volcano. Its hard rock once lay on the inside of an ancient mountain that erupted 350 million years ago. Once cooled and firm, that foundation was carved by ice and sculpted by rain into the landscape under your feet.

Leaving the peak behind, drop down its south side into the saddle between Arthur's Seat and Nether Hill (778 feet). Pick the safest of the many social trails, which is wider with a gentler grade. The open grass meadow between the hilltops is quieter than the summit and can feel surprisingly remote. If Arthur's Seat is the head of a lion, Nether Hill is the backside (it was called "Lion's Haunch" on an 1880s map of the area). There are trails that go around Nether Hill, but this route goes straight over the broad top and down the other side, taking a sharp right turn onto the so-called Zig Zag Path. While this junction is just 0.2 mile from the top of Arthur's Seat, it feels more distant and rugged.

From the top of the Zig Zag, you'll see your next destination—the dark dolerite and basalt cliffs of the Salisbury Crags, which were formed when magma forced its way in between existing rock layers, resulting in multicolor creases and columns. Descend gradually until the trail turns to many rock stairs, reaching an intersection in 0.2 mile. Make a right, then follow the trail as it curves up to your left, ascending a flight of stone stairs. A number of trails branch off to your left, through the gorse and toward the top of the Salisbury Crags. Choose one and continue up to the high point, roughly 0.5 mile along the ridge, and carefully peer over the 150-foot high cliffs. From there practically all of Edinburgh is visible.

Down below is an area of the Salisbury Crags called the "Hutton's Section" for the founder of modern geology, James Hutton, who studied them in the eighteenth century while forming his revolutionary theories on earth's history. In Hutton's day, most learned people believed the earth was six thousand years old. But through careful observations and experiments, he hypothesized that heat, pressure, sedimentation, and erosion acted together to shape landscapes over a period of time unimaginable to most people of that era. "The result, therefore, of our present enquiry is that we find no vestige of a beginning—no prospect of an end," Hutton wrote in 1788. While his landmark ideas were not fully appreciated in his lifetime, some credit him with freeing scientific inquiry from religious orthodoxy, and opening the door to ideas like Charles Darwin's theory of natural selection.

From the high point, follow the trail along the edge of the plateau as it curves north and east, then head downhill on a wide, grassy track. Enjoy the tremendous views from atop the crags before continuing 0.5 mile to an intersection. Make a left to rejoin Volunteer's Walk and retrace your steps to Holyrood Palace.

EXTEND IT

Extend your loop roughly 3 miles by huffing it up to two more of Edinburgh's high points—Calton Hill (330 feet) to the northwest and Castle Rock (430 feet), the rock formation upon which Edinburgh Castle stands—both fascinating for their histories, architecture, and views.

47 WATER OF LEITH

Explore a miles-long urban oasis along the river that flows through the heart of Edinburgh.

Distance: 9.6 miles
Elevation Gain: 420 feet
High Point: 240 feet
Rating: ★ ★ ★ ★
Difficulty: Easy to moderate
Year-round: Yes

Family-friendly: Yes
Dog-friendly: Yes, leashed
Amenities: Restrooms and cafe in museum; many restaurants and shops along the way
Map: OS Explorer Map 350, Edinburgh
Agency: Water of Leith Conservation Trust

GETTING THERE

GPS: 55.950961°, -3.227667°
Postcode: EH4 3DR
Driving: The scarcity and high cost of parking are legendary and, along with congestion, should deter you from driving.
Public Transit: Edinburgh Coach Lines Service 13 travels through the city center,

stopping on Belford Road in front of the Scottish National Gallery of Modern Art (Modern One).
Before You Go: This route is predominantly off-road, but short sections are on sidewalks alongside roads. As in any urban area, caution is recommended.

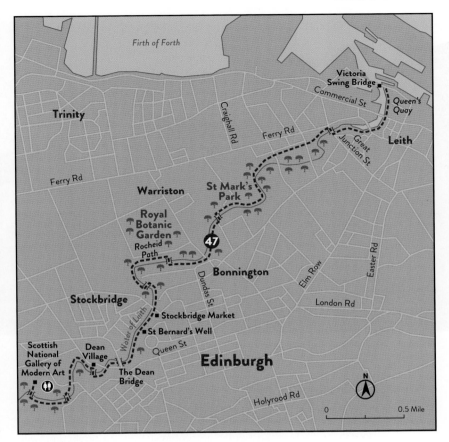

ON THE TRAIL

Start this walk between the pillars of the Scottish National Gallery of Modern Art (Modern One), looking out at *Landform*, the stepped serpentine mounds reflected in three pools, designed by Charles Jencks. Take a left and walk for 400 feet around the back of the museum and parking lot, then go through the large green gate. Cross the cobblestones to a dirt path heading downhill, and descend several staircases, about 70 feet in elevation over roughly 300 feet, to the Water of Leith. Edinburgh's main river flows 24 miles from the Pentland Hills to the Firth of Forth. Coursing through the hills and folds of outer Edinburgh and then directly through the city, the Leith has been a lifeline for many generations of Scots. The Water of Leith Walkway follows the river for nearly 13 miles, from Balerno in the suburbs to the Firth of Forth (this route covers its final five miles).

The small milling hamlet of Dean Village along the Water of Leith enchants with red-tile roofs and cobblestone streets.

Go through the gate and go over the wooden bridge, then take an immediate left where the sign points to "Dean Gallery / Stockbridge / Leith." (This is the first of many brown signs indicating "Leith" that you will follow.) Already the area feels like a parallel universe, so close to the city buzz but isolated and untamed. The riverbanks burst with grasses and wildflowers beneath leafy canopies of beech, birch, Scots pine, and yew. On your left in the distance is what's left of the Bell's Mill complex, an eleventh-century mill site and one of the oldest on the river. The last of the eighty mills that once produced flour, fabric, and paper on the Leith, closed in 2003.

Take the wide path east as it curves along the river for 0.4 mile to a blue metal footbridge, and cross back over the river. Continue for another 0.4 mile, making a tight S curve to arrive at storybook Dean Village. You can take a quick diversion here to explore Dean Village's narrow cobblestone lanes and unique architecture (note its red roofs). In past centuries, the area hummed with several grain mills, a brewery, a distillery, and a cannery. (It's now a desirable residential area.)

Pick up the route again by crossing the footbridge at Dean Village to meet the path running alongside the south bank. Continue for 0.2 mile through Dean Gorge, following the brown signs toward Leith. This section is Millers Row, and on your left are several millstones (with the 1838 Rhema Church beyond). While most grinding stones were made from locally quarried stone, these are French quartz, which were needed to cut tougher grain imported from the US. Cross under the four-arched Dean Bridge—the 106-foot-high stone span was completed in 1831 and carries Queensferry Road over the leafy oasis you're immersed in.

Continue for 0.5 mile beneath rowan and willow, watching for colorful kingfishers and leggy herons hunting for trout and minnows on the river, as you head toward Stockbridge. This stretch, one of the most tranquil on the Water of Leith, takes you past St. Bernard's Well, a Greco-Roman temple-like structure made of stone. Inside it, encircled by eight pillars, is a sculpture of the Greek goddess of health, Hygeia. The monument was built in the late eighteenth century to protect a mineral spring that was believed to have medicinal properties. (The temple, which has a spectacular mosaic ceiling, is generally only open on Sundays in August and on "doors open days" in September.)

When you reach the popular shopping district at Stockbridge, ascend the stone stairs and cross the busy paved road. Follow the signs on the opposite side to descend again (beneath the clocktower) to the riverside, where you'll meet the Deanhaugh Path. Here, river and track run close together in a dense thicket of tall trees, shrubs, and flowers.

Within 0.2 mile you'll leave the riverside, curve to your right (follow the brown signs), and head north onto a trail alongside Arboretum Avenue. Follow the river for 0.2 mile, then take a sharp right, passing through stone pillars and a green gate onto the Rocheid Path. A few hundred feet north is Edinburgh's Royal Botanic Garden.

This section of the route follows the 61-mile St. Margaret's Way, a pilgrim's route from downtown Edinburgh up the coast to St. Andrews in the north. It was inspired by Margaret (1045–1093), the English princess and Scottish queen who was celebrated for her piety and care of orphans and the poor. Pilgrimages have pagan roots in the UK, and many people still walk the forty-eight major routes, and many lesser known tracts. The reasons for pilgrimage may have shifted somewhat, but the main intention remains consistent—connection—to self and others, to nature and supernature, to regret and gratitude.

Continue for 0.3 mile, enveloped in stately oak and London plane, to the Tanfield Footbridge marked with a red-and-yellow sign. Make a right, leaving the Rocheid Path, to cross the river. Keep an eye out for a pair of resident white swans, the occasional cormorants, and tufted ducks as you continue 0.2 mile to a staircase leading away from the river onto Brandon Terrace. Go right at the top of the stairs (there's a brown sign there to guide you) and follow the sidewalk for 0.4 mile along Warriston Road to the grassy slopes of St. Mark's Park.

Keep to the well-marked main track for the next 1.5 miles to enter Leith. Cross Commercial Street onto a pedestrian path called the Shore, and continue straight. This area has been settled since Roman times and was Edinburgh's principal port for centuries (its piers and docks are still used today), home to timber yards, soap, and sugar factories. Ships were built here from the sixteenth century through the 1980s, and the *SS Sirius*, the first steamship to cross the Atlantic, launched from the port in 1837.

Leith's motto has long been to "persevere," but you'll only have to do that for another 0.3 mile to the blue iron Victoria Swing Bridge, which marks the official end of the Water of Leith Walkway, and where the river itself empties into the Forth estuary and on to the Firth of Forth. Watch for plovers, oystercatchers, and terns (which breed near here during the summer). Either retrace your steps on foot or hop on a bus, many of which serve the immediate area.

EXTEND IT

Add a mile-long walk around the perimeter of the "Botanics," as locals call the 350-year-old Royal Botanic Garden Edinburgh. In addition to the can't-miss sculptures at its center, this 70-acre garden is home to one hundred thousand plants and ten glasshouses, each with its own climatic zone, supporting three thousand exotic plants from around the world. (The garden is free, but the glasshouses charge admission.)

48 PENTLAND PEAKS TRIPTYCH

This loop, a great introduction to hillwalking in Scotland, crosses the three highest summits in Pentland Hill Regional Park and a variety of habitats and history—with a side dish of epic views.

Distance: 7.6 miles
Elevation Gain: 1820 feet
High Point: 1900 feet
Rating: ★ ★ ★ ★
Difficulty: Moderate to challenging
Year-round: Yes

Family-friendly: Yes; appropriate for hillwalkers-in-training
Dog-friendly: Yes, leashed for most of the year
Amenities: None
Map: OS Explorer Map 344, Pentland Hills
Agency: Pentland Hills Regional Park

GETTING THERE

GPS: 55.860360°, -3.331974°
Postcode: EH14 7JT
Driving: From central Balerno, take Bavelaw Green (which turns into Mansfield Road after 0.3 mile) for 1.8 miles. Make a left into the Threipmuir Reservoir car park.

Before You Go: The car park can fill up early on summer and fall weekends. Heather usually blooms in early and late summer, peaking in August.

ON THE TRAIL

Walk to the end of the car park and straight onto the trail. Curve right almost immediately and cross a quiet, paved road before ducking back into the trees. In roughly 0.2 mile, reach a seldom-used tarmac road and turn left. In 0.1 mile reach and cross the Redford Bridge, pausing to take in views of the teeming Bavelaw Marsh on your right and the gleaming Threipmuir Reservoir on your left.

The marsh and reservoir were created in 1890 when a nearby stream (or "burn," as they're called in Scotland) was dammed; there are a dozen such reservoirs in the Pentlands that once powered mills and now provide drinking water to surrounding communities. They are also an important breeding ground for one hundred bird species, including waterfowl. In the early fall, watch for the glossy blue-and-red heads and long, forked tails of swallows as they dart around agilely, gulping down insects in preparation for migration to their wintering grounds in Africa.

From the bridge, walk 0.3 mile uphill along a beautiful, pin-straight lane lined with old beech trees. At a T intersection, take a sharp right onto a wide dirt track. After 250 feet, still beneath the tree canopy, go left at a sign pointing toward "Nine Mile Burn." Pass through two gates soon after, careful to leave them as you found them. People have lived here since prehistoric times, and these are still largely working lands.

Emerge from the trees and walk straight ahead, keeping a strip of conifers and a stretch of ancient rock walls, called "drystane dykes," to your left. Admire the skill required to craft these walls—heavy stones stacked together roughly four-to-five feet high, without cement or mortar—over countless miles of moor. This type of enclosure, which dates back at least to the Iron Age, is also a sprawling habitat for mosses, lichens, stoats, and voles.

As the landscape opens up to grasslands, with butterflies fluttering by in flashes of green and orange, follow the rock walls 1 mile uphill to pass through another gate marked by a "Welcome to the Moor" sign. The next stretch of trail is dominated by heather moorland, a rare habitat, which looks like a prickly, purple blanket tossed over the rolling hills. Roughly three-quarters of the world's remaining heather moorland lies in the UK, much of which is in Scotland. Walking by huge thickets of the tightly packed plants can have a hypnotic effect. Heather is tough, with coarse, woody stems—it has to be to survive cold, windy winters—but when you get up close, its flowers are tiny, delicate, and abundant. In addition to benefiting wildlife, such as mountain hares, healthy moorland controls erosion and acts as a natural reservoir.

From the gate, continue straight in the direction of a sign reading "Nine Mile Burn, 2.5 miles." In 0.3 mile, cross a small rock bridge over the burbling Logan Burn. Enjoy views of the Pentland peaks—a 15-mile-long range of lowland hills—which look like a string of green pearls. Turnhouse Hill, Carnethy Hill, Scald Law, East Kip, and West Kip (called "Edinburgh's lungs" by some) are closest, most dramatic, and best known.

An unfurled ridge of Pentland Hills awaits for unwinding—and peak bagging.

The Pentland Hills' tens of thousands of acres are threaded with dozens of miles of trails. Its violent, volcanic beginnings are a distant thought amid the now-tranquil countryside, which has inspired poets and storytellers for centuries. Robert Louis Stevenson, the Scottish, Victorian-era novelist (*Treasure Island*), poet, and travel writer lived nearby for a dozen years. He called the Pentlands the "Hills of Home," writing, "A crying hill-bird, the bleat of a sheep, a wind singing in the dry grass, seem not so much to interrupt, as to accompany, the stillness; but to the spiritual ear, the whole scene makes a music at once human and rural, and discourses pleasant reflections on the destiny of man."

From Logan Burn, walk 0.6 mile more to reach a junction. Go left, in the direction of a post pointing toward both the "Pentland Way" and "Pentland Path," and start up the steep, grassy flanks of West Kip (1808 feet). On a clear day, the terrain will open up beneath you in an undulating expanse of green, grey, blue, and pink. Carry on to reach the rounded apex of West Kip, with views of its sister, East Kip (1752 feet)—your next stop.

Descend the hillside on a wide, well-worn path to reach the saddle between the Kips. A narrow mountain pass is called a "bealach" in Scottish (pronounced "beh-lick").

Continue 0.4 mile to reach the top of East Kip, where you'll enjoy views northwest of Hare Hill and Black Hill (1640 feet) and Threipmuir Reservoir beyond.

The hike down, east toward the next planned peak, is steeper, with some scree under foot, so take your time. When you reach a junction, follow the trail straight ahead toward a post marking the "Pentland Way." Where the trail splits again, follow the left fork with a yellow arrow indicating "Pentland Way." From here, start the real climb up 1900-foot Scald Law: 360 feet over just 0.4 mile.

At the summit of Scald Law, pause at the survey marker to see Edinburgh 8 miles distant, the Firth of Forth, and the Fife coast beyond. Stevenson wrote about the Pentlands that "the shadow of a mountainous cloud, as large as a parish, travels before the wind; the wind itself ruffles the wood and standing corn, and sends pulses of varying colour across the landscape. So you sit, like Jupiter upon Olympus, and look down from afar upon men's life."

Continue straight off Scald Law in the direction of the next peak, watching out for sure-footed, free-ranging sheep on the ground, and peregrine falcons overhead. Reach a junction in 0.4 mile, pass through a gate, and go left. Here you'll likely see more people, traveling from nearby Carnethy Hill (1880 feet), and you may appreciate this quieter approach to the Pentland Way, a 20-mile footpath from Swanston to Dunsyre, crossing West Kip, East Kip, Scald Law, Carnethy Hill, Turnhouse Hill, and Allermuir—a total ascent of 3630 feet.

Go downhill on a loose stone path (the Kirk Road) for 0.1 mile to a ladder stile on your left. Cross over the fence onto a narrower dirt track, cutting through a sea of copious heather, and descend gently 0.4 mile to reach a stone bridge. Ignore the bridge, turning left instead to walk alongside Logan Burn. Follow the trail for 0.4 mile, curving to your right and crossing over a small wooden footbridge. Take note of Logan Waterfall on your left just past the bridge. This area is a Site of Special Scientific Interest because of its unique flora that thrives on the lime-rich soil, including golden saxifrage, rock rose, and yellow pimpernel.

Follow the trail straight to enter Green Cleugh—a narrow, picturesque valley running in between Hare Hill, to your left, and Black Hill, on your right. This is arguably the prettiest glen in the Pentlands, once scoured by glacial ice and now sheltering myriad quiet spots and complex histories. Green Cleugh has a primordial feel—it's a place where modern cares are easily set aside and one can imagine the preoccupations of someone walking here millennia ago: Do I have enough food to make it through the winter? Can I defend myself against raiders? Do I honor my ancestors with my actions?

From the waterfall, it's 0.4 mile to a gate on your left. Pass through that and another gate in about 400 more feet. Continue for 0.6 mile to a stone wall at the edge of a wooded area and go through another gate. Walk along a shady stretch of trail,

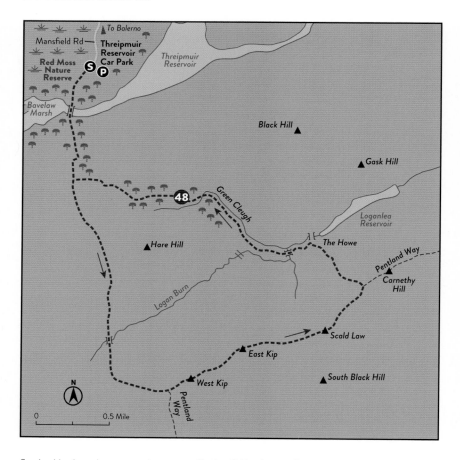

flanked by beech trees and stone walls, for 0.3 mile to a final gate. Cross through and follow the trail as it curves right and then left. Continue for 0.2 mile and turn right to retrace your steps downhill toward the car park.

EXTEND IT

Go left just before the car park on the return to enter the Red Moss Nature Reserve (a 0.5-mile boardwalk circles its center). This raised bog, one of the few remaining in Lothian, has been accumulating for thousands of years and is 20-feet deep in some spots. As the biggest carbon sink in the UK, peat plays an important role in mitigating climate change. On a planetary scale, peat stores more carbon than all other types of vegetation combined.

49 TURNHOUSE HILL

Spend a morning exploring the rolling expanses and historical folds of this climb on the eastern side of Pentland Hills Regional Park.

Distance: 3.2 miles
Elevation Gain: 1000 feet
High Point: 1660 feet
Rating: ★ ★ ★
Difficulty: Moderate
Year-round: Yes
Map: OS Explorer Map 344, Pentland Hills

Family-friendly: Yes, though final stretch to summit is steep
Dog-friendly: Yes, leashed when livestock is present
Amenities: Restrooms, picnic tables, and snack bar at Flotterstone Information Point
Agency: Pentland Hills Regional Park

GETTING THERE

GPS: 55.855124°, -3.226846°
Postcode: EH26 0PP
Driving: Heading south on A702 from Edinburgh, turn right at the Flotterstone Inn sign and follow the road for about 300 feet. Turn right again when you reach the inn, and continue another 300 feet to the Flotterstone car park.

Public Transit: It's about thirty-five minutes to the Flotterstone Inn by bus from central Edinburgh, then a 0.1 mile walk to the trailhead.
Before You Go: The car park fills quickly on summer weekends. Some steep sections are slick when wet. Keep your distance from livestock, and leave gates as you find them.

ON THE TRAIL

Pick up the trail on the south end of the car park, keeping the information point on your right. Pass in between an ornately carved wood bench and a semicircle made of stones, now a seating area, on a straight, graveled trail. It was once a nineteenth-century sheep corral, a reminder that the surrounding hills are still sheep pasture and you'll likely encounter some on this walk. Carry on along the path through a small, dense pocket of woodland. Pause at the blue plaque attached to the fence on the right, commemorating C. T. R. Wilson, born locally, who won the Nobel Prize in Physics in 1927 for inventing the cloud chamber, which was used to track ionizing radiation.

Roughly 0.3 mile from the car park, cross a paved road toward metal gates. Go through the narrower of the two gates, on your left, in the direction signed to "Scald Law." Join a wide dirt track and enjoy expansive views of the rolling hills ahead of you. In about 500 feet, the trail branches left and passes through another gate (also signed toward Scald Law). Reach a wooden bridge almost immediately and cross Glencorse Burn (meaning "valley crossing stream" because it marks the best low elevation route through the Pentlands).

Bear right (still toward Scald Law) and climb for 0.3 mile along a rocky track heading west toward the hump of Turnhouse Hill. Watch for robins and wrens in the gorse scrub as the landscape unfurls below in countless shades of green. Keep a look out, too, for a parliament of rooks perched on fences or tree limbs along the trail. Similar to crows, these birds are even more raucous, with thinner beaks and somewhat pointy heads. Rooks are extremely social; the name "parliament" comes from their tendency to circle collectively around one or two individuals that are vocalizing. And they're clever, able to work in teams and solve complex problems. There is a well-known rookery, or nesting colony, in the treetops of nearby Glencorse Reservoir, just a half mile north of the trail.

Continue uphill, passing through two gates within about a tenth of a mile of each other. After the second gate, follow the track left—this is where the real climb begins. You'll gain roughly 300 feet in elevation over the next 0.2 mile to reach a copse of conifers and broadleaves sculpted by the wind. From there it's just 0.7 mile to the top of Turnhouse Hill, but with roughly 530 feet in elevation gain. Continue past the Scots pine, with Glencorse Reservoir coming into view downhill to the north and Bell's Hill (1320 feet) behind it. The 20-acre reservoir was formed in the 1820s to supply fresh water to Edinburgh during a cholera epidemic. The valley of Glencorse Burn and everything in it, including a fourteenth-century chapel, St. Catherine's, was flooded in the process. The chapel now lies beneath 50 feet of placid water.

Push on to the cairn at the top of Turnhouse Hill for "a good spy" (as they say in Scotland) of the panorama of grass-and-heather-clad hills scoured by an ice sheet

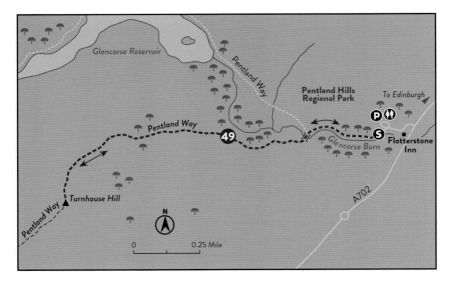

A copse of larch trees shelters walkers near the summit of Turnhouse Hill, a peak popular with locals and visitors alike.

long ago. To the north lies the Edinburgh skyline and Firth of Forth. Loganlea Reservoir is visible to the northwest, backed by Black Hill. To the southwest is one spine of the Pentland Hills—the next vertebrae is Carnethy Hill, then Scald Law, East Kip, West Kip, Green Law, Spittal Hill, and Paties Hill. After taking in this view in the late eighteenth century, poet and novelist Sir Walter Scott wrote, "I think I never saw anything more beautiful than the ridge of Carnethy against a clear frosty sky."

To the west, ancient roads—with evocative names like Monks Road, Old Roman Road, and The Thieves Road—can be seen coursing through the valleys. The Pentlands are peppered with archaeological remains, including Bronze Age burial cairns and Roman fortifications. Ten miles or so distant lies the watershed of Scotland, an invisible but important boundary that runs the length of the country (a 745-mile trail, one of the country's toughest, follows it). Water flowing off the watershed either goes west to the Atlantic Ocean or east to the North Sea.

Before turning back, look for buzzards (a medium-sized hawk) overhead, with their sunflower-yellow legs, talons, and upper beak, and big, dark eyes set against cream-and-dark-caramel plumage. Return to the trailhead the way you came.

EXTEND IT

Add 2.8 miles and make the walk a loop by following the trail down the other side of Turnhouse Hill (toward Carnethy Hill). At the gap between the two peaks, go right on the trail heading north and downhill. Go right after Logan Burn and follow the trail around the north shore of Glencorse Reservoir, then follow signs back to Flotterstone.

50 NORTH BERWICK LAW

The green, rocky slopes of "The Law," as it's known locally, can be seen standing sentinel over a quaint, seaside village from miles around. Climb to the top to earn some of the best views in East Lothian.

Distance: 3.2 miles
Elevation Gain: 560 feet
High Point: 614 feet
Rating: ★ ★ ★
Difficulty: Moderate
Year-round: Yes
Map: OS Explorer Map 351, Dunbar & North Berwick

Family-friendly: Yes, but steep in spots; Lodge Grounds have children's play area and plenty of green space
Amenities: Cafe on the Lodge Grounds; public restrooms downtown
Dog-friendly: Yes, leashed
Agency: Town of North Berwick

GETTING THERE

GPS: 56.058136°, -2.716055°
Postcode: EH39 4LG
Driving: The car park entrance is on the north side of the Lodge Grounds on East Road in downtown North Berwick.
Public Transit: Buses and trains frequently run from Edinburgh to North Berwick.

The rail station is 0.7 mile from the Lodge Grounds in central North Berwick, and buses stop in the center of town.
Before You Go: The grassy parts of the trail can be slippery with mud and, when windy at sea level, it can be gusty on the summit.

ON THE TRAIL

Start this walk by heading south out of the car park. In about 200 feet, turn left at a T intersection, following the trail as it curves right, then left, and ignoring any trails branching off. If you lose your way in the Lodge Grounds, just keep heading south-southwest uphill toward the only hill around—North Berwick Law. (*Law* is actually a Scottish Lowlands word for "a hill alone on the landscape.")

Reach the top of the Lodge Grounds in 0.2 mile, where two sets of signs indicate different directions for "The Glen," "North Berwick Law," and "John Muir Way." Follow the John Muir Way, which leads onto Lady Jane Road where the trail exits the south side of the park and soon crosses St. Baldred's Road. In less than 0.1 mile, look for a public footpath (still the John Muir Way) branching right to leave the road. Follow that for a little over a quarter mile toward North Berwick Law, crossing three roads—Couper Avenue, Gilbert Avenue, and Lochbridge Road. Once across Lochbridge, bear left for roughly 100 feet, then pick up a dirt trail heading right.

This spot has great views of the conical hill, a reminder of the area's once tumultuous geological activity. North Berwick Law is actually what remains of an extinct volcano that formed at least three hundred million years ago when its neck became choked with magma, which then solidified. That igneous rock is tough and, while a lot of its adjacent rock and ash were worn away over the years, this mass survived even the scraping glaciers of the last ice age.

Continue through the fields for 0.2 mile to a trail junction just before busy Haddington Road. Go left to join the track heading uphill, still in the direction of the Law. In 0.1 mile reach a car park at the base of Berwick Law (you could park here if you're short on time, but that means missing the beautiful Lodge Grounds). From here it is roughly 0.7 mile to the summit.

Big views from North Berwick Law include the town's twelfth-century harbor, the scene of notorious witch trials in 1590.

Cross the car park to reach a gap in the stone wall and pass through. Follow the wide, rocky trail as it runs around the west side of the Law. There are small signs along the way with arrows indicating the "Path to summit." Pass through a forested area briefly before beginning the steeper part of the route, where you'll gain about 500 feet

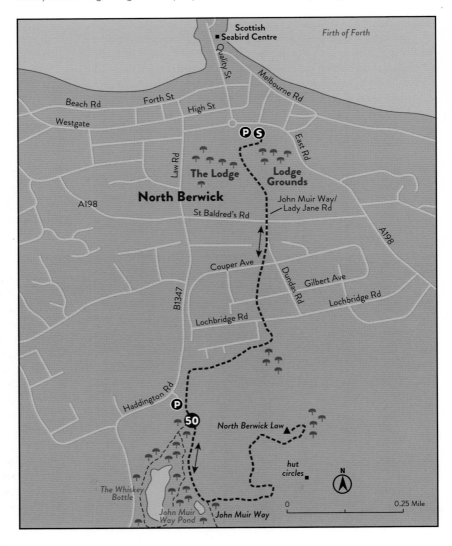

in elevation over the next 0.5 mile. Follow the trail as it narrows, curves tightly around the southern base of the hill (ignore any trail branching off to your right), and makes a series of switchbacks to the top. Try your best to ignore the many steep "shortcut" scrambles along the way.

North Berwick Law is a smallish hill with a big history. While on its south side, keep an eye out for what look like stone circles—the ruins of at least twenty-one Celtic roundhouses. Two thousand years ago, this was a peaceful farming spot for the Gododdin, who managed to survive the onslaught of the Romans but not the Angles. Back then, tendrils of smoke would have risen from each roundhouse, as the Gododdin tended fires to offset the chilly North Sea air.

The trail winds among crags of grey-black phonolite, also called "sounding stone," due to the metallic clang it makes when struck. This is vital habitat for rare mosses and lichen, and the roots of wood sage and wild thyme can be found in its cracks. In summer, the Law's slopes burst with bright yellow gorse and buttercups, purple milk vetch, and snow-white meadow saxifrage. Look overhead for kestrels, peregrine falcons, or buzzards. The area is also home to rabbits, hares, stoats, and deer.

The Law has a lengthy history as a naval lookout and signal station. On the summit, there are ruins of an Iron Age hillfort and other military buildings dating from the Napoleonic Wars (the best specimen dates from 1800) through World War II. In 1544 fires were lit here to warn of English ships entering the Firth of Forth. (By some accounts, this was done by a nun living in a nearby convent.) Hundreds of years later, soldiers on North Berwick Law would scan the horizon endlessly for French, then German, ships. Look for the jawbones of a whale, rising from the hilltop like a giant wishbone, as you approach the summit—a sign of Scotland's former whaling industry. There have been bones here since 1709, to guide homecoming sailors. The most recent set was removed in 2005 for safety (the present set is a replica made of fiberglass, wood, and steel).

At the top, unless you're socked in by clouds, the entire region is open before you. To the south is farmland and the Lammermuir Hills beyond. Out to the east are more farms and Tantallon Castle along the coast. In the distant west, you may see Arthur's Seat in Edinburgh, the Pentland Hills, and the Fife coastline. Off the coast of downtown North Berwick are many islands in the Firth of Forth including, most prominently, Craigleith and Bass Rock. From the summit, follow the route back the way you came.

EXTEND IT

Explore the Lodge Grounds, a 30-acre public park, created by the prominent Dalyrymple family in the seventeenth century and made into a split-level public park in 1939. Start first in the lower park (with a formal garden and aviary) and continue into the upper early Victorian area, a wide-open green space lined with big trees, wildflowers, and lavender gardens.

51 NORTH BERWICK SHORE

Amble from the town center along the lovely, storied coast, with views of rocky isles, to a fourteenth-century castle.

Distance: 6.8 miles
Elevation Gain: 780 feet
High Point: 120 feet
Rating: ★ ★ ★ ★
Difficulty: Moderate
Year-round: Yes
Family-friendly: No; steep and along roads

Dog-friendly: No
Amenities: Restrooms at Scottish Seabird Centre and Tantallon Castle; cafes and restaurants in North Berwick
Map: OS Explorer Map 351, Dunbar & North Berwick
Agencies: Town of North Berwick, Scottish Seabird Centre

GETTING THERE

GPS: 56.061568°, -2.717356°
Postcode: EH39 4SS
Driving: The Scottish Seabird Centre is at the end of Victoria Road in North Berwick.
Public Transit: Buses and trains frequently run from Edinburgh to North Berwick. The rail station is 0.7 mile from the Scottish

Seabird Centre in central North Berwick, and buses stop in the center of town.
Before You Go: This route, which is most fun at low tide, has a couple of steep ascents and descents. A 0.5-mile stretch near the end is on a road that can be busy in summer.

ON THE TRAIL

Start this walk at the Scottish Seabird Centre on the isthmus north of town. The center's back deck has panoramic views of Milsey and North Berwick bays and countless islands where there's always "some birdy" in residence. The height of colonization is May and June, when half a million seabirds populate the Forth islands, including 90,000 puffins and 150,000 gannets. In late fall, grey seals peak when several thousand hang out on the Isle of May.

Leave the Seabird Centre and, within a few hundred feet, pass the remnants of St. Andrew's Old Kirk (marked by signs). In the seventh century, a simple wooden chapel would have stood here as a beacon for pilgrims en route to St. Andrews to pray over religious relics. They believed that, if they offered enough of themselves, the relics could vanquish illness and sin. Centuries later a stone church was built on this site, and then expanded in the pilgrim-intensive Middle Ages (there were a lot of plague victims to pray for), but was nearly destroyed by a storm in 1656. Today what remains is the south porch and the outline of much of the central and western parts of the church.

From the church ruins, walk down onto East Beach, following the track through tall grass. Continue on packed sand for about three quarters of a mile, keeping a lookout for shorebirds, like gulls and guillemots, and tide pools teeming with sea anemones and hermit crabs. This was volcanic terrain 340 million years ago, and along the way, you'll see the remnants of this era in the black igneous rock boulders and red ash tuffs. The tallest of these is Yellow Craig Rock (25–30 feet high), named for the lichen that grows on it. The green-grey, bowl-shaped cliffs at the end of the beach are another volcanic remnant, made up of solidified ash imbedded with rock fragments (the material that collapsed into the volcano's vent as it went extinct). As you trek across the beach, you are walking inside what's left of a volcanic crater.

At the end of the beach, head uphill onto a trail through the dunes. Within roughly 100 feet you'll emerge onto a narrow paved street (Haugh Road), where there are several picnic tables on your right. Follow the grass track alongside the street for about a tenth of a mile (until just before a small parking lot), and take a left onto the narrow dirt path heading downhill. There are some nice benches on this stretch with great views of the islands of the Firth of Forth, the biggest of which (from west to east) are Fidra, Lamb, Craigleith, and Bass Rock. They are all volcanic in origin and heave with nesting birds. Robert Louis Stevenson's book *Treasure Island* was based on Fidra.

Boats sailing north from the North Berwick coast to St. Andrews once ferried ten thousand religious pilgrims each year.

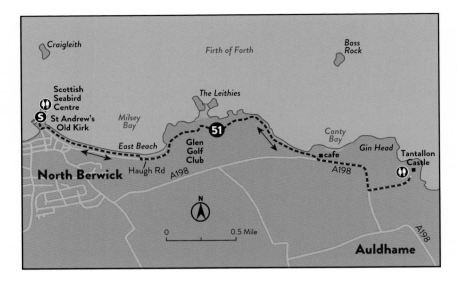

Continue for 0.2 mile to where the path forks. Head down to your left on a 0.1-mile steep spur trail to a beautiful, secluded-feeling beach cove. Follow the sand for a few hundred feet to curve right for excellent views of Bass Rock (351 feet), about two miles offshore. It is a premiere breeding site for gannets, and tens of thousands of them take over the island in summer. Gannets appear both tough and elegant, predominantly white with black-tipped wings, an orange-tinted head, and piercing blue-rimmed eyes. Look for them plunging into the sea at speeds of up to 60 miles per hour. Seals, dolphins, and whales are also regularly spotted nearby.

Return to the main trail and take the fork to your right. Hug the top of the cliff as you wind around a golf course for 0.8 mile to arrive at a short stretch of white sand. Cross to the end of the beach and take the path up the grass-covered slope (beware of thistles and stinging nettles off the path) to reach the headland separating the beach from Canty Bay, a lovely curved inlet on your left.

Pass a small parking lot and cafe, then go left (east) to continue along the coast. Follow A198 for 0.5 mile (there is a wide sidewalk or grass track for most of the way, but you will be walking close to traffic) as it curves right. Turn left onto the well-marked access road to Tantallon Castle. Take the grass path alongside the narrow road for 0.5 mile to the fortress entrance (fee required). Because of its location, this fourteenth-century castle only ever needed one 50-foot-high defensive wall on its southwest perimeter: the other three sides drop from 100-foot cliffs to the sea. Still, the castle was attacked multiple times and essentially destroyed in 1651 during the Third English Civil War. Oliver Cromwell sent thousands of troops to blow a hole in Tantallon and expel his enemies. There were fewer than one hundred men within the castle walls, but they managed to hold off Cromwell's forces for nearly two weeks.

Climb to the top of the castle ruins to get a sense of its truly dramatic architecture and setting, as well as 360-degree views of the region. Leaving the battlements behind, return to North Berwick the way you came.

52 DUNBAR CLIFF WALK

Explore windswept cliffs, tranquil bays, and a picturesque Scottish fishing village with a special connection to conservationist John Muir.

Distance: 4.3 miles
Elevation Gain: 400 feet
High Point: 82 feet
Rating: ★ ★ ★ ★
Difficulty: Easy to moderate
Year-round: Yes
Family-friendly: Yes; kids will love the tide pools; note that route includes several flights of stairs and spots with sheer cliff drops

Dog-friendly: Yes, leashed during nesting season at John Muir Country Park
Amenities: Restrooms in central Dunbar and near car park in John Muir Country Park; many shops and cafes on Dunbar High Street
Map: OS Map 351, Dunbar & North Berwick
Agency: John Muir Country Park

GETTING THERE

GPS: 56.005851°, -2.517183°
Postcode: EH42 1HX
Driving: From the roundabout in central Dunbar, follow Victoria Street onto Victoria Place and down to Victoria Harbour (0.1 mile in total). The closest off-street parking to Dunbar Castle is at the Dunbar Leisure Pool.

Public Transit: Regular buses and trains run from Edinburgh to Dunbar.
Before You Go: This walk is best done at low tide to beachcomb. Storms can be intense here, especially in winter, so be aware of wind and waves.

ON THE TRAIL

"Dunbar" derives from the Scottish Gaelic *Dùn Barra*, meaning "summit fort," so it's fitting that this walk begins near the ruins of Dunbar Castle. People began building crude fortifications on this basalt promontory jutting out into the North Sea thousands of years ago. The first stone castle was likely built in the twelfth century and, in the centuries since, it has been dismantled, rebuilt, expanded, reinforced, defended, and invaded countless times. Dunbar Castle was also the stage for many royal dramas between Scotland and England (and, occasionally, France), including that of Mary Queen of Scots, who lived there in the mid-sixteenth century.

The castle ruins, now inaccessible to all but nesting kittiwakes (the colony here is one of the most prolific in Britain), can be seen from where this walk starts at Victoria Harbour. There has been a harbor here since the eleventh century, but this version was built in the nineteenth century to support the town's booming fishing and whaling industry. (The project's engineer was the uncle of author Robert Louis Stevenson who wrote *Treasure Island*.) Victoria Harbour is still a busy, working port with trawlers coming and going. Look for seals, some of which are known to hang out, looking for a handout from fishermen.

With the castle ruins behind you, walk straight for about a tenth of a mile toward, and then around, the large glass-enclosed Dunbar Leisure Pool, keeping it to your right (a small, tree-lined park is to your left). Follow a brown "John Muir Link" signpost pointing right and, in 0.1 mile, descend some stairs to a small bay overrun with lumpy volcanic outcroppings, part of John Muir Country Park, and continue on the 134-mile coast-to-coast John Muir Way. At low tide, you can diverge from the paved path to get a better look at Doo Rock, the prominent dark sea stack in the middle of the bay, and to peek into rock pools teeming with seaweed, colorful crabs, and barnacles.

So much in this area is named for uberconservationist John Muir because he was born in downtown Dunbar. This landscape, and seascape, sparked his curiosity and fed his passion for wild places. In *The Story of My Boyhood and Youth*, he wrote, "With red-blooded playmates, wild as myself, I loved to wander in the fields to hear the birds sing, and along the seashore to gaze and wonder at the shells and seaweeds, eels and crabs in the pools among the rocks when the tide was low; and best of all to watch

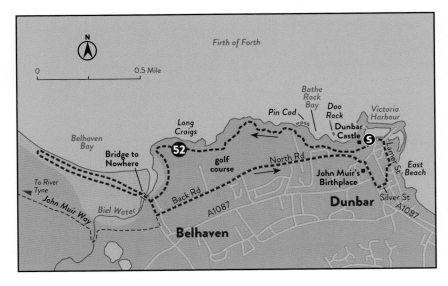

The Belhaven Bridge, aka the "Bridge to Nowhere," spans Biel Water as it empties into the North Sea but is stranded at high tide.

the waves in awful storms thundering on the black headlands and craggy ruins of the old Dunbar Castle when the sea and the sky, the waves and the clouds, were mingled together as one."

Keep the rocky shoreline to your right as you continue (with no turns) for the next 1.5 miles. The path turns to dirt and zigzags down a flight of stairs, across a set of wooden planks, and out onto Tarry Ship headland, where you may see fishing vessels and cargo ships plying the blue-grey waters. Almost immediately ascend a steep set of stairs, pass under a stone arch, head through a short tunnel, and emerge to see the cove of Bathe Rock Bay. The most prominent chunk of sandstone in this red-rock garden is called Pin Cod. Though you are still close to town on this stretch, boisterous gulls or mute swans, pumping their powerful wings, may be your only company.

Here the path widens and is flanked by a high, red sandstone wall on your left (beyond it lies a golf course) and, on your right, grassy expanses that ultimately drop off into the sea, requiring caution. Look northwest over the water to see hulking Bass Rock (351 feet), an important breeding spot for a massive colony of northern gannets (learn more on Trail 51). On a clear day, beyond the Bass, you can spot the conical bulk of North Berwick Law (614 feet), a conspicuous hill roughly seven miles away (learn more on Trail 50).

Drop down some stairs and gentle slopes, skirting the edge of the golf course, to round a headland for wide, sweeping views of Belhaven Bay. Here, the rust-hued rock gives way to low, grass-studded dunes and a broad sand beach. Walk along the beach for 0.1 mile to cross the metal so-called Bridge to Nowhere, taking care on the (quite slippery) rock walk that leads to some stairs. (The bridge is inaccessible at high tide, unless you want to get your feet wet.) Take the bridge over Biel Water, a large stream that flows to the sea, and walk 0.3 mile across the cove to enjoy vast views of the Forth Estuary. These waters are a popular spot for surfers and kayakers.

Walk back across the bridge and onto Shore Road (the only street around), heading south for 0.1 mile. Go left onto Back Road and follow the quiet, shady paved road for 1 mile to where it joins Bayswell Road. Bear right soon after onto High Street. In less than 0.1 mile you'll arrive at John Muir's Birthplace, a small but excellent museum.

Here you can learn about how Muir's early, somewhat feral days of local exploration inspired his later work as a champion of untamed places. He left Dunbar for America as a boy, but it never left him. In his late twenties, Muir took a 1000-mile trek from Indiana to the Gulf of Mexico and, when he neared the water, his thoughts were of Scotland. The smell of the sea, he wrote, "suddenly conjured up Dunbar, its rocky coast, wind and waves; and my whole childhood . . . dulse and tangle, long-winged gulls, the Bass Rock in the Firth of Forth, and the old castle, schools, churches and the long country rambles in search of bird's nests."

Turn right out of the museum and continue up High Street—which looks similar in many ways to Muir's day—for 0.1 mile. Turn left onto Silver Street and follow it 0.1 mile steeply downhill to East Beach. Pause to take note of Barns Ness Lighthouse, 3 miles southeast of Dunbar before, keeping the shore to your right, continuing for 0.3 mile past historical warehouses and granaries to Victoria Harbour where the walk began.

EXTEND IT
Continue across the sands of Belhaven Bay for another mile to a dynamic estuary at the mouth of the River Tyne. Be aware that the bay fills quickly near high tide.

53 ABERLADY NATURE RESERVE TO GULLANE BENTS

A birding hot spot, Aberlady was designated as Britain's first local nature reserve in 1952, to protect diverse habitats, such as estuaries and dunes, and the unique species that rely on them.

Distance: 7 miles
Elevation Gain: 660 feet
High Point: 317 feet
Rating: ★ ★ ★ ★
Difficulty: Moderate
Year-round: Yes
Family-friendly: Yes, with dunes and coves to explore

Dog-friendly: No, prohibited in Aberlady Bay Local Nature Reserve
Amenities: Restrooms at car park
Map: OS Explorer Map 351, Dunbar & North Berwick
Agency: East Lothian Council

GETTING THERE

GPS: 56.014213°, -2.849713°
Postcode: EH32 0QB
Driving: From Aberlady, go east on High Street (A198) for 120 feet and turn left to stay on A198. Continue for 0.6 mile before turning left into the Aberlady Bay car park.
Before You Go: Sections of this route are not well signed and require some wayfinding. Before you venture too far out, keep in mind that tides advance rapidly here.

ON THE TRAIL

From the car park, walk north on the boardwalk for about 500 feet over the estuary where Peffer Burn flows into Aberlady Bay. Depending on the time of year, many different resident and migrant birds may be seen. Aberlady Bay Local Nature Reserve is just 1500 acres, but it's home to a recorded 250 species, and packed with a diversity of coastal habitats—salt and freshwater marsh, grassland, woodland, freshwater pools, mud flats, dunes, and sea—that make it feel at once vacant and abundant. Continue straight past reed beds onto the wide dirt path. In a little under half a mile, pass through a tunnel of sea buckthorn, heavy with orange berries in autumn. When the path emerges, North Berwick Law (614 feet) will be visible straight ahead, roughly 6 miles distant to the northeast. Glance back to see Marl Loch, a freshwater lake popular with a local herd of roe deer.

Continue 0.5 mile through tall grasses and abundant wildflowers (there are over 500 species of the latter at Aberlady) rippling outward in swells of green, purple, and white. When you reach a brown sign that says "Footpath" with an arrow, go left. Looking west on a clear day, you may be able to see Edinburgh (and Arthur's Seat) across the Firth of Forth, and the Pentland Hills south of that. To the north across the Firth are the rolling hills of Fife.

In another 0.2 mile the trail forks. Head right, following the sign that says "Footpath" with two arrows, and continue through the grasslands for about a third of a mile. When you arrive at the lumpy, grass-covered dunes, stay to the established path between the marking posts. While this is part of one of the largest naturally developing dune systems in southeast Scotland, this area is nevertheless fragile. In a couple hundred feet you'll emerge onto Gullane Sands, a wide, golden beach, where you'll turn right and continue for 0.5 mile. Offshore lie the wrecks of several nineteenth- and twentieth-century fishing boats, and a couple of midget submarines (part of which may be visible at low tide). Before the rocky outcropping (called The Old Man) that juts into the water at the end of the beach, pick up the path on your right that climbs into the dunes. Ascend gently (about 50 feet in elevation gain) to the top of the bluff, and follow the trail as its hugs the coast.

In 0.2 mile arrive at The Old Man rock, where there's a wonderful view of the sea and surrounding terrain. The dark igneous rock outcrops that populate the shoreline give it a rugged, unfinished feel. Look for the long legs and tapered bills of godwits as well as gannets, with their penetrating gaze and dagger-like beaks. Continue on, reaching Gullane Point (rough rocks on your left) in about 500 feet. There are many social trails here, so stick to the coast as safely as you can.

In 0.3 mile leave Aberlady Nature Reserve to drop down slightly into Ironstone Cove, named for the iron compound, at one time mined and smelted, in its sedimentary rock. Continue over shells and sea glass toward Hummell Rocks at the end of the cove. Look up to see huge concrete blocks—some anti-tank remnants from World War II. Climb steeply to your right on an established track through tall dune grass, cutting in between the concrete blocks. When the trail splits in roughly 500 feet, keep left to follow along the clifftop. Offshore you can see the alternating pale and dark bands of the Bleaching Rocks jutting out perpendicular to the coast. It is a 30-foot-thick bed of sandstone whose cliffs drop dramatically to the sea.

Skirt the edge of a golf course for the next 0.3 mile to intersect a dirt road. Go left and then follow the wood sign pointing toward "Gullane Bents" along a grassy track

In fall, Aberlady hosts more than thirty thousand cartoonish, pink-footed geese migrating from Iceland to roost on the East Lothian coast.

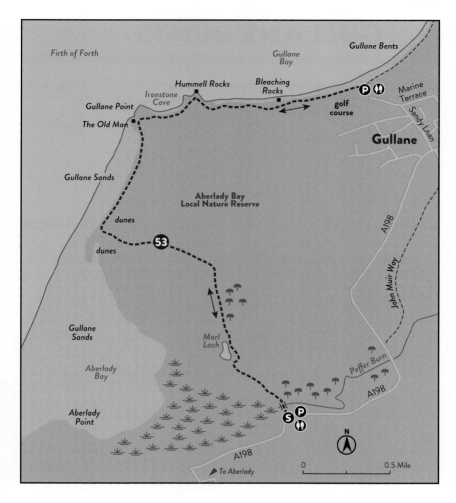

for 0.2 mile. Head left and downhill for 0.1 mile to the beach and car park. If you want to go into the village of Gullane (about 0.5 mile away), take a right here on the path between the walls. Arrive at Gullane Bents, another beautiful beach, at the bottom of the slope. Return the way you came.

EXTEND IT

Tack on the 3.2-mile Gullane Bents loop (Trail 54) which heads east from the beach where this walk finishes.

54 GULLANE BENTS

Explore some of Scotland's surprisingly exotic sand beaches, intriguing geology, and a very cool forest.

Distance: 3.2 miles
Elevation Gain: 340 feet
High Point: 85 feet
Rating: ★ ★ ★ ★
Difficulty: Easy
Year-round: Yes
Dog-friendly: Yes

Family-friendly: Yes, with sandy beaches and coves to explore
Amenities: Restrooms, viewpoint, picnic tables, and potable water at start
Map: OS Explorer Map 351, Dunbar & North Berwick
Agency: East Lothian Council

GETTING THERE

GPS: 56.038012°, -2.839392°
Postcode: EH31 2BE
Driving: Head southwest on Main Street (A198) for 0.3 mile, then turn right onto Sandy Loan. Go 0.3 mile and take a left onto Marine Terrace, which ends in 400 feet at the Gullane Bents car park.

Public Transit: There are buses from Edinburgh through North Berwick to Gullane.
Before You Go: The rock formations at the west end of Gullane Bents can only be explored before high tide. Tide tables can be obtained from the UK Hydrographic Office.

ON THE TRAIL

Gullane Bents is one of the most popular beaches in eastern Scotland, and it's immediately clear why. From the viewpoint overlooking the sea, you can see a gentle, perfect crescent of sand hemmed in by the Hummell Rocks to the west and the Black Rocks to the north, all backed by impressive grass-covered dunes ("bent" means a tough, reedy kind of grass).

Begin at the north end of the car park and follow the well-established path, flanked by sea buckthorn and marram grass, for 0.1 mile to the beach. Take an immediate left at the sand and follow the curve for about a quarter mile to reach two interesting rock formations—Bleaching Rocks and, farther on where the beach ends, Hummell Rocks. Bleaching Rocks is a huge, exposed sandstone bed upward of 30 feet thick. The grey-white rock with its dark iron stains looks like the swirls and curves of a giant topographical map. Hummell Rocks, which is composed of dark grey mudstone, has exposed trace fossils of bark (most likely lycopod) and insect burrows.

Turn around and go back the way you came along the beach, then follow the sand all the way to the eastern end of the bay (roughly 0.8 mile from Hummell Rocks). Just before the beach becomes rocky, take a trail on your right to ascend slightly through the grass. Arrive at a shallow cove in 0.4 mile and walk along its edge, continuing straight to follow the shoreline. In another 0.1 mile, you'll reach the Black Rocks—scattered boulders of olivine basalt that act as an anchor for seaweed species. This is a good, quiet spot for birdwatching, especially in winter when a large number of waders and waterfowl are hanging out.

Continue following the shoreline as it curves right and meets some stone ruins (what's left of the one-room Red House) on the edge of another sandy cove on Broad Sands Bay. That's Elliot Beach, also known as West Links Beach (because of the famous nearby golf course). At low tide, there are many rock pools with barnacles, anemone, and mussels, which attract crabs. Beyond the ruins are countless dune humps covered in sea lyme and marram grasses, as well as sea buckthorn and the occasional elder and hawthorn, that provide shelter for foxes, roe deer, rabbits, weasels, shrew, and voles. While not a part of this walk, there are public footpaths through the dunes that can be explored. In summer, look for showy stalks of viper's bugloss, a strangely austere name for a wildflower with papery blue-purple blooms.

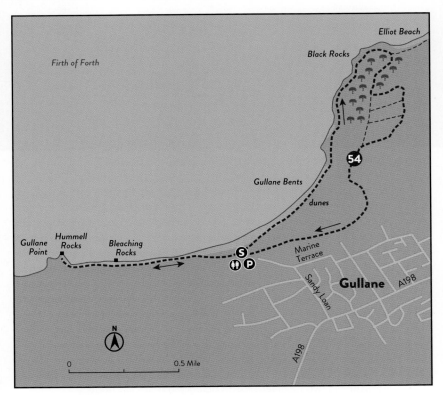

The tranquil passage to Gullane Bay cuts through huge dunes where discovery awaits.

Reach a stone wall roughly 0.1 mile from the ruins. Keep it to your left as you continue toward a stand of evergreens. This is one of two small plantations in the area seeded with lodgepole and Scots pines. The woodland feels surprisingly dense and can be filled with song from the resident nesting birds including wren, song thrush, blackbird, bullfinch, chaffinch, great tit, and blue tit. Summer nesters include several warblers, while in the winter there can be huge flocks of redwing and fieldfare, enjoying the buffet of orange berries on the sea buckthorn.

Continue straight for 0.3 mile, first along and then through the woodland, until the trail splits. Take a left to exit the tree canopy, heading east toward some farm buildings. Make a right when you reach them, and follow the trail as it narrows and cuts through some dunes. Continue for 0.9 mile, winding through the grass and brush, and crossing several boggy areas on planks (ignoring any trails on your right heading back toward the coast). Keep an eye out in summer for rare flower species, such as the purple milk vetch and frog orchid (whose green blooms actually look like tiny frogs).

Join a flat, wide dirt track heading west in the direction of some houses on a hill for 0.2 mile back to the Gullane Bents car park and beach.

EXTEND IT
Instead of passing by Elliot Beach, cross it and continue along the quiet coast for 7 miles to North Berwick (where you have the option to pick up Trails 50 and 51).

SCOTTISH HIGHLANDS

The less-populated but mountain-crammed northern part of Scotland, with the highest seventy-five peaks in the British Isles, includes many of the UK's greatest hits—tallest peak (Ben Nevis, 4413 feet), largest lake (Loch Lomond), and coolest kilts (obviously). It covers an immense and diverse area with ancient forests, glacial cirques, lonely peaks, and sprawling shorelines.

CAIRNGORMS NATIONAL PARK

The largest national park in the UK (Trails 55–58), established in 2003, has a mountain range of the same name at its center. The Cairngorms are the best known—and generally considered the most challenging—mountains in the Highlands to ascend, due to their remoteness, elevation, and changeable weather. Called *Am Monadh Ruadh* in Gaelic, or the Red Hills, they were named when the grey granite still had a rosy tint following the last ice age. Since then, the once-jagged peaks have been rounded by snow and frost, and now look more like a series of high, domed plateaus. It's a tundra-like environment that is home to many of Britain's rarest plant, bird, and animal species (including its only reindeer herd). Equally alluring areas of the national park include more rugged ranges, tranquil valleys, and gushing rivers.

LOCH LOMOND & THE TROSSACHS NATIONAL PARK

Scotland's first national park (Trail 59), established in 2002, encompasses 720 square miles of rumpled hills, lovely lochs, and shady forests. It's a land of contrasts and a hiker's heaven with twenty-one Munros (mountains over 3000 feet) and nineteen Corbetts (hills between 2500 and 3000 feet), as well as twenty-two large lochs—and many smaller ones—and roughly fifty rivers channeling abundant snow and rain to lake and sea.

OPPOSITE: *The steep climb to the base of Ben Nevis, Trail 60, crosses primordial terrain.*

FORT WILLIAM & GLENCOE

The town of Fort William and nearby valley of Glencoe (Trail 60) both dwell in the shadow of the behemoth, Ben Nevis. From there, head up any of the area's lung-busting hills for breathtaking panoramas or, if getting up high isn't on the agenda, revel in the region's lush glens (used in many scenes in the *Harry Potter* films), lengthy lochs, and profusion of waterfalls.

ISLE OF SKYE

The so-called Misty Isle (Trails 61–63), known for its frequent low clouds, is the largest and most northerly of the Inner Hebrides and is, quite simply, a magical place. At 50 miles long, the island boasts some of the most technical peaks in Scotland—sometimes referred to as having "shark's tooth" summits with "dragon's back" ridges. It's a rugged, windswept landscape that feels wilder than most places in Britain. But getting Skye-high doesn't require climbing gear; its quirky rock formations, abundant wildlife, and colorful history are accessible to all.

55 LOCH AN EILEIN & LOCH GAMHNA

This wooded stroll by Loch an Eilein, at the edge of the mountains and with nice views of the hills and the lakes, is one of the prettiest walking spots in the Highlands.

Distance: 4.5 miles
Elevation Gain: 440 feet
High Point: 940 feet
Rating: ★ ★ ★ ★
Difficulty: Easy
Year-round: Yes
Family-friendly: Yes
Dog-friendly: Yes, under voice control

Amenities: Restrooms on approach trail to Loch an Eilein; picnic spots around Loch an Eilein
Map: OS Explorer Map OL57, Cairn Gorm & Aviemore
Agencies: Rothiemurchus Forest, Cairngorms National Park

GETTING THERE

GPS: 57.154859°, -3.824739°
Postcode: PH22 1QP
Driving: From Aviemore, go south on Grampian Road for 1.3 miles to B970, and turn left at roundabout. Go 1.8 miles on B970, then turn right to stay on B970. Go

another 2 miles to turn right into the car park.
Before You Go: The trail to Loch Gamhna is unmaintained and can get boggy. The low elevation makes this a good choice for days when adverse weather prevents higher altitude wandering.

ON THE TRAIL

Walk to the well-marked trailhead at the south end of the car park. Continue straight for a few hundred feet, past the restrooms on your right. When you arrive at a T inter-section at the edge of Loch an Eilein, go left to start a clockwise loop around it. Follow the wide dirt track as it skirts the edge, with views south across the lake to the hills beyond, including Creag Fhiaclach and Creag Dhubh (2780 feet). The serene fresh-water lake lies within Rothiemurchus Forest at the western edge of the rugged Cairn-gorms plateau. Much of the forest forms part of the Rothiemurchus Estate, which has been owned by the Grant family since the 1540s.

Continue into a wooded area shaded by mature Scots pines and speckled with wildflowers and heather, ignoring any tracks branching left. These woods are a rem-nant of the Caledonian woodlands, a temperate rainforest that formed at the end of the last ice age and once covered most of the Scottish Highlands. Back then, broadleaf

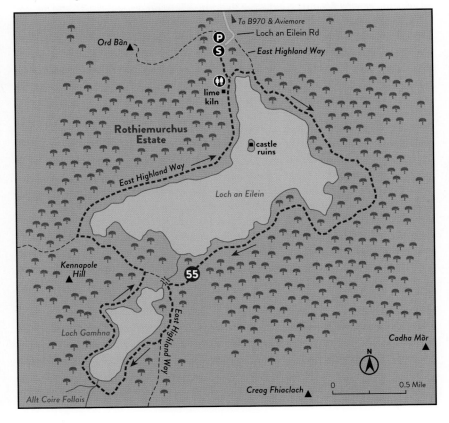

trees and immense ferns would have been the haunt of lynx, wolves, and wild boar. The Romans called Scotland "Caledonia," or "wooded heights," but a changing climate and human activity took their toll. Today less than 5 percent of the old-growth forest remains.

Red squirrels, roe deer, pine martens, and red foxes now top the remaining charismatic fauna, along with the Scottish wildcat, a fascinating species that evolved from European wildcats stranded on the British isles when the sea level rose nearly ten thousand years ago. There are very few "pure" wildcats left, since they have bred with domestic felines over time, and sightings are extremely rare. But the fierce kitty is still something of a national obsession and an icon, and many prominent clans use its image on their crests. In addition to being roughly twice the size of a house cat, Scottish wildcats—a.k.a. the Highlands tiger—can be identified by their thick fur, broad heads, banded tails (with perfect black rings), and kilts (just kidding about that last one). Like all wildcats, they look pretty cuddly, but they are vicious predators.

In roughly 0.5 mile, the trail veers away from the lakeshore and climbs gently into a forest with thigh-high ferns and birds darting from tree to tree. The Scots pines here are direct descendants of the first pines that sprung up thousands of years ago after the ice receded. The woods maintain a primeval feel, and are important habitat for jays, wrens, Scottish crossbills, and plump, pointy-beaked tree creepers. The latter are tiny and susceptible to the cold, so they'll cleverly smooth a groove into a tree trunk and then press themselves inside to escape the wind. Scottish crossbills are a small, poufy finch with peachy feathers and odd beaks and nest exclusively in Scots pines. They are named for the unusual way the top half of their beak crosses over the bottom half.

Follow the dirt track for another 0.5 mile as it presses closer to the lakeshore, with plenty of spots to rest or explore the water's edge. Climb away from the lake through a dense section of tall pines over the next 0.7 mile to intersect with the East Highland Way, an unofficial 83-mile route that spans the Highlands from Fort William to Aviemore. Go left (south) to leave the main loop around Loch an Eilein, and head toward the shore of Loch Gamhna on your right. In 0.2 mile go right at another trail junction to stay close to the lakeside.

It may be hard to picture now, but centuries ago, when the pines were first poking up out of the ground, Loch Gamhna was teeming with outlaws. The cattle rustling got so bad that ranchers would tie some of their cows to the trees here as an offering to raiders. Rob Roy was one of the most famous outlaws in the area during the late seventeenth and early eighteenth century. Some mix of fact and fiction solidified his place in popular folklore as a red-haired Robin Hood. In "Rob Roy's Grave," English poet William Wordsworth wrote, "Say, then, that he was wise as brave; / As wise in thought as bold in deed: / For in the principle of things / He sought his moral creed."

Continue for 0.3 mile, where the trail can get a bit swampy as it fords a small stream, Allt Coire Follais. Follow the track as it wraps around the southern end of Loch

Water and woodlands define Loch an Eilein, once voted "Britain's Favorite Picnic Spot."

Gamhna to hug the lake's edge. In about two-thirds of a mile, rejoin the main track around Loch an Eilein. Go left and continue for 0.3 mile to a T intersection. Head right to stay on the trail following the lakeshore.

In 0.7 mile you'll see where the name "Loch an Eilein" (Scottish Gaelic for "Lake of the Island") came from. Take the short spur trail down to the water's edge to get a look at the small island just offshore, crowned by castle ruins. The striking structure is believed to have been the fourteenth-century home of the so-called Wolf of Badenoch, a.k.a. Alexander Stewart, who became an earl by forcing an heiress into marriage. The island has shrunk due to rising lake levels, and the causeway that used to lead to it is now submerged. But its tower and the outer wall surrounding a small courtyard remain visible.

Rejoin the main trail from the spur and continue for 0.2 mile to finish the lake loop. Toward the end you'll see what's left of a lime kiln from the late eighteenth or early nineteenth century. Limestone was quarried from the abundant outcrops in the area, and nearby trees were logged as fuel to burn the rock in the kilns. That lime powder was then used to improve soil fertility on farms and in construction. Just past the kiln, go left to return to the car park.

EXTEND IT

Add the summit of Ord Bàn (1400 feet) for an additional 0.5 mile and 500 feet in elevation gain. Pick up the trailhead in the north corner of the car park and go over the stile next to the locked gate.

56 COIRE AN T-SNEACHDA

This out-and-back walk crosses high, haunting terrain in the central Cairngorms to arrive at a sheer and spectacular high mountain corrie.

Distance: 4.3 miles
Elevation Gain: 1100 feet
High Point: 3060 feet
Rating: ★ ★ ★ ★ ★
Difficulty: Moderate
Year-round: No
Dog-friendly: Yes

Family-friendly: Yes, but last stretch crosses a field of large boulders with big drops
Amenities: Restrooms and restaurant at the start
Map: OS Explorer Map OL57, Cairn Gorm & Aviemore
Agency: Cairngorms National Park

GETTING THERE

GPS: 57.134901°, -3.672010°
Postcode: PH22 1RB
Driving: From Glenmore, go east for 4 winding miles on Cairngorm Road to the Cairngorm Mountain Upper car park at the road's end, near the Snowsports Centre complex.

Public Transit: There are buses to the car park from Aviemore.
Before You Go: This is a high, exposed, treeless route in an area with changeable weather. The trail ends at a huge boulder field that must be navigated to reach the small lakes (but isn't required to achieve the "wow" factor on this walk).

ON THE TRAIL

Walk to the Base Station (the building that says "Cairngorm Mountain Scotland") at the south end of the car park. Veer right of the structure, past the sculptures, and bear right onto the wide gravel path toward the ski tows. When the trail forks to three narrower paths, head right to follow the track uphill, ascending some steps, for 0.1 mile. In a little over a tenth of a mile, bear left where the trail forks and start the climb toward Coire an t-Sneachda.

As the trail curves south, you'll have your first peek at the destination ahead. Gentle, stream-streaked green slopes rise to rock walls draped with snow and ice. Ahead lie the three glacial cirques on the northern slope of the Cairngorm plateau—Coire Cas, Coire an t-Sneachda, and Coire an Lochain. This route winds its way to the central one, Coire an t-Sneachda, or "Corrie of the Snow." Its sheer cliffs drop from the summits of Cairn Lochan (3990 feet) and Stob Coire an t-Sneachda (3860 feet). The coire is north-facing, which means snowfields persist year-round (Scotland has no true glaciers).

Climb more than 400 feet in elevation over the next 0.7 mile, with views of what may be the wildest land tract in the British Isles. The winds, low temperatures, and snow cover of the Cairngorms plateau translate to an Arctic-Alpine environment not seen elsewhere in the UK. This route, which ascends from roughly 2000 feet above sea level to 3000 feet, is representative of the stark, but far from barren, landscape that characterizes much of the area. Alpine grasses line the path, and hardy moss and

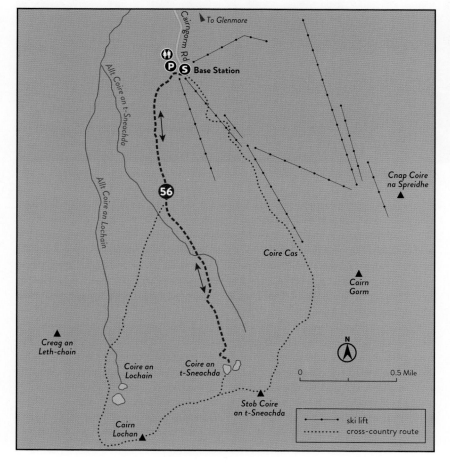

The tumbled-down glacial rock corrie of Coire an t-Sneachda is at once a stirring and restful place.

lichen decorate trailside boulders. Clumps of purple heather brighten the slopes alongside wildflowers like Scottish bluebell and alpine azalea.

Climb alongside a stream, the Allt Coire an t-Sneachda, for 0.3 mile to cross it on giant stepping stones. The rushing meltwater flows from the north-facing slopes of the corrie, cutting down through boggy terrain to the lakes and woodlands below. Pause to look behind you at a huge lake, Loch Morlich, to the northwest, and the vast green forest that encircles it. Beyond that are the town of Aviemore and the peaks of the Monadhliath Mountains.

Continue alongside the stream for 0.6 mile, gaining another 400 feet in elevation. Between the boulders strewn across the terrain are mats of heath bedstraw, distinctive with profuse clusters of tiny white flowers. As you near the coire, the trail gets harder to follow among large slabs and rocks. Continue south into the craggy basin, working your way toward the lochans, or small lakes, at the foot of the cliffs.

Glacial moraine piled up here, creating a meltwater basin. Upward of ten thousand years ago, there was a glacier in the 500-foot-high, half-mile-wide gap hollowed out of Caledonian granite. The frost-shattered upper headwall of the coire is fractured with chimneys and gullies, and its four main buttresses are popular climbing routes year-round. The huge scree, or talus, slopes beneath the cliffs continue to grow with each new rockfall.

This beguiling terrain is reminiscent of the imagery captured by Scottish poet Nan Shephard, who wrote achingly and meaningfully of her relationship with the Cairngorms in "Summit of Corrie Etchachan" in 1934: "But this grey plateau, rock-strewn, vast, silent / The dark loch, the toiling crags, the snow / A mountain shut within itself, yet a world / Immensity." Rest awhile, if weather permits, in desolate beauty. Reflect on the forces, both immense and minute, shaping this impressive place, while watching for some of the hardy species that thrive on life's periphery—ring ouzel and rock ptarmigan, bearberry and reindeer lichen. When you're ready, retrace your steps to the start.

EXTEND IT

Create a loop back to the car park by either going east over Stob Coire an t-Sneachda from Coire an t-Sneachda and down Coire Cas, or west over Cairn Lochan and around Coire an Lochain. These loops should only be attempted by experienced hikers.

57 CREAG BHEAG

This classic hillwalk ascends to Creag Bheag, a small, steep hill in the Cairngorms above the River Spey, that affords panoramic views of the surrounding lakes, peaks, and valleys.

Distance: 3 miles
Elevation Gain: 900 feet
High Point: 1600 feet
Rating: ★ ★ ★
Difficulty: Moderate
Year-round: Yes
Dog-friendly: Yes

Family-friendly: Yes, but descent of back side of Creag Bheag is steep
Amenities: Restrooms at car park
Map: OS Explorer Map OL56, Badenoch & Upper Strathspey
Agency: Cairngorms National Park

GETTING THERE

GPS: 57.080868°, -4.054932°
Postcode: PH21 1LR
Driving: From Newtonmore, take Main Street (A86) for 2.8 miles northeast to Gynack Road in Kingussie. Turn left and continue 400 feet to turn left into Ardvonie car park.
Public Transit: Trains run from Edinburgh, Glasgow, Inverness, and London along the Highland Main Line. The Kingussie train station is 0.3 mile from the trailhead.
Before You Go: Walking this route clockwise involves a steep descent; reverse it if you prefer a gentler descent. Even if it's calm in Kingussie, it can be very windy at the top of Creag Bheag.

ON THE TRAIL

Head for the trailhead on the west side of the car park, by the placards and signpost to "Creag Bheag Summit." Walk a couple hundred feet up a grass track, through a gate, and then along a narrow dirt path to a tarmac road (Tait's Brae). Turn right and continue for a little over a tenth of a mile as the road turns to gravel. When the road ends, follow the path heading left and uphill into the woods.

Go straight for less than a tenth of a mile and, when the trail forks, veer left onto the wider track. Follow that for 0.4 mile as it curves through Scots pine and birch around the base of 1600-foot Creag Bheag. When the trail reaches a gate, pass through it and continue a little farther to an intersection at a signpost. Go straight (north), heading uphill toward the rock cliffs at the base of Creag Bheag, which are popular with climbers.

A short hill climb up Creag Bheag yields views across the River Spey and Speyside, a region spanning mountains, forests, villages, and lochs.

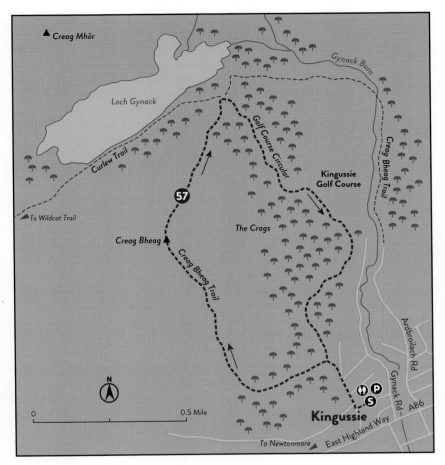

Walk along the remnants of a stone wall, through gorse and bracken, toward the heather-coated flanks of Creag Bheag, or "The Mound." In summer some wonderful wildflowers, including many cheerful wild pansies, line the narrow, rocky trail. From there head up a short stretch of stone steps, and around some rocky crags, for 0.6 mile to the top. Look back to the southeast for views of Kingussie and the Ruthven Barracks ruins beyond.

The ruins, which sit atop a hillock surrounded by floodplain, are easy to spot. The barracks were built to house British troops after the Jacobite uprising in 1715. Those soldiers suppressed unrest in the area, or at least tried to, until another Jacobite uprising thirty years later. At that point, the English were driven out by siege and fire. To this day, the barracks are a high-profile reminder that there have been dark days in this now-peaceful valley.

The apex of Creag Bheag is not well defined, but when you reach the plateau, go right to follow the sporadic path across the narrow, cracked-stone cap of the summit. There are a few cairns, the larger of which marks the true top, and a stone shelter with a bench that is a welcome respite from the sometimes-wicked wind. The shelter offers excellent views of Kingussie to the south.

Kingussie (pronounced "King-yoo-see"), which translates roughly as "Head of the Pine Forest," lies on the River Spey. Over 100 miles long, the Spey is one of the fastest-flowing rivers in Scotland. Salmon and trout fishing are big on the river, as is whiskey production; apparently, the water's high quality has attracted some of the most famous distilleries to Speyside. Kingussie is also somewhat famous for a sport called "shinty" that resembles field hockey and has been played in the Highlands since ancient times. The town sits in a broad mountain valley, or "strath," as it's called around here. "Strathspey" is the name for the area around the River Spey. While you may hear it referred to by its anglicized name, "Spey Valley," that moniker is a bit controversial. Scotland is a country with a strong national identity and unique traditions. With ongoing rumblings about gaining independence from Britain, any loss of individuality (linguistic or otherwise) is not well received.

Beyond Kingussie to the east are the foothills and high peaks of the Cairngorm Mountains, including Ben Macdui (4295 feet), Scotland's second-highest peak, and its neighbor, Cairn Gorm (4085 feet). To the northwest is glittering Loch Gynack, backed by Creag Mhòr (2170 feet) and Creag Dhubh (2580 feet). They are some of the Monadhliath Mountains, a largely treeless and trackless wilderness (the majority of which is outside the national park) that encompass some of the most ancient landscape in Britain. The popular Munro group of Càrn Dearg, A' Chailleach, and Càrn Sgulain can be seen to the northwest.

In about 0.2 mile cross the top of Creag Bheag, and begin to descend sharply toward Loch Gynack. In another 0.2 mile veer right into the woodland. Reach a trail junction in 0.1 mile and go right (a left here would bring you to Loch Gynack along the Curlew Trail). Continue for 0.7 mile along the Golf Course Circular through birch and pine woodland, listening for birds such as jays and woodpeckers in the branches.

Climb slightly into the forest and, in 0.3 mile when the trail splits, go left. Rejoin the track you began on in 0.1 mile and retrace your steps to the car park.

EXTEND IT

To complete a wide loop around Creag Bheag, go left at the junction for Loch Gynack on the Curlew Trail. Continue for 2.8 miles to link with the Wildcat Trail. Follow that for 0.8 mile to intersect the East Highland Way (A86), and go left to walk 1.8 miles east into Kingussie.

58 RYVOAN PASS, AN LOCHAN UAINE & MEALL A'BHUACHAILLE

This loop in the Cairngorms National Park pairs a steep climb up a Corbett with a walk deep into ancient pine forest and along the shores of a magical green loch.

Distance: 5.5 miles
Elevation Gain: 1740 feet
High Point: 2540 feet
Rating: ★ ★ ★ ★
Difficulty: Moderate to challenging
Year-round: No
Family-friendly: Yes, though ascent of Meall a'Bhuachaille is steep

Dog-friendly: Yes, leashed to protect ground-nesting birds
Amenities: Restrooms and cafe at start
Map: OS Explorer Map OL57, Cairn Gorm & Aviemore
Agencies: Glenmore Forest Park, Cairngorms National Park

GETTING THERE

GPS: 57.167685°, -3.692238°
Postcode: PH22 1QU
Driving: From Aviemore, follow Grampian Road (B9152) south for 1.3 miles. At the second roundabout, take B970 for 1.7 miles to a junction. Continue straight (where B970 turns left) on Cairngorm Road for 4.2 miles to the Glenmore Forest Park Visitor Centre car park on the left.

Public Transit: Buses run from Aviemore to the Glenmore Forest Park Visitor Centre.
Before You Go: To skip the steep ascent of Meall a'Bhuachaille, do the first section of the featured walk as an out-and-back. The paths are mostly good, but with plenty of exposed roots and rocky steps. Steer clear of adders, the UK's only venomous snake, which live here.

ON THE TRAIL

Start facing the Glenmore Forest Park Visitor Centre and go right (east) along a foot-path for 0.1 mile to a trail junction. (Follow the wooden posts with blue blazes.) Turn left at the junction onto a wide, gravel path and, when it intersects another path in 500 feet, bear right to climb modestly, with some great views south of the peaks of the Cairngorm plateau.

Like much of Glenmore Forest Park, these woods are mainly Scots pines, the trea-sured fragments of the ancient Caledonian forest that once covered much of the High-lands. Under pressure from people and the shifting climate, the temperate woodlands have receded to less than 5 percent of their original footprint. Still, half of the UK's remaining native pinelands are found in the Cairngorms, making this an unusual

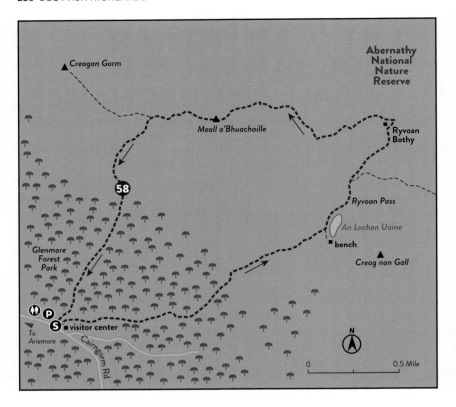

and important landscape for many species such as red squirrels and red deer. Wind through the ancient-feeling forest for 1.5 miles, past dwarf juniper and astonishing pine specimens, some hundreds of years old. Their wide crowns, accompanied by heather, grasses, blaeberry (Europe's version of a blueberry), and crowberry, form an iconic portrait of the Highlands. In spring, these woods burst with Scottish primrose blooming in small fuchsia bouquets. In summer, sun-warmed pines emit a strong resin tang. In fall, the heather casts a purple haze.

Descend some rocky steps to arrive at the western shore of An Lochan Uaine ("Small Green Lake"). Against the blue-green water, the scree-strewn slopes of Creag nan Gall (2040 feet), the hill behind it, are a dramatic backdrop. Bear to the right of An Lochan Uaine (pronounced "Oo-an-yi") to follow a spur trail that runs along its western shore to a lookout with a carved wooden bench. On the bench a quote reads, "And again in the dusk of evening / I shall find once more alone / The dark water of the green loch / And the pass beyond Ryvoan." The excerpt is from a poem left in the

Ryvoan Bothy (a shelter you'll pass a little farther along the trail). The poet scratched out the words sometime during World War II, when the area must have provided a much-needed mountain refuge from the air raids in London. The poem, which has been attributed to a woman named A. M. Lawrence, continues: "For tonight I leave from Euston / And leave the world behind; / Who has the hills as a lover, / Will find them wondrous kind." Traditionally, a copy of the whole poem is posted on the door of the hut.

Return to the main trail and go right to continue past the placid waters and sandy shores of the emerald loch. Some believe the lake gets its magical hue from the reflection of the trees lining its banks, or the silt deposited from the surrounding hills, but there is another perfectly plausible explanation. Local lore maintains that the color comes from pixies who wash their clothes there.

Head up a gentle incline thick with birch and pine to Ryvoan Pass, a low, wide passage through the hills running from Glenmore to Nethybridge. Here, the landscape

Placid Lochan Uaine is, in more ways than one, a place for reflection.

opens up again, and the views down the glen, back toward the loch, take in big hills and bigger skies. But keep an eye out for adders—a distinctive snake with a black zig-zag on its back—which can slither boldly across the path in broad daylight.

In 0.8 mile enter Abernathy National Nature Reserve—a diverse jewel that spans 32,000 acres from the River Nethy to the top of Ben Macdui. Watch overhead for yellow siskins, Scottish crossbills, and even the occasional osprey or golden eagle. Look too for the largest of all grouse species—the western capercaillie is an almost comically huge, colorful game bird that lives in pinewoods. Beyond the reserve sign, arrive at Ryvoan Bothy, a shelter maintained by volunteers for any and all walkers.

Once past the hut, turn left to start up the steep east side of Meall a'Bhuachaille (2660 feet). This peak is a "Corbett," or Scottish mountain ranging from 2500 to 3000 feet. Pronounced "Meal a Voo-cal" and meaning "the Herd's Hill," walkers here follow in the footsteps of the shepherds who drove their flocks across these slopes each summer for centuries. Ascend rough steps and wind across the heather-crammed slopes for roughly 1.2 miles and nearly 1000 feet in elevation gain.

As you climb, there are views over several lakes and beyond to the higher ground of the Cairngorm plateau. Cross over the top of the summit heath, past a large rock cairn that doubles as a wind break, and continue heading west. Follow the track for 0.4 mile through more heath with stunning views. At the junction, go left to head downhill into the sheltered pass between Meall a'Bhuachaille and Creagan Gorm. Drop through forest, bracken, and grasses for 1.3 miles back to the Glenmore Forest Park Visitor Centre.

EXTEND IT

Add the summit of Creagan Gorm (2400 feet), west of Meall a'Bhuachaille. Continue past the summit of Meall a'Bhuachaille, into a saddle, and up the east side of Creagan Gorm. This optional climb adds 1 mile and about 300 feet elevation gain.

59 BEN LOMOND

Walk through woodland and moorland to the tundra-like top of a popular Munro for a bird's-eye view of the biggest lake in Britain.

Distance: 7.6 miles
Elevation Gain: 3500 feet
High Point: 3195 feet

Rating: ★ ★ ★ ★
Difficulty: Challenging
Year-round: No

Dog-friendly: Yes, leashed near livestock and otherwise under voice control
Family-friendly: No
Map: OS Explorer Map OL39, Loch Lomond North

Amenities: Restrooms and a few picnic tables at start; tap water when information center is open
Agency: Loch Lomond & The Trossachs National Park

GETTING THERE

GPS: 56.152129°, -4.642262°
Postcode: G63 0AR
Driving: Ben Lomond is one hour northwest of central Glasgow. The trailhead lies at the end of the road (West Highland Way) to Rowardennan, 11 miles beyond Drymen.
Public Transit: Buses and trains frequently run from Glasgow to Tarbet, where you can

take the water taxi across Loch Lomond to Rowardennan.
Before You Go: Arrive early to find parking. The "tourist" route that this walk ascends is exposed, and the summit can be wickedly windy. The return "Ptarmigan Ridge" route is steep, rocky, and boggy in places. Walking poles may be helpful. Take extreme caution in foggy conditions.

ON THE TRAIL

Pick up the trail (signposted as "Ben Lomond Hill Path") behind the information center to cross a small footbridge. Climb steadily through birch and oak woods, with ferns and wildflowers giving this stretch a rainforest feel. Continue straight through a gate and cross a wider track, gaining about 200 feet in elevation over the next 0.3 mile.

Continue climbing to get your first view of Loch Lomond. At 23 miles long and 5 miles wide, it is the largest lake in Britain. A glacier scoured out the lake bed over ten thousand years ago—to an eerie depth of 623 feet on its north end—and meltwater filled it. Straddling the border of the central Scottish Lowlands and the Highlands, Loch Lomond has a backdrop of numerous high peaks crowding its northern and western shores. To the north is Beinn Bhreac (2234 feet) and Ben Reoch (2169 feet) and to the south are Coire na h-Eanachan (2156 feet) and Beinn Dubh (2106 feet). Today the loch, which has thirty islands to explore, is popular for a variety of water sports.

In 0.6 mile, and after another 400 feet in elevation gain, pass through a gate and exit the forest. Gain 1200 feet over the next mile, and even better views up and down Loch Lomond. On your left you'll pass Sròn Aonaich (1890 feet). As you follow its ridge north, the broad shoulders and conical cap of Ben Lomond will come into view (when not covered by clouds). The hill has had the name Ben Lomond (from the Welsh word "llumon"), or Beacon Hill, since the middle of the first millennium, and it stuck even as Gaelic took over as the dominant language. The reason for the name has been lost to history, but it's likely the summit, which is visible for many miles around, was used as a signal tower of sorts. Ben Lomond is the country's most southerly Munro, or mountain with a summit of more than 3000 feet. (Loch Lomond & The Trossachs National Park hosts twenty-one Munros in all.)

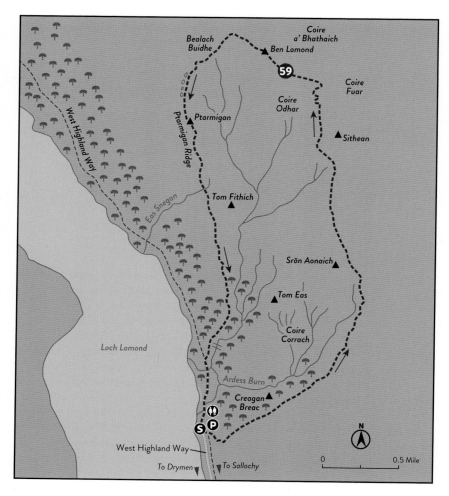

Switchback up 1000 feet of elevation over the next 1.5 miles to where the trail turns west toward the peak. Make a last push over the steep shoulder of the mountain before the gradient backs off for the final 0.3 mile. To the east, the mountain drops away into a wide, rocky cirque, Coire a'Bhathaich. Beyond that, admire views of Loch Chon and Loch Ard, two lakes surrounded by woodland, and multiple peaks to the north and east. Reach the triangulation pillar on the (often crowded) summit at mile 4, with panoramic views that give the impression of standing on the roof of the earth. If weather permits, there are some decent lunch spots. In the rain, however, you get a firsthand look at Ben

Lomond's unique position in the Scottish watershed. All water draining west and north of the peak flows to the Firth of Clyde (and, ultimately, the Atlantic Ocean), while water draining east flows into the Firth of Forth and out to the North Sea.

To pick up the return route along Ptarmigan Ridge (which is tougher than the way up), take the path heading northwest off the peak. The initial descent requires some scrambling as it drops nearly 500 feet over the first 0.3 mile. This route offers an up-close look at some of the mountain's layers of metamorphic and igneous rock, which hint at how, millions of years ago, ice sheets scoured cooled magma.

The gradient eases over the next 0.4 mile to arrive at a series of small, pretty ponds. The path can get somewhat swampy here, but there are some helpful stepping stones. Past those, in about a quarter mile, the trail crosses over the top of Ptarmigan (2400 feet), then starts down its ridge. Switchback down a steep grade, which then mellows out somewhat, over the next 0.7 mile and roughly 800 feet of elevation loss. In spots the track is quite narrow and winding as it hugs the hillside and drops below some crags. Take extreme caution if cloud cover is obscuring the route. The views to the west along this stretch are spectacular, across the northern tip of Loch Lomond to the peaks of the Arrochar Alps. This cluster of mountains ranges in elevation from 1280 feet to 3320 feet, and one of the most famous, 2900-foot Ben Arthur (better known as "The Cobbler"), has three summits said to resemble a shoemaker stooped over a foot. Keep a look out for ravens spiraling overhead and, on the ground, the plump rock ptarmigan, a greyish grouse with a red cap that breeds in the tundra-like landscape of the Highlands. Occasionally merlins, golden eagles, and peregrine falcons are spotted scoping out the terrain, likely for a hearty meal of mountain hare.

Roughly 5.7 miles into the hike, you'll round a few small hills and cross a small stream, Eas Snegan, on stepping stones. Over the next 0.3 mile, drop gradually through grasses, heather, and wildflowers before the trail steepens again. Among the bracken are cheerful yellow roseroot and delicate pink moss campion. In 0.7 mile—and another 800 feet of elevation loss—enter a wooded area. Listen for the high-pitched song of the streaky brown skylark, which often sits on boulders or fence posts. While they are known to sing the day away, their name comes from the extraordinary show they put on. Male skylarks will fly nearly vertically, sometimes upward of 1000 feet, and hover there singing, before careening back down (hopefully to meet a willing mate). For centuries, and perhaps longer, they have been a source of awe for poets and pilgrims alike. These woods are also home to red deer and pine marten, a rare weasel about the size of a house cat.

Pass a pretty waterfall before intersecting a road in about a third of a mile. Go left (south) to walk along the road and over a bridge. You are now on the West Highland Way, which runs along the western base of Ben Lomond and eastern shore of Loch Lomond on its 96-mile course from Milngavie (north of Glasgow) to Fort William.

Loch Lomond has its own mythical monster to rival Nessie—a giant crocodile-like creature.

In 0.3 mile, arrive at a little beach on the shore of Loch Lomond. In 0.2 mile more, hug the shore to see a circular stone and granite sculpture dedicated to those lost in both world wars. From that peaceful memorial, follow the path as it curves inland to the car park.

EXTEND IT

Take the West Highland Way south from Rowardennan to Sallochy, a roughly 3-mile route through oak woodland and along the lakeshore, for more outstanding views of Loch Lomond and Ben Lomond.

60 NORTH FACE OF BEN NEVIS

Walk through a forest and along a gushing stream to a dramatic cirque beneath the awe-inspiring North Face of Ben Nevis.

Distance: 7.5 miles
Elevation Gain: 2200 feet
High Point: 2332 feet
Rating: ★ ★ ★ ★
Difficulty: Moderate to challenging
Year-round: No
Family-friendly: Yes, but use caution at stream crossings

Dog-friendly: Yes, leashed
Amenities: None
Map: OS Explorer Map 392, Ben Nevis & Fort William
Agencies: John Muir Trust, Loch Lomond & The Trossachs National Park

GETTING THERE

GPS: 56.842278°, -5.041362°
Driving: From Torlundy, go south on A82 for 0.2 mile, then turn left at the sign for North Face parking. Go straight for 0.5 mile to the North Face car park on your right.

Postcode: PH33 6SS
Before You Go: The trail is well maintained but rocky and boggy in spots. Expect to cross some small streams, mostly on carefully placed rocks.

ON THE TRAIL

Pick up the path signed "North Face Trail" on the south end of the car park (next to the information signs). Head down the wide, shady path and soon cross over the Allt na Caillich ("the stream of the old woman" in Gaelic). In 0.1 mile, bear right at the fork to stay on the North Face Trail. When the trail splits again in another 0.1 mile, carry on straight through the forest on a gentle grade that turns into a more rigorous ascent. Leanachan Forest is held in the palm of a wide valley shaped by ice age glaciers. Since the Iron Age, people have frequented this area, eking out lives, making tools, and hunting on the flanks of the looming massifs. Today Scots pine, oak, and birch harbor species like red deer, pine martens, osprey, and even golden eagles.

In 0.6 mile and roughly 400 feet in elevation gain, bear right at the intersection. Walk uphill through the trees, glancing back for views—south to Fort William and the head of Loch Linnhe, and west down the length of Loch Eil, and to the hills beyond. Continue on toward the sound of rushing water. In roughly 1 mile, the path runs alongside the Allt a'Mhuilinn, the stream that will stay on your right for the rest of the walk. Pronounced "Allt-a-Vollin," and meaning "mill stream," this waterway gushes forth from the northern slopes of Ben Nevis, where it once powered a mill and distillery and now supplies hydroelectric power to a factory downstream. You'll soon pass the hydro dam and a small waterfall on your right. When the trail splits, go right to keep to the stream. In a few hundred feet, cross a tall wooden stile.

Up ahead are the precipitous black rock walls and crags of Ben Nevis and Coire Leis. At 4409 feet, Ben Nevis—or "*the* Ben" as it's well known—is the tallest mountain in the UK. That moniker is anglicized from "Beinn Bibheis," which means something like the "venomous" or "terrible" mountain. Exposed to the full wrath of weather systems blowing in off the Atlantic, the peak can indeed be a furious spot. But, on a clear day, someone on the summit can see for 125 miles—all the way to Ireland!

Ben Nevis sits at the western end of the Grampian Mountains (which include the Cairngorms). Its most hikeable faces—the south and west sides—are still impressively craggy with steep-sided corries. But this, its northeast face, is a dramatic interplay of sheer gullies, ridges, and buttresses—a landscape straight out of a J. R. R. Tolkien novel. It's also Britain's premier crag for rock and ice climbers, and for over a century people have traveled from around the world to test themselves on its classic routes.

Over the next 0.5 mile, climb a gentle ascent through high, open country. At the next, and final, junction, head right to stay next to the stream. (The left route is the start of the challenging Càrn Mor Dearg Arête trail.) Continue straight for 1.7 miles, climbing roughly 1110 feet in elevation into the belly of the cirque.

Fern-lined crags to your left fall away to moss- and lichen-covered boulders. There are a few small streams to ford along this stretch, but most have large boulders to cross on. On your right the powerful, tree-lined stream cuts through squishy peat bog and radiant pink heather and hums with bees, butterflies, damselflies, and dragonflies. Heather thrives in tough, wet landscapes where other daintier botanicals would wither. The hardy shrub, which covers millions of acres in Scotland, comes in three main varieties—common, bell, and cross leaved—all distinct in shape and color.

The Scots romanticize heather—it's a symbol of independence, confidence, passion, and even luck—but it's had many practical uses over time as well. The Celts and Druids used it medicinally, and the Picts fermented it to make ale. Early Scottish Highlanders mixed heather with peat, mud, and dry grass to build huts, and it's still used as thatch for roofs. It's also been used for fuel and fashioned into brooms, brushes, baskets, and bedding.

And, of course, like most things Scottish, heather has legends attached to it. One popular myth maintains that wherever you see heather flowers blooming, there are fairies living nearby. (If that's true, there is a *large* pixie population living in the shadow of Ben Nevis!) Another tale is that, when the Vikings invaded what is now Scotland, the Pictish King preferred to be thrown off of a cliff rather than reveal the secret recipe for their heather ale.

As you approach the corrie, rocky greyness dominates the landscape (especially on a cloudy day). But this rare and fragile Arctic-Alpine ecosystem has plenty of variety

One oft-accurate translation of Ben Nevis is "a mountain with its head in the clouds."

if you look closely—there are seventy-two lichen species in this area alone. Look for patches of heath spotted-orchid—a long-stemmed wildflower capped by a cluster of small lilac flowers with purple spots. Despite its exotic, delicate facade, this is the most common wild orchid in Scotland, and it thrives in the wind and cold.

Where the main trail ends, you may be able to cross the stream to a cabin. If the allt is "in spate" (British-speak for "overflowing"), however, do not attempt to ford and instead veer left along the water, over a little hummock, to a sheltered spot with big views. There is a thrilling chaos to this hodgepodge of rock, which is the product of a collapsed caldera that was eroded away by glaciation roughly two million years ago. As you face south, the sheer rock walls of Coire Leis look like a fierce lower jaw with jaggy teeth. To your left are the scree-littered slopes of three peaks—Càrn Beag Dearg, (3300 feet), Càrn Dearg Meadhonach (3870 feet), and Càrn Mòr Dearg (4000 feet). On your right, montane cliffs rise to the rock fins and steep gullies of Coire na

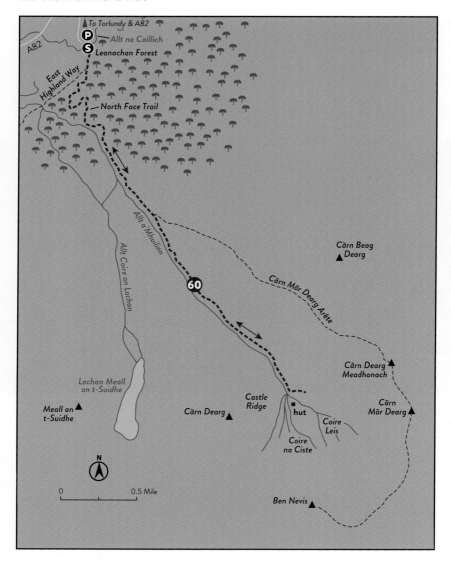

Ciste. Above those lies the zenith of Ben Nevis. All around, semipermanent snowfields dissolve into multiple waterfalls.

When you've had your fill of the brooding north face of Ben Nevis, turn around and retrace your steps back to the start.

EXTEND IT

Experienced mountaineers can take the long, challenging Càrn Mòr Dearg Arête trail to summit Càrn Dearg Meadhonach, Càrn Mòr Dearg, and, finally, Ben Nevis. The 11-mile loop from the North Face car park gains roughly 5000 feet.

61 COIRE LAGAN

This walk on the Isle of Skye piles on superlatives—the most impressive glacial cirques at the foot of the largest mountains, with peaceful lakes and a 150-foot waterfall.

Distance: 6 miles
Elevation Gain: 1900 feet
High Point: 1900 feet
Rating: ★ ★ ★ ★ ★
Difficulty: Moderate to challenging
Year-round: No

Family-friendly: Yes, but not suitable for young children
Dog-friendly: Yes
Amenities: Restrooms at trailhead
Map: OS Explorer Map 411, Skye–Cuillin Hills
Agency: Visit Scotland

GETTING THERE

GPS: 57.202967°, -6.291409°
Driving: From Glenbrittle, follow C1237 south for 0.7 mile over a cattle grate and past several farms to a parking area facing the beach, just before the Glenbrittle Campsite & Cafe.

Postcode: IV47 8TA
Before You Go: A couple of stream crossings can be tricky during or after rainfall. The last 0.6 mile of the route is steep and crosses scree, with some scrambling necessary.

ON THE TRAIL

From the end of C1237, go straight for 0.2 mile past the campsite on your left to a gate. Go through the gate and head toward the small, white building (restrooms) directly ahead. Go left around the building to access the trailhead. Bear left uphill and cross a rough track in a few hundred feet. In 0.5 mile bear left where the trail splits. In another 0.1 mile cross a stream, Allt a'Mhuilllinn, on rocks. At this point you have gained 500 feet in elevation, and the views are already spectacular. Behind you is Loch Brittle with its wide, sandy beach and beyond, out in the Sea of the Hebrides, are three large islands—from right to left—Canna, Rùm, and Eigg (a fourth island, Muck, is just out of sight). Loch Brittle is a sea loch, or fjord—though a relatively shallow one—fed by the River Brittle, which flows out of the hills and across Glen Brittle to the loch. (Scots say "loch" with an aspirated *k*, something like "lockkh." You may not nail it the first time, but locals will toast you for trying!)

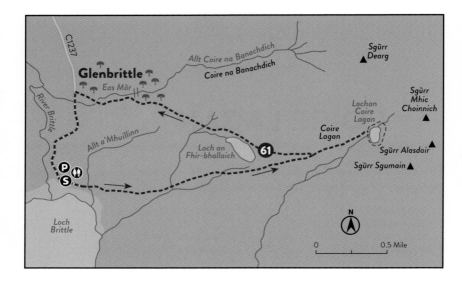

Over the next 0.4 mile the narrow, stony trail gains another 300 feet in elevation and crosses another burn. Ahead, to the east, are the mountains of the Black Cuillin, the remnants of an eroded magma chamber from an enormous, bygone volcano. Considered by many to be the most beautiful in the British Isles, these mountains are also the most challenging to climb. Continue toward an arc of serrated peaks surrounding Coire Lagan, including Sgùrr Dearg (3234 feet), Sgùrr Mhic Choinnich (3111 feet), and Sgùrr Alasdair (3255 feet). The Cuillins (pronounced "coolins") is one range with two main ridges—the Black and the Red. In general, the Red Cuillin (east of here beyond the Blacks and across Glen Sligachan) are sloping and gentle, though still impressive, while the Blacks are much steeper and more dramatic. The Cuillins include fifteen peaks topping 3000 feet, and some of the Black Cuillin didn't log successful first ascents until the end of the nineteenth century.

In a little under half a mile, when a trail branches right, continue straight through grasses and heather. As you climb, look for Loch an Fhir-bhallaich on your left; you'll get a close-up of the beautiful and mysteriously named "lake of the spotted man" on the return. In 0.3 mile, go right at a junction (the trail to your left is the return route of the loop). The wall of mountains ahead appears impenetrable as boulders begin to accumulate across the terrain. While they are called the "black" hills, their color shifts with the light to greyish-green and salmon-streaked.

In 0.2 mile enter a gully with loose rocks, which require some ankle endurance. Over the next 0.4 mile, cross boulders with some moderate scrambling, then run close to the stream flowing from Lochan Coire Lagan. Waterfalls tumble down a rocky chute to your right. This, as well as some of the huge, flat rocks you pass as you near the lake, are good examples of gabbro—coarse-grained, igneous rock formed by the slow cooling of magma that endured the glacial onslaught that shaped this cirque (its grippiness is popular with climbers). There's also basalt here, the result of magma that cooled more quickly, which is much slicker and more susceptible to erosion. The chimneys and gullies lining the coire were formed from eroded basalt.

Reach the shore of Lochan Coire Lagan, where there are picnic spots aplenty, and take in the incredible scenery. The clear, cold waters reflect the bare rock summits encircling it. This is the starting point for climbers intent on summiting many of the peaks on the ridge above. The Black Cuillin span roughly 7 miles, but from Coire Lagan you can see some of the most spectacular of its many hills. To your left (northwest) is Sgùrr Dearg, topped by the Inaccessible Pinnacle (that's its actual name), a basalt fin that can only be reached with rock climbing gear. Straight ahead is Sgùrr Mhic Choinnich, an exposed, wedge-shaped chunk of rock. To your right (southeast) is the Great Stone Shute (yet another illustrative name), a huge scree gully used to access the col below the main ridge of Sgùrr Alasdair, the Black Cuillin's highest peak, on the way to its summit.

Leave the lake and its sentinel rocks behind to retrace your steps 0.6 mile to where the trail splits, and bear right. Work your way downhill for 0.5 mile along a rocky track, passing the peat-encircled Loch an Fhir-bhallaich. Continue for roughly 1 mile,

Eas Mòr meaning "Great Fall," is a simple but truthful name.

catching glimpses east into the mouth of Coire na Banachdich—the cirque west of Coire Lagan with its own guardian peaks.

Arrive at an Eden-like patch of forest surrounding a gorge cut by the Allt Coire na Banachdich. Continue along the ravine to a vantage point roughly level with where the stream runs out of land and plunges into a chasm more than 150 feet below. It looks like something out of a daydream when the sun glints off the Eas Mor waterfall and illuminates the rocky ramparts that are its backdrop.

Carry on past the waterfall and, in 0.4 mile, cross a footbridge over the Allt Coire na Banachdich. In 0.2 mile the trail ends at the road. Go left and follow the road for 0.7 mile back to the parking area. If you have time, head to the beach on Loch Brittle to look for ringed plovers, grey herons, oystercatchers, and even puffins.

EXTEND IT
Follow the 0.3-mile loop around Lochan Coire Lagan.

62 FINGAL'S PINNACLES & THE QUIRAING

This route, on the north of the Isle of Skye, passes through Fingal's Pinnacles on a quieter approach to the popular Quiraing area with its sculptured mountains and weird, wonderful rock formations.

Distance: 4.6 miles
Elevation Gain: 1670 feet
High Point: 1160 feet
Rating: ★ ★ ★ ★
Difficulty: Moderate
Year-round: Yes
Dog-friendly: Yes, leashed near livestock

Family-friendly: Yes, but drop-offs and steep sections near rock formations
Amenities: None
Map: OS Explorer Map 408, Skye, Trotternish & The Storr
Agency: Visit Scotland

GETTING THERE

GPS: 57.658055°, -6.254297°
Postcode: IV51 9HZ (Flodigarry)
Driving: From Flodigarry, take A855 south for 0.6 mile and, after rising over a hill, look for the parking lay-by on your right (there's a boulder with a placard on it marking the spot).

Public Transit: Take a bus from Portree toward Flodigarry and ask the driver to stop at the base of the Loch Langaig footpath.
Before You Go: The track can be muddy, and the loop around The Needle is not well defined.

Fingal's Pinnacles epitomize the Isle of Skye's fairytale look and feel.

ON THE TRAIL

From the parking lay-by, go right (southwest) uphill on the worn, grassy track toward Loch Langaig (there's a sign pointing the way). Continue through bracken and heather toward the lumpy landforms that look like huge piles of discarded grey-green clay. In 300 feet, pass lupine-lined Loch Langaig ("lake of the long bay") and look for the humps rising to rocky ramparts beyond. Birds of prey, including kestrels, buzzards (hawks), golden eagles, and even white-tailed eagles (a.k.a. sea eagles), can be seen here. At this point the bulk of the Quiraing—an area of cliffs, pinnacles, and peaks—starts to come into view (at least in clear weather), topped by Meall na Suiramach (1781 feet), which looks like the smooth back of a whale. The peak, though it is more like a plateau, is the northernmost summit of the Trotternish Peninsula. There's an interplay of light and cloud, sea and summit here that makes the area feel remote and otherworldly.

Walk on toward the grey, guarded cliffs of Leac nan Fionn (1250 feet), or Fingal's Tomb, on your right. According to different accounts, Fingal the Fair-haired may have been myth or reality—a giant, or just a really big guy, who was both a prolific hunter and warrior. Regardless, at some point, he became larger than life and, when he died, Fingal was laid to rest in these hills. The huge, nearly flat-topped stone sentry ahead marks his grave.

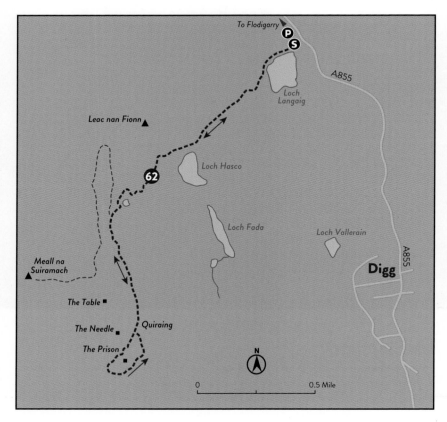

Continue straight uphill along the rocky track and, in 0.7 mile and roughly 300 feet of elevation gain, pass along the base of Fingal's Tomb past picturesque Loch Hasco. In 0.1 mile, cross a tall, wooden stair stile. The terrain starts to gets craggy here as the spires and hummocks of Fingal's Pinnacles rise to the north and west like the ruins of a castle from another time. In about a quarter mile, swing right and then left around another small lake. When the trail forks soon after that, bear left (south) among springy mounds of moss and heather toward the high, wonky rock towers.

If you get the sense that this ground is impermanent, or unfinished, you're right. The rock formations here are part of the 20-mile-long Trotternish Ridge, which was formed by landslips so massive the scale is hard to grasp. Long ago, ancient lava flows that had cooled to heavy basalt crushed older, softer sedimentary rock beneath it. Gravity, time, and sometimes ice led to cycles of sliding, slumping, and tumbling, resulting in the Lord of the Rings landscape all around you. While the rest of the escarpment has settled down, the Quiraing is still on the move (as the people who repair the roads nearby can attest).

In 0.2 mile, go left (south) at a T intersection along the base of The Quiraing. On a clear day, the coast to the east is visible, as are Staffin Bay and Staffin Island, and some peaks on the mainland may even be seen. Ahead on your left are two of the better-known features of the maze-like Quiraing—The Needle, a 120-foot basalt spire, and The Prison, an invulnerable, triple-layered crag.

Go straight for 0.5 mile and pass a steep, rocky spur trail to your right that leads into a labyrinth of rock that can be explored (carefully) off-trail for views up to The Table—an improbably flat, rectangular area of rock and grass roughly the size of a soccer field. The plateau is so well concealed that local people are said to have hidden cattle up there from Viking raiders.

When the trail forks beneath The Needle, continue straight with The Prison on your left. Continue on the main route for 0.2 mile as you pass the pyramidal Prison, which looks like an inland Alcatraz, to a fork. Go left to loop around the bottom of The Prison, and, in 0.3 mile, arrive back at the track you were on earlier beneath The Needle. From here, follow the trail back to the start.

EXTEND IT

Add Meall na Suiramach on a 2.2-mile out-and-back with 700 feet of elevation gain. On the return, instead of going right to drop down past the lake, continue straight for 0.3 mile, then make a sharp left to start climbing. In 0.6 mile, turn right on a spur trail and continue for 0.2 mile to the top.

63 PASS OF KILLIECRANKIE

Spend a day hillwalking and river rambling in the Perthshire countryside, which has a deeply remote feel. This route goes through a wooded gorge, along the confluence of two rivers, and up a small, quiet peak that features some of the best scenery in the region.

Distance: 9 miles
Elevation Gain: 1400 feet
High Point: 1290 feet
Rating: ★ ★ ★ ★
Difficulty: Moderate
Year-round: Yes
Family-friendly: Yes, but on-road sections require caution

Dog-friendly: Yes, leashed
Amenities: Restrooms, shop, and refreshments at the start
Map: OS Explorer Map OL49, Pitlochry & Loch Tummel
Agencies: National Trust for Scotland, Killiecrankie Visitor Centre

GETTING THERE

GPS: 56.743133°, -3.772196°
Postcode: PH16 5LG
Public Transit: Buses run from Pitlochry to Killiecrankie.
Driving: From Pitlochry, take Atholl Road (A924) northwest for 1.1 miles. Continue onto B8019 for 1.6 miles, and then onto B8079 for 1.1 miles. Look for the Killiecrankie Visitor Centre parking on your left.
Before You Go: This area is particularly popular in the autumn.

ON THE TRAIL

Walk around the visitor center to a brick pillar marked "Pass of Killiecrankie." Head straight down the stairs through a tunnel of greenery. Follow the trail 0.1 mile as it curves and climbs another short flight of stairs. Bear left and follow the path for about two-tenths of a mile, with views of the gorge opening on your left. Just past a viewpoint with a bench, descend more stairs.

The Pass of Killiecrankie, meaning "wood of the aspen trees," is a narrow, steep-sided glen cut by the River Garry, roughly 1.5 miles long. It's a designated Site of Special Scientific Interest because of its variety of flora and fauna. The densely wooded gorge shelters mature ash, beech, birch, hazel, oak, and a huge variety of wildflowers, like cheerful golden primrose and delicate white wood anemone. You may hear birdsong from wood warblers, woodpeckers, or nuthatches, or some of the many other species that nest in the gorge or visit seasonally. For the last few centuries, at least, Killiecrankie has awed visitors. Some were intimidated by its grandeur, while others roundly appreciated its dramatic good looks. In 1844, Queen Victoria wrote in her journal, "I cannot describe how beautiful it is. [Prince] Albert was in perfect ecstasies."

At the bottom of the steps, go right (you'll return to this junction later). Follow the trail for 0.1 mile to where it intersects the road, B8079. Carefully cross the road and head slightly left to pick up the trail (marked by a green footpath sign) behind the Killiecrankie Hotel placard. Continue on a shady stretch for 0.2 mile before, again, intersecting the B8079 at the small center of Killiecrankie village. Cross back over and bear right and downhill along the sidewalk for about 200 feet.

Go left to follow an unnamed side road downhill and over a stone bridge spanning railroad tracks. Continue for 300 feet to another stone bridge over the River Garry as it squeezes through a small canyon. Downriver, the water courses powerfully between rock walls topped by dense forest and is backed by Tom Dubh (820 feet), while upriver, it rushes around rocky bends and alongside a wide gravel beach.

Continue straight on a tarmac road along a high stone wall for 0.1 mile. Bear left at a fork marked "Killiecrankie Path: Garry Bridge." Follow the narrow road for 0.2 mile to a T intersection. Turn right (signed "Craig Fonvuick" hill route), and continue along the gravel track past a small parking area opposite a drystone wall.

At a signpost with a blue arrow, bear left and begin to climb. Continue for 1.2 miles—and 800 feet up—through several gates and over one stile as it circumnavigates Craig Fonvuick (1355 feet). Pass through several wonderful pockets of woodland, including spindly birches and sturdy oaks, an area famous for its intense autumn show. Climb through open grassland and onto heathland as you near the peak. When it's in bloom, the heather casts a hypnotic purple blur across the landscape. Watch for a narrow track on your left and follow it for 0.1 mile to the top of Craig Fonvuick, marked

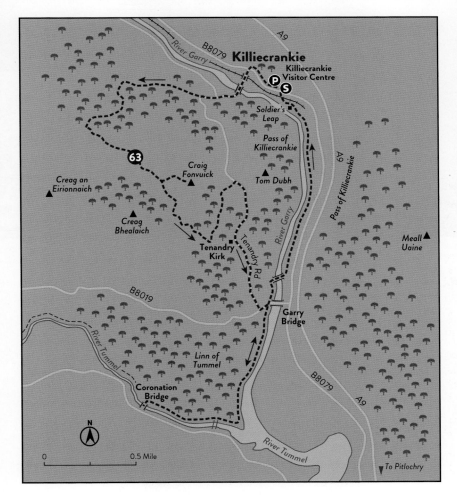

After the wide and calm River Garry squeezes through the Pass of Killiecrankie, it flows into the more rambunctious River Tummel.

by a cairn. Looking east over the Pass of Killiecrankie, admire woods and waters intertwined like blue and green ribbons to the impressive stone precipice of Ben Vrackie (2760 feet).

Retrace your steps off the peak and turn left to continue along the main track. Follow that for roughly 1 mile through fields of bracken and moss-draped trees. This is part of the Tulach Hill Special Area of Conservation, a Natura 2000 wildlife site of European importance, notable for its dry heath, dry grasslands, and alkaline fens, which are rich in mosses and flowering plant species. Along the way pass the ruins of a homestead.

When the trail intersects Tenandry Road, go right. Follow the narrow road flanked by farms and pastures for 0.5 mile, passing the Tenandry Kirk, with lovely views of the surrounding hills. In the 1830s this simple Chapel of Ease, as it was colloquially known, was built for nearby residents who, up to then, had to walk many miles to a house of worship. Carry on for 0.4 mile beyond the church, through a forested area lined with rock walls. When Tenandry Road intersects B8019, go left and walk along the path for roughly 400 feet, past a small car park, to a set of stairs at the Garry Bridge (marked "Linn of Tummel").

Descend the stairs and, at the bottom, go right in the direction signed to Pitlochry. Cross beneath the bridge on the wide dirt track, alongside the River Garry, lined with trees. The impressive, 130-foot-high bridge is a popular bungee-jumping spot. This crossing lies at the junction of ancient and important routes that once connected east to west, and the Scottish Highlands to the Lowlands. It is humbling to imagine the volume and variety of travelers over the centuries.

Follow the track for 0.5 mile to an opening in the trees. (A short spur trail on your left leads to a rocky beach on the river's edge.) In 0.3 mile curve right where the rushing River Tummel rounds a bend to join the lazy River Garry. (Go straight on a short spur trail to get a good look at the rushing confluence where hearty souls ride inner tubes down a rocky gully.) Here, in the heart of the Linn of Tummel, the two rivers link arms to feed Loch Faskally. Linn of Tummel in Gaelic translates roughly to "deep pool of tumbling stream," capturing the spot's duality, its calm drama.

Follow the trail, with the River Tummel on your left, for 0.7 mile to the Coronation Bridge. The narrow suspension footbridge commemorates the coronation of King George V in 1911. While the trail continues, the bridge is the turnaround point for this route.

Make your way back to the Garry Bridge, but instead of going up the stairs, continue straight along the river. In 0.1 mile, follow the track right, over a footbridge spanning the river. Keep the river on your left for 1 mile through the Pass of Killiecrankie. Be on the lookout for rare red squirrels and pine martens. At the turnoff for Soldier's Leap, go left and continue 200 feet to a rocky precipice with a view of the River Garry.

This peaceful spot overlooking the gorge belies a bloody past. The story of Soldier's Leap starts with the 1688 ouster of (Catholic) King James in favor of (Protestant and Anglican) William and Mary. Scots loyal to King James, called Jacobites, assembled a force of Highlander rebels—who knew the land well—to fight government troops. In late July 1689, English troops marched to intersect the Jacobites at Killiecrankie Pass, but the rebels had gotten there first.

As night fell, the Jacobites charged the government troops and, though massively outnumbered, secured the Battle of Killiecrankie as their first victory. (The campaign went more or less downhill from there.) While the redcoats were retreating, one soldier with Jacobites on his heels reportedly leapt from a large rock across the river—a distance of 18 feet. After you've surveyed the spot and decided whether the feat was possible, return to the main trail and, in roughly 200 feet, go right to ascend the stairs and return to the visitor center.

ACKNOWLEDGMENTS

To my husband, Juan Castro, for sharing *your* Cambridge, then heeding every call for "Adventure!" You make everything better.

To my sister, Alison Baukney, for the Cornwall days and the boundless support. To my UK family—Andrew, Netta, Maya, and Ari—for the many explorations of Oxford, Blenheim, London, and the Lake District.

To Rebekah and Matthew, in Isleham, for the Peak District introduction. To Sue Saalau, for your tips on Snowdonia. To Maureen Ryan, for your Edinburgh insights. To Chris Pye, of the Fellowship of the Fells, for your good cheer and knowledge.

To family and friends from California to Massachusetts—and beyond—for your encouragement, especially Nicole Friederichs, for introducing me to Hampstead over twenty years ago. It's still a favorite!

And last but never least, to the dedicated and talented team at Mountaineers Books, including Kate Rogers, Laura Shauger, Laura Lancaster, Janet Kimball, Jen Grable, Callie Stoker-Graham, Debbie Greenberg, and Bart Wright. Thank you.

OPPOSITE: *Follow in the footsteps of Charles Darwin and Edmund Hillary into Cwm Idwal, Wales's finest natural amphitheater.*

RESOURCES

LAND MANAGERS

Alexandra Palace: www.alexandrapalace.com
Blenheim Palace: www.blenheimpalace.com
Brecon Beacons National Park: www.breconbeacons.org
Cairngorms National Park: cairngorms.co.uk
Cambridge Botanic Gardens: www.botanic.cam.ac.uk
Cambridge City Council: www.cambridge.gov.uk
Christ Church College: www.chch.ox.ac.uk
City of London: www.cityoflondon.gov.uk
City of London, Parks, Green Spaces and Biodiversity: www.london.gov.uk
Cotswolds National Landscape: www.cotswoldsaonb.org.uk
Cotswolds Tourism Partnership: www.cotswolds.com
Dartmoor National Park: www.dartmoor.gov.uk
Dunwich Greyfriars: www.dunwichgreyfriars.org.uk
East Lothian Council: www.eastlothian.gov.uk
Edinburgh City Council: www.edinburgh.gov.uk
English Heritage: www.english-heritage.org.uk
Exmoor National Park: www.exmoor-nationalpark.gov.uk
Friends of the Parkland Walk: www.parkland-walk.org.uk
Glenmore Forest Park: forestryandland.gov.scot
Gloucestershire Wildlife Trust: www.gloucestershirewildlifetrust.co.uk
Haringey Council: www.haringey.gov.uk
Historic Environment Scotland: www.historicenvironment.scot
Holkham National Nature Reserve: www.holkham.co.uk/nature-reserve-beach
Islington Council, Parkland Walk: www.islington.gov.uk
John Muir's Birthplace: www.jmbt.org.uk
John Muir Trust: www.johnmuirtrust.org

OPPOSITE: *From the modest, heather-covered summit of Craig Fonvuick (Trail 63), Ben Vrackie dominates the eastern viewshed.*

Jurassic Coast Trust: jurassiccoast.org
Lake District National Park: www.lakedistrict.gov.uk
Lizard Lighthouse Heritage Centre: www.trinityhouse.co.uk
Loch Lomond & The Trossachs National Park: www.lochlomond-trossachs.org
Minsmere Nature Reserve: www.rspb.org.uk/Minsmere
National Parks UK: www.nationalparks.uk
National Trust: www.nationaltrust.org.uk
National Trust for Scotland: www.nts.org.uk
Oxford University Parks: www.parks.ox.ac.uk
Peak District National Park: www.peakdistrict.gov.uk
Pembrokeshire Coast National Park: www.pembrokeshirecoast.wales
Pentland Hills Regional Park: www.pentlandhills.org
Rothiemurchus Forest: rothiemurchus.net
Royal Oak Foundation: www.royal-oak.org
Royal Parks: www.royalparks.org.uk
Scotland's Great Trails: www.scotlandsgreattrails.com
Scottish Seabird Centre: www.seabird.org
Snowdon National Nature Reserve: naturalresources.wales
Snowdonia National Park: www.snowdonia.gov.wales
Sudeley Castle: sudeleycastle.co.uk
Suffolk Coast Path: www.suffolkcoastandheaths.org
Town of Kingussie: www.kingussie.co.uk
Town of North Berwick: www.northberwick.org.uk
Visit Scotland: www.visitscotland.com
Water of Leith Conservation Trust: www.waterofleith.org.uk
Woodland Trust: www.woodlandtrust.org.uk
Yorkshire Dales National Park: www.yorkshiredales.org.uk

LAND SURVEY

Ordnance Survey: www.ordnancesurvey.co.uk

LEGAL CODES

Countryside and Rights of Way Act 2000: www.gov.uk/guidance/
    open-access-land-management-rights-and-responsibilities
Countryside Code: www.gov.uk/government/publications/the-countryside-code
Freshwater Rod Fishing Licenses: www.gov.uk/fishing-licences/buy-a-fishing-licence,
    0344 800 5386
Freshwater Rod Fishing Rules: www.gov.uk/freshwater-rod-fishing-rules
Land Reform Act (Scotland) 2003: www.legislation.gov.uk/asp/2003/2/contents
Scottish Outdoor Access Code: www.outdoraccess-scotland.scot

LONG-DISTANCE PATHS
Long Distance Walkers Association: ldwa.org.uk
National Trails: www.nationaltrail.co.uk

PUBLIC TRANSIT
National Express: www.nationalexpress.com, 0871 781 8181
National Rail: www.nationalrail.co.uk, 0345 748 4950
Stagecoach: www.stagecoachbus.com
Transport for London: tfl.gov.uk, 0343 222 1234
Traveline: www.traveline.info, 0871 200 2233

TIDES
Met Office: www.metoffice.gov.uk, 0370 900 0100
United Kingdom Hydrographic Office: www.ukho.gov.uk, 0182 348 4444

WEATHER
Met Office: www.metoffice.gov.uk, 0370 900 0100
Mountain Weather Information Service: www.mwis.org.uk

INDEX

ABOUT THE
AUTHOR

Heather Hansen is an award-winning science and travel journalist and author of *Wildfire: On the Front Lines with Station 8* and *Prophets and Moguls, Rangers and Rogues, Bison and Bears: 100 Years of the National Park Service.* She is the recipient of awards from the American Society of Journalists and Authors, the Society of American Travel Writers, and the Colorado Authors League. Hansen is a member of the National Association of Science Writers and the Society of Environmental Journalists.

For several years Hansen has split her time between the UK and the US, and while she has bridged the linguistic and cultural gap in many ways, she'll never get used to going clockwise through a roundabout, or calling potato chips "crisps." She is currently researching and writing about solitude, including her time in Great Britain's backcountry.

MOUNTAINEERS BOOKS

SKIPSTONE   BRAIDED RIVER

recreation · lifestyle · conservation

MOUNTAINEERS BOOKS, including its two imprints, Skipstone and Braided River, is a leading publisher of quality outdoor recreation, sustainability, and conservation titles. As a 501(c)(3) nonprofit, we are committed to supporting the environmental and educational goals of our organization by providing expert information on human-powered adventure, sustainable practices at home and on the trail, and preservation of wilderness.

Our publications are made possible through the generosity of donors, and through sales of more than 700 titles on outdoor recreation, sustainable lifestyle, and conservation. To donate, purchase books, or learn more, visit us online:

MOUNTAINEERS BOOKS
1001 SW Klickitat Way, Suite 201 • Seattle, WA 98134
800-553-4453 • mbooks@mountaineersbooks.org • www.mountaineersbooks.org

An independent nonprofit publisher since 1960

Mountaineers Books is proud to support the Leave No Trace Center for Outdoor Ethics, whose mission is to promote and inspire responsible outdoor recreation through education, research, and partnerships. The Leave No Trace program is focused specifically on human-powered (nonmotorized) recreation. For more information, visit www.lnt.org.

YOU MAY ALSO LIKE: